Learning Love from a Tiger

Learning Love from a Tiger

Religious Experiences with Nature

Daniel Capper

UNIVERSITY OF CALIFORNIA PRESS

University of California Press, one of the most
distinguished university presses in the United States,
enriches lives around the world by advancing scholarship
in the humanities, social sciences, and natural sciences. Its
activities are supported by the UC Press Foundation and
by philanthropic contributions from individuals and
institutions. For more information, visit www.ucpress.edu.

University of California Press
Oakland, California

Library of Congress Cataloging-in-Publication Data

Names: Capper, Daniel, 1962.
Title: Learning love from a tiger : religious experiences
    with nature / Daniel Capper.
Description: Oakland, California : University of
    California Press, [2016] | ©2016 | Includes
    bibliographical references and index.
Identifiers: LCCN 2015042583 (print) | LCCN 2015046714
    (ebook) | ISBN 9780520290419 (cloth : alk. paper) |
    ISBN 9780520290426 (pbk. : alk.   paper) |
    ISBN 9780520964600 ()
Subjects: LCSH: Human-animal relationships—Religious
    aspects—Comparative studies. | Human-animal
    relationships—Philosophy. | Animals (Philosophy) |
    Animals—Religious aspects—Comparative studies. |
    Nature—Religious aspects—Comparative studies.

Classification: LCC BL439 .C36 2016 (print) | LCC BL439

    (ebook) | DDC 202/.12—dc23

LC record available at http://lccn.loc.gov/2015042583

25   24   23   22   21   20   19   18   17   16
10 9 8 7 6 5 4 3 2 1

CONTENTS

ILLUSTRATIONS

Introduction

Into Muir's Forest

The snowy peaks of the Sierra Nevada shimmered in the California sunrise as John Muir arose from his wilderness bed of oak leaves. Because he was helping to drive a flock of more than two thousand sheep up Yosemite Creek Valley to their summer highland pastures, Muir usually slept under the stars, or "sky lilies," as he affectionately called them. After finishing a simple breakfast of tea, sugar, and bread, he quickly packed up his few possessions and was ready for a long day of climbing. The sheep moved at only one mile per hour, leaving Muir with plenty of time to investigate, sketch, and collect from the multitude of plants, animals, and geologic formations within his pristine mountain habitat. Unshackled from the urban-human social realities that he found so alienating, and freely communing with his forest environment, for the first time in his forty-one years the nature-loving Muir felt truly himself.

Born in Scotland on April 21, 1838, Muir immigrated with his family to Wisconsin when he was eleven. Eastern settlers had only recently come to Wisconsin, and Muir as a boy adored the wilderness setting into which he had been thrust. He went on to study botany and geology at the University of Wisconsin, but the upheavals caused by the Civil War led to his becoming a successful machinist and inventor. Then an industrial accident left him temporarily blind. At that time he feared above all not being able to see a flower again, and his desire to become a nature explorer like his hero, Alexander von Humboldt, burned hotter than ever. Thus, after he recovered his eyesight, he surprised even himself by quitting his job and enacting a plan to undertake a thousand-mile botanical "saunter" through the wilds stretching from Louisville, Kentucky, to Florida.

What Muir called his "floral pilgrimage" began on September 1, 1867, and he purposefully traveled by "the wildest, leafiest, and least trodden way" that he could manage. Over the next few weeks he would enter the first real mountains that he had ever seen; visit Savannah, Georgia, to resupply; and contract malaria in northern Florida. From Florida in January 1868 he sojourned to Cuba to find a ship to take him to South America in order to explore Amazonian foliage. But finding no transport to South America available, instead he traveled to San Francisco in March 1868 in order to explore the natural world at Yosemite, which had also been calling him.[1]

Muir was no ordinary lover of nature (by which, of course, I mean nonhuman nature). In addition to the scientific side of his personality, he was a nature mystic who experienced the natural world as God in the flesh. He approached nature first and foremost spiritually, with the impassioned intellectual aspect of the experience coming along with the spiritual. For him, encountering nature meant directly embracing the sacred, or the awesome, fascinating, and numinous supernatural reality that the theologian Rudolf Otto described. Throughout his life Muir ecstatically bathed in holiness through his profound, unbounded immersion in the natural world. As he wrote in his journal, "I only went out for a walk, and finally concluded to stay out till sundown, for going out, I found, was really going in."[2]

Even as a child he spoke not of flowers but of "flower people," and as a young man he explained that alligators were not Satan's handiwork, as was sometimes believed, but rather were beautiful expressions of God's noble intentions. But he failed to find his true personal religion until he moved to Yosemite. Awed by the overwhelming size and ethereal beauty of his surroundings, Muir felt a strong sense of interconnection with his environment in general as well as with innumerable individual natural beings that his sharp eye spied. Part of this feeling of interconnection was fueled by his ongoing studies in botany and geology, to be sure, but part of it arose from a special spiritual sensibility that had always been part of his makeup.[3]

In Yosemite he worshipped effortlessly: since "everything turns into religion, all the world seems a church and the mountains altars." With trees and boulders as his spiritual colleagues, he said that Yosemite "is by far the grandest of all the special temples of nature I was ever permitted to enter." Muir's natural world was suffused with the presence of divinity, so that hares served as his priests and cool mountain streams offered sacramental wine. Embracing yet exceeding the common idea that the natural world provides a beautiful example of God's handiwork, for Muir nature didn't just point to a deity; nature *was* the deity. He said: "Nature like a fluid seems to drench and steep us throughout, as the whole sky and the rocks and flowers are drenched with spiritual life—with God." Mountains had "spiritual power," the sky had "goodness," and the majestic sequoia was a divine "King."[4]

Thus always in church, so to speak, Muir also had alpine scripture to read. Finding the "divine manuscript" of nature to be richer than the many books that he had laboriously memorized from the Bible, Muir spoke to his dear friend Jeanne Carr of "glorious lessons of sky and plain and mountain, which no mortal power can ever speak." A comforting lesson came in Bonaventure Cemetery, in Savannah, where John learned from live oak teachers not to fear death. Other lessons involved nature's tough love, including a frightening experience in a storm on Brady Glacier in Alaska with his dog pal Stickeen, an experience that led Muir to exclaim that nature "gains her ends with dogs as well as with men, making us do as she likes, shoving and pulling us along her ways, however rough, all but killing us at times in getting her lessons driven hard home." Still, for Muir, nature, "so replete with divine truth," was a better teacher of spirituality than any Sunday-school parson or professor of theology.[5]

But for Muir it was not enough simply to attend this church of nature or to ponder these bucolic spiritual teachings intellectually. Like many mystics before him, Muir by temperament was driven to experience this sacredness as completely as he could. Exhibiting the classic mystical theme of an experience of holy unity, he said of a moving experience in Yosemite: "You cannot feel yourself out-of-doors; plains, sky, and mountains ray beauty which you feel. You bathe in these spirit-beams, turning round and round, as if warming at a campfire. Presently you lose consciousness of your own separate existence: you blend with the landscape and become part and parcel of nature."[6]

Interestingly, Muir's mysticism was quite expansive, including sacred experiences not just of living beings but also of supposedly inanimate things like rivers and stones. In *My First Summer in the Sierras* he wrote: "The happy plants and all our fellow animal creatures great and small, and even the rocks, seemed to be shouting, 'Awake, awake, rejoice, rejoice, come love us and join in our song. Come! Come!' ... Everything seems equally divine—one smooth, pure, wild glow of Heaven's love, never to be blotted or blurred by anything past or to come."[7]

Thus Muir was not just a scientific naturalist, as he is sometimes described; he was also an active worshipper of what he considered the divinity of the natural world. Like other inspired mystics, he wanted to share his religion, where bears were ministers and mountains were monks. Of fulfilling his self-appointed task to "preach Nature like an apostle," he said: "Heaven knows that John [the] Baptist was not more eager to get all his fellow sinners into the Jordan than I to baptize all of mine in the beauty of God's mountains." Yet Muir built no church nor started any religious movement. Instead he channeled his spiritual energies into the late-nineteenth-century conservation movement. To this end he published a number of scientific pieces in newspapers and periodicals, was a motive force in the establishment not just of Yosemite but of the entire National Park system in the United States, and helped

Figure 1. Muir Woods National Monument is named for John Muir. (Photo: Author.)

to found the Sierra Club, thus becoming the greatest American naturalist living in the late nineteenth and the early twentieth century. Today his voice continues to influence and energize scientists, environmental activists, and lovers of nature alike.[8]

Muir embraced nature mysticism, which is the direct experience of sacredness in and through nature, and his lasting impact cannot be clearly understood apart from this. Muir's nature mysticism calls our attention to the manifold ways in which nonhuman nature, humans, and religions interact. These myriad interactions are not surprising, given that the religions of the world inform us about who we are as individuals and as a species, and so do our interactions with natural beings, although this latter movement is not always recognized.

Every human interacts with natural entities, as is easy to see with rural folks surrounded by many animals, plants, minerals, and water.

But even urbanites dwelling in the most developed cities interact with natural forms, since city residents on a daily basis will contact pets, other domestic animals, birds, insects, fish, bodies of water, and natural beings used for food. To be human is to coexist with natural beings, so that they shape how we understand ourselves, others, the world in which we live, and how we approach religious questions regarding meaning and proper living. As the philosopher Mary Midgley said: "Had we no other animate life-form than our own, we should have been utterly mysterious to ourselves as a species. And that would have made it immensely harder for us to understand ourselves as individuals, too." Because we share a planetary habitat with natural beings, they strongly color how we approach life, including religious life, and for *Homo sapiens* this has always been true.[9]

The environmental scientist Paul Shepard argues eloquently that interactions with animals directly resulted in our humanness. He tells us that "the hunt made us human," as hunting and the eating of meat resulted in larger human brains, the development of cognitive and symbolic powers, and the necessity for human social organization. These aspects of our humanness led in part to the development of human language and religion. Cultural forms then emerged both as praises of nature and as reactions to natural dangers. Using animals as our mirrors, we defined our goals and reflected upon our achievements and shortcomings. Of the influence of dogs alone, David Gordon White tells us that they "no doubt played a significant role in the rise of Homo sapiens to dominance over our planet, in the human transformation of environment into world.... We cannot overestimate the importance of this relationship to the 'humanization' of the human species." Human beings would not be the same today without animals.[10]

It is not just natural beings like dogs who influence humans, as humans obviously have reciprocal strong impacts on natural beings, such as can be seen in the human creation of the dog in the first place. Genetic data indicate that dogs likely were the first domesticated animals, appearing in East Asia or perhaps Africa around fifteen thousand years ago, whereas fossil data indicate a European origin around thirty thousand years ago. Most scholars believe that hungry wolves with the lowest status in their packs would have sought food near human settlements. Such wolves likely would have been smaller, weaker, and more docile as compared with their fiercer wolf colleagues, and for these reasons they were hungry and were therefore willing to conform to human lifestyles. Because of their capacities to guard, help with the hunt, shepherd, aid transportation, and so on, over generations humans chose the wolves mildest in behavior and smallest in size (as many people still seek with dogs today), fed them, and interbred these meeker, dogs-in-the-making wolves. For their part, many of these wolves knew a good thing when they saw it—as dogs now vastly outnumber wolves—and volunteered for domestication. This artificial evolution caused such physical changes as the smaller skulls, teeth, and brains in dogs, as well as dogs' floppy ears and sickle-shaped tails. Selective genetics appears to have resulted in the submissive behavior that is greater in domestic dogs than in wolves. Furthering this human-controlled species process, the plethora of dog breeds seen today is of relatively recent occurrence, as the breeding of fancy dogs became widely fashionable only in the Victorian era and led to an explosion of new varieties. Dogs are a human development, as are all other domestic animals—as sheep and cattle, for instance, have been bred specifically to be more barrel-shaped and have lighter bones, benefiting human meat-eaters.[11]

Of course these mutual influences between humans and natural beings often take a religious hue, as we see with the bear. Religious regard for bears among numerous Eurasian and indigenous American peoples is so ancient that the anthropologist A. Irving Hallowell describes bear ceremonialism as possibly the first form of human religion. Although bear veneration varies widely by time and place, there appear to be a few universal themes. In many places, a bear serves as the Master of Animals, the spirit leader of all animals and therefore the controller of the hunt. The anatomy and behaviors of bears sometimes so strongly resemble those of humans that sacred bears commonly serve to specify simultaneously the boundaries between humans, animals, and the sacred. This results in elaborate bear-hunting rituals, which include apologies to the bear, ceremonial handling of the body, and special treatment for ursine body parts, so that bears color the religious forms observed by humans. Bears, too, are affected by this ritual complex, as they foremost have served as religious sacrifices through which (it is commonly but not universally believed) they are liberated from their earthly limitations and become pure spirit. In these ways bears and humans have shaped each other's lives and deaths precisely through the medium of religions.[12]

Humans and natural entities strongly impact each other, and religions mediate these processes. Interactions with nature and the existence of religion are human universals, so that across times and places humans and nature have encountered each other in diverse, religiously charged ways. On one hand, in various religions, natural beings may be recipients of the sacred, divine messengers, bringers of spiritual or material gifts, gods, vehicles or protectors for gods, guardian spirits, or sacred ancestors. On occasion natural beings possess spiritual insight superior to the human and function as religious teachers. Animals, plants, minerals, and water may be models for emulation, kin who share human souls, or partners in the project of existence. Real and symbolic natural beings may direct ethical mores and define virtue or vice. Conversely, sometimes flora and fauna are sacrificed, shedding their sap and blood for the religious sake of humans, whereas at other times natural beings provoke distinctions that solidify notions of humanity's separation from the rest of the natural world. Numerous researchers tell us that our relationships with nature typically are tinged with ambivalence, and this remains true with religious experiences with nature, in which natural beings appear in positive and negative forms.

Unfortunately, instances of these spiritually charged interactions between humans and nature often get overlooked in discussions of other things, perhaps because of a bias in Western culture that generally portrays religion as a human-only affair. But these interactions leave us with two fundamental questions unanswered: Why are religious experiences with nature so diverse? And what does this diversity mean in terms of real-world outcomes for humans, animals, plants, minerals, and water? These are the central questions of this book.

What I will do is shift the discussion of religious experiences with nature from background to foreground, in order that we may better understand the essences and influences of such experiences. Because different religions shape and are shaped by a variety of approaches to the natural world, the discussion will be comparative, finding similarities and differences among several religious forms in context. By doing this, we can better understand how variations of individual religions encourage or deny certain spiritual interactions with nature while we can also better behold the reverse process, in which spiritual experiences with nature may alter the paths taken by individual religious forms.

To illustrate what I mean, take ordinary cows. Many Christians experience cows as soulless sources of food but not as religious sacrifices; Muslims may experience them both as food and as acceptable for religious sacrifices; millions of Buddhists experience them as inappropriate for both food and sacrifices; and Hindus often experience them as living symbols of a divine Mother, worthy of their own rituals, festivals, and bovine old-folks' homes. Why are these experiences of the same animal so diverse?

When we look into an answer to this question, we find that the doctrines and rituals of Christianity guide some followers into experiencing cows as provided by God for human use and therefore perfectly acceptable to kill for food. It never occurs to many Christians that they might venerate a cow instead of eating it or its milk products. On the other hand, Hindu doctrines and rituals lead to experiences of cows as our sacred mothers, so that many Hindus think of cows only in terms of nurturance and never as hamburger. In such and similar ways religions alter how we experience nature. For decades scholars like Steven Katz have argued that religions shape the experiences of their followers, and we see this dynamic with experiences of nature. Paying attention to these processes helps us to answer the question why experiences with nature are so diverse.[13]

If we peek into other religious worlds, we find illustrations of this dynamic of religion's effects on experiences with nature. Take, for instance, the traditional religion of the indigenous Ojibwa group of North America, whose word *ototem* gave us the English word "totem." According to Ojibwa legend, one day long ago several powerful, god-like great beings suddenly appeared from the sea and happily assimilated into the Ojibwa people, becoming totems. Although today we can identify more than twenty-one Ojibwa totems, they are all thought to be variations of the first five: Catfish, Crane, Loon, Bear, and Marten. These totems divide Ojibwa society into smaller clans as holy badges of identity, as one is a Catfish person, Crane person, and so on, as part of one's sense of self. Totems are not chosen but inherited from one's father and ordinarily cannot be changed.

The totems themselves, although in animal form, should not be thought of strictly as physical animals, because their most important aspects are their powerful spiritual essences. Nonetheless the totem's natural characteristics help to create certain personal qualities in humans: Catfish people are expected to have fine hair and long lives; Crane people should be expert orators; Loons are premised to be regal; Bears are expected to have thick, dark hair and be ill-tempered; and Martens should be excellent providers of food.[14]

Ritually, traditional Ojibwa will respect taboos by not eating their totem and by choosing a marriage partner from a different totemic clan, and these practices inform the Ojibwa how to experience nature. For instance, a Catfish-clan woman likely will experience catfish, unlike other animals, as kin so sacred that they cannot be eaten. And because catfish are kin, she may not experience other Catfish-clan people as prospects for marriage but, rather, as extended-family members. Yet a Bear-clan man may have no problem experiencing catfish as a food source and Catfish people as possible spouses. So we see in Ojibwa totemism how specific religious forms encourage specific experiences of nature, helping us to appreciate why religious experiences with nature are so diverse.

Having briefly discussed approaches to the question of why experiences with nature differ so, we should approach the question about alternative outcomes for human and nonhuman beings that arise from experiences with nature. To do this, let us consider leopards: as with all animals, mainstream Christians typically may experience leopards as soulless and religiously irrelevant; in Islam, experience generally instructs us that leopards have souls but will not go to heaven; in Buddhist Tibet, stories inform us that holy men may shape-shift into leopard form to teach disciples; and in Hindu India, sad experience shows us that leopards may be nefariously controlled by the angry ghost of their last human victim and thus need to be managed through religious ritual.

When these diverse experiences express themselves in cultural forms, ripple effects may significantly alter outcomes for leopards and humans alike. For instance, although people respond in a variety of ways, if a dangerous leopard lurks near a human settlement, it could be that a Christian grabs a gun and shoots it without a thought other than for hunting laws, whereas a Hindu may prefer having a holy man perform an exorcism. In this way alternative experiences of leopards create differential practical outcomes for leopards and humans alike, providing us with an approach to the question of what significance differences in natural religious experiences may have. Katherine Wills Perlo studied this dynamic with respect to animals, especially animals used for food; in this book I extend this perspective to include a much broader array of natural beings.[15]

Briefly turning to the Indian religion of Jainism provides a rich example whereby experiences with nature spark real-world outcomes like these. Based on the religious experiences of nature of the saint Mahavira, Jainism teaches that all elements of the natural world, including water and stones, possess a soul, or *jiva*. Because all tangible things have souls, the natural world forms one holy community, and humans are spiritual kin to water, stones, plants, insects, and animals.

But beings can still be distinguished in terms of having one to five senses. One-sense beings have the faculty of touch and include earth, water, fire, and air bodies, microorganisms, and plants. Notice that in the Jain universe, all these one-sense beings are technically animate, as they have souls, unlike in Western discourse. Two-sense beings add the faculty of taste and include worms, leeches, conches, and snails. The sense of smell occurs among three-sense beings, such as most insects and spiders. Vision is added at the fourth level of being, as in flies, scorpions, crickets, and bees. At the level of five-sense beings one finds hearing, as in birds, fish, mammals, reptiles, and humans. Because of reincarnation, all humans likely have been born or will be born as any of these life forms with one to five senses, leaving Jains to experience a deep tie to all forms of existence. Jains experience this kinship through empathy and respect for a broad array of life forms in terms of the dominant value of *ahimsa,* or nonharm to others.

Such experiences have resulted in several cultural outcomes for the Jains, including the establishment of facilities for animal health care. Several hundred Jain animal hospitals are scattered around India, especially in the north. These facilities offer charity health care and nutritive support to a wide variety of animals. Such a facility, for example, is the Jain bird hospital in Delhi, where daily hundreds of birds are fastidiously fed, watered, cleaned, and medicated. Jains maintain similar hospitals for insects and also provide hermitages for lost, ailing, or aged cattle. The exceptional Jain experience of nonviolent kinship also results in notable cultural food rules. The flesh of commonly eaten animals, all of which are five-sensed, is avoided, and so Jains are expected to be vegetarian. Jains should also avoid agriculture, as tilling the soil may harm microorganisms; thus the earth is preserved from plows.

But, as extraordinary as Jain compassion for the natural world is, it has limits. Just like humans, animals in the Jain universe must work off their negative karma through suffering, which acts as a karmic cleanser. This means that animals in Jain hospitals are not euthanized, and in some cases this practice may be perceived as uncaring.

In these ways Jain experiences result in a variety of outcomes for humans and other beings alike. Birds, insects, and cattle enjoy enhanced health-care opportunities, although they may go without compassionate euthanization. Animals are not slaughtered for food. The earth is not tilled under Jain farm implements. And some Jains have become quite wealthy by entering the fields of finance and banking instead of traditional Indian farming.

Of course these two processes, wherein religions alter human and nonhuman experiences and these experiences alter religions, dialectically influence each other. We will see many examples of this mutual influence as we "saunter," as Muir would say, through numerous different forms of religious experience with nature. But before we do this, it would do us good to be armed with four useful terms from the philosophy of nature. These concepts appear in a lot of environmental discourse, because they are helpful paradigms for understanding relationships between humans and nonhuman natural beings.

First, often we find humans asserting their superiority to nature in a way that environmentalists and philosophers call *anthropocentrism*. Anthropocentrism is a point of view that values the human more dearly than any other species or form and favors humans in thought and action. To demonstrate anthropocentrism, I offer the following thought experiment: Imagine that your home is engulfed in flames. You have little time and can save only either your best human friend, Jane, or Sugar, the beloved family cat who is your best animal friend, but not both. Whom do you choose to save, and why? If you choose to save Jane because she is human and Sugar is not, you have favored humanity above another species and thus have chosen anthropocentrically. Many people will make this choice.

When an anthropocentric perspective is advanced most strongly, only humans are valued intrinsically, for themselves, without concern for usefulness, and everything else is valued simply for its use to humans. Weaker versions of this perspective will value some nonhuman things for themselves, like family pets, but still insist that humans retain substantially greater intrinsic value. Either way, with anthropo-centrism the nonhuman natural world in whole or part is valued instru-mentally, simply for whatever service it may provide to humans, and the typical human-to-nature relationship is one of superiority and dominance.

Biocentrism represents another paradigm for understanding human interactions with nature. With biocentrism, all beings considered in Western discourse to be living or animate, such as humans, animals, and plants, are valued for themselves, without concern for human use, although the worlds of minerals and water remain valued significantly less. When people say that they care for all *living* things, they express a sense of biocentrism. Biocentrism expresses a living moral community shared between humans and animals, and on occasion plants, and the typical form of relationship involves cooperation between humans, ani-mals, and plants.

Plants often mark boundaries in biocentric perspectives. Given that humans frequently treat plants unreflectively, as lifeless objects that we may use as we please, sometimes we encounter statements of respect for all living things that, on closer inspection, reveal respect for ani-mals but not for plants. Even among some vegetarians, who claim to be nature-friendly but in fact sometimes have a limited vision of the natu-ral world, plants remain forgotten or rejected from value. Consider a codicil in the Statement of Faith of the Unity School of Christianity, which argues for a vegetarian lifestyle: "We believe that all life is sacred and that humans should not kill or be a party to the killing of animals for food." Although this statement is friendly toward animals used for human food, it clearly, if implicitly, does not embrace plants within its understanding that "all life is sacred," despite plants' being living enti-ties. If eating meat implicitly condones the killing of animals, this state-ment of the Unity School (and others like it) likewise implicitly con-dones the killing of plants, which is not very nature-friendly from a botanical point of view. The fact that we must eat plants to live does not change this formulation's narrow inclusion of intrinsic value for animals that are used as food but exclusion of plants from such value, a limit that we will explore more extensively in chapter 6.[16]

Often, but not always, arguments for excluding plants from value ground themselves on the preciousness of animals because of their similarities with humans. Animals, having locomotion, specialized sensory organs like eyes, and central nervous systems, look more like us, and the philosopher Montaigne taught us that, for some people, "Nothing is worth anything if it does not look like us." But however one may choose to argue the point, the commonly found limited biocentric position that asserts substantial intrinsic value for animals but not plants may better be described as *zoacentrism,* or human-and-animal-centered, as the Greek *zoa* denotes animals, both human and nonhuman. Zoacentrism is not fully biocentric in terms of finding nonuse value for *all* forms of life.[17]

Full biocentrism, on the other hand, regards all forms of plant life as intrinsically valuable, on par with humans and other animals. Full biocentrism potentially avoids pitfalls commonly found with zoacentrism because it more fully embraces the phrase "all living beings." As an example, Manichaean Christians, vegetarians like members of the Unity School, differ from the latter by not justifying vegetarianism by overlooking plants. On the contrary, Manicheans practice vegetarianism because, in their perspective, plants are more pure and sacred than animals; and so if one wishes a blessing from nature, one should eat only plants. But full biocentrism like this faces difficulties of its own. Should we allow other plants to choke out the wheat crop because all plants have an equal right to live? Should we use antibiotic substances to kill bacteria, which are living things?

One more philosophical position demands mention. *Ecocentrism* is an approach to nature that values all existent things in the natural world, including inanimate things like rocks and lakes, for themselves, without concern for human use. The center of value is not just in particular entities, such as humans alone or humans and animals, but in the natural world in its entirety. Philosophically holistic, an ecocentric attitude intrinsically values all (or almost all) natural forms, including humans, animals, plants, bodies of water, and stones big and small. Humans are still valued as part of the larger natural world but as rough peers with, rather than masters over, other forms in nature. Within ecocentric perspectives, images of relationship with the natural world tend to include notions of partnership and sometimes express a sense of human-nature kinship. In Muir's case, his valuation of rivers, stones, animals, and flowers as peers, "brothers," "friendly, fellow mountaineers," "God's people," and "so-called lifeless rocks" reflects an ecocentric philosophy.

It is of interest that ecocentric worldviews sometimes understand things like stones and lakes to be living, conscious beings, as we saw with the Jains, thus making problematic familiar words in English such as "living," "animate," or "person." For instance, a river that is a goddess is "living"; a stone with a soul literally is not "inanimate," a word derived from the Latin for " soulless"; and the sun is a "person" when reverentially addressed as "Grandfather," as many indigenous humans do. Further, although in this book I use terms like "humans," "nature," and "natural world" within the context of dominant Euro-American paradigms in order that I may connect with my presumed reader, these terms too take on different meanings within ecocentric worldviews that regard the human world and the natural world as one and the same reality. If humans truly *are* nature, then we cannot speak of humans and nature as separate realities, as is common in Western discourse.

Perhaps an analogy will help to clarify the meanings of anthropocentrism, zoacentrism, biocentrism, and ecocentrism. If we understand the natural world as a complete jigsaw puzzle, consisting of many pieces, anthropocentrism may regard humans as spectators outside of and looking down upon the puzzle. Zoacentrism may regard humans as part of a puzzle that includes animals but not plants, minerals, or water, whereas full biocentrism would include plants in this puzzle. An ecocentric view would regard humans as just one among many puzzle pieces that comprehensively include the human, animal, plant, mineral, and water realms.

We can see how these concepts help us to understand religion if we return to Muir's life. John Muir was not raised to be a nature mystic, since his father, Daniel Muir, strictly followed Calvinist Christianity before enthusiastically joining the new, at the time, denomination of Disciples of Christ. When John was a boy, his father coerced the entire Muir household into daily Bible study as well as rigid adherence to his own biblical interpretations. Daniel Muir's severe understanding of the Protestant Christian tradition included a strong transcendental element, in which the invisible God remains aloof from creation and thereby does not incarnate in earthly forms, aside from Jesus. Moreover, the Muir family's beliefs embraced a traditional reading of Genesis 1:26–28, the biblical verses in which God grants humanity "dominion" over animals and plants, as well as permission to use nature for human benefit. As with many Christians, to the Muirs nature was devoid of any religious relevance aside from, perhaps, as an example of God's magnificent handiwork for human benefit. Thus, to the rest of his family, John's talk of meeting "flower people" seemed eccentric, even crazy. For most of the Muirs, nonhuman natural forms possessed no value except as means to human ends.

Such religious attitudes toward the natural world took tangible shape at Fountain Lake, the Muir family farm in Wisconsin. Following his interpretation of the biblical view that the natural world exists for the sake of humans to use as they please, John's father, Daniel, heedlessly rode a horse literally to death, blithely shot an innocuous puppy, and nearly shot a horse simply for harassing cattle. Moreover, not only did he destroy rich forests by inefficiently clearing land for farming; within a few years he had exhausted that cleared soil by overplanting. At least in part because of his religious beliefs regarding human superiority, John's father carelessly drove his natural environment to its demise.

These actions fueled animosity within his sensitive son John, who came to hate the "dreary work" of clearing land. He had loved the family land at Fountain Lake best when it was untamed "pure wildness" that offered "baptism in Nature's warm heart." In response, he mentally escaped while at home by reading travelogues of the natural worlds of South America and Africa. Later, at the University of Wisconsin, he began to revise his inherited worldview by embracing more liberal Christian views as taught to him by his mentors, Professor Ezra Carr and his botanist wife, Jeanne.[18]

Muir fully developed as a nature mystic only after he had left home for good as an adult. His wanderings first on the "floral pilgrimage" to Florida and later in Yosemite not only offered him constant reminders of nature's magnificence; they also allowed him plenty of time to reconsider his beliefs and, most especially, to alter his mode of experience of nature's sacredness. Although he had always been a spiritual partner with the natural world, it was only in the freedom from his upbringing in his late thirties that his encounter with nature as divine maximally blossomed, resulting in what he described while in Yosemite as a "conversion." The therapists Aaron Katcher and Alan Beck tell us that "the active contemplation of the natural world" enables "the ability to reduce tension and to integrate the sense of self," and this description fits Muir's development. The man who invented a better sawmill and the "early-rising machine" now invented a new, heterodox, entirely personal form of nature mystical Christianity.[19]

His new religion diverged in significant ways from that of his childhood. Although he retained a measure of distant-God transcendence in his concept of the deity, Muir's new god also manifested immanently by dwelling in worldly, physical forms. Muir disposed of the remote deity of his Protestant heritage in favor of a living divinity that resided in and oozed sacred energy through animals, plants, rivers, and mountains. In a decidedly un-Calvinist manner, the adult Muir was a panentheist, as he regarded nature and God as linked and overlapping yet not identical, like the rings of the logo for the Olympic Games.

As well, long gone was the sense of human superiority of his inherited form of Christianity in favor of an ecocentric philosophy. His later ecocentrism regarded humanity as just one facet of a vast, interconnected natural world. Rather than anthropocentrism's projection of human superiority and dominance over nature, his nature-centered perspective embraced a wealth of natural beings as partners. Philosophically, this was a major shift.

These personal religious innovations of Muir's—an immanent God in the world and an ecocentric web of peerlike connections with nature—coalesced in his personal, noninstitutional, and Christian nature mysticism. Although he worshipped alongside redwoods and spiders, he revealed that he grounded his experiences within a Christian framework when, in a letter to his friend Professor Catherine Merrill, he wrote:

> I wish you could come here and rest a year in the simple unmingled love fountains of God. You would then return to your scholars with fresh truth gathered and absorbed from pines and waters and deep singing winds, and you would find that they all sang of fountain Love just as did Jesus Christ and all of pure God manifest in whatever form.

Describing his stay in Yosemite as "revival time," he spoke not of bathing in waterfalls but instead of being "baptized" by them. He cited Matthew 6:28 in following and encouraging others to follow Jesus's advice to "consider the lilies." And he even implicitly compared the sequoia to Jesus in calling it "King" (of the Jews) and by saying: "The King tree and I have sworn eternal love—sworn it without swearing, and I have taken the sacrament with Douglas squirrel, drank Sequoia wine, Sequoia blood." Yet Muir told us that his new Christianity opposed biblical anthropocentrism:[20]

> You say that good men are "nearer to the heart of God than are woods and fields, rocks and waters." Such distinctions and measurements seem strange to me. Rocks and waters, etc., are words of God and so are humans. We all flow from one fountain Soul. All are expressions of one Love. God does not appear, and flow out, only from narrow chinks and round bored wells here and there in favored races and places, but He flows in grand undivided currents, shoreless and boundless over creeds and forms and all kinds of civilizations and peoples and beasts, saturating all.

Muir in fact trenchantly criticized his contemporaries' sense of human superiority:[21]

> The world, we are told, was made especially for humans—a presumption not supported by all the facts.... It never seems to occur to these farseeing teachers that nature's object in making animals and plants might possibly be first of all the happiness of each one of them, not the creation of all for the happiness of one [humanity].

Because of this, "No wonder the hills and groves were God's first temples, and the more they are cut down, and hewn into cathedrals and churches, the farther off and dimmer seems the Lord himself."[22]

Muir's Druidlike respect for hills and groves as places of worship reflects both the naturalistic immanence and the sincere ecocentrism that fused into his revised nature mystical religiosity. He already possessed the ascetic habits of a monk, as he lived simply and hardily, and he traveled light. With these habits he combined a meditator's concentrated attention upon what he considered holy. Always an opponent of hunting, he also voluntarily adopted the value of nonharm, which is so common among mystics. For instance, he once visited the Grand Canyon with members of the nascent National Forestry Commission, a forerunner to the United States Forest Service, and during the tour one commissioner, Gifford Pinchot, wished to kill a large tarantula. Muir restrained him, saying: "It has as much right there as we."[23]

The conjunction of these forces resulted in a series of profound mystical experiences for Muir of nature as incarnate divinity. As he wrote in *My First Summer in the Sierras:* "More and more, in a place like this, we feel ourselves part of wild nature, kin to everything." Muir supported this ecocentric sense of kinship biblically, by highlighting that all natural forms, including stones and water, are the differently clothed sons and daughters of the same creator. He claimed: "The very stones seem talkative, sympathetic, brotherly. No wonder when we consider that we all have the same father and mother."[24]

But to Muir, natural beings were not just kin; they were sacred kin in the process of constant revelation of their holiness, "pulsing with the heartbeats of God." As he put it: "All the wilderness seems to be full of tricks and plans to drive and draw us up into God's light." Experiencing this vibrant, sacred kinship led him to a spiritual communion with the totality of his natural surroundings. In his journal Muir wrote: "The trees, the mountains are not near or far; they are made one, unseparate, unclothed, open to the divine soul, dissolved in the mysterious incomparable spirit of holy light!"[25]

These mystical stirrings were highly emotional for Muir, as he once "shouted and gesticulated in a wild burst of ecstasy" at a gorgeous vista across the Sierras. On another occasion, contemplation of the holy beauty of his surroundings caused him to spring to his feet and shout: "Heaven and earth! Rock is not light, not heavy, but is transparent and unfathomable as the sky itself. Every pore gushes, glows like a thought with immortal life." In Muir's nature religion, a true encounter with nature demands a direct, numinous, whole-being experience of the divinity of the entire natural world. The philosopher of mysticism W. T. Stace showed us that one of the hallmarks of nature mysticism is strong emotion, whether it be bursting joy, placid serenity, or some other affect, and we see this emotional power in Muir's religiosity.[26]

It was this heterodox Christian nature mysticism that drove Muir for the rest of his life as a prolific author about nature, founder of the Sierra Club, and advocate for the national park system in the United States, as these influential conservation activities were an outgrowth of his effort to "preach Nature." As such, Muir's life teaches us several lessons. To begin with, Muir's spirituality highlights the process in which religions shape experiences with nature. From the time as a child when he used the Bible to learn to read and until his last day, Muir remained a self-identifying Christian, if a heretical one compared with the mainstream. If he wished as an adult to abandon the Christianity of his childhood, he could have approached nature purely technically and scientifically, without a spiritual side, as so many other biologists have done; yet this was not his path. Perhaps he learned indigenous natural mysticism from one of his many Native American acquaintances, but Muir, to my knowledge, never expressed himself in this way. Instead Muir described experiences that were Christian upon occurrence and Christian in later interpretation, even if it was a Christianity somewhat of his own devising. Thus Muir arguably experienced two types of Christianity, the Protestant version in which he was raised and the heterodox nature mystical variety that he developed within himself. The natural world in which the adult Muir was so completely immersed was a Christian natural world, a physical embodiment of the Christian God. His religious upbringing powerfully shaped how he perceived nature, and it helps to explain why he had the experiences that he did.

If we peer at the outcomes of Muir's experiences with nature, we recognize that his childhood religious experiences, informed as they were by notions of human superiority, would have made a poor platform for his later conservation efforts. It is logically incoherent to argue that nature exists solely for the sake of humans and simultaneously maintain that national parks should exist to preserve trees for their own sake. Even if, as it seems, Muir always had the seed of a mystic within him, if he had obediently maintained the religion of his childhood, he might not now be recognized as a great naturalist. Instead he developed his own unique and very personal form of Christian belief and practice oriented toward sacred animals, plants, minerals, and water, and the resulting passion fueled a vigorous life spent in defense of the wilderness. In Muir's case, different experiences of Christianity and nature created alternative outcomes. Thus if we inquire about the meaning of his religious experiences with nature for humans and nonhumans, we need look no further than the National Park System of the United States.

Over the rest of this book I tease out other examples of the dialectical processes in which religions help to determine experiences with nature while experiences with nature alter the shapes of religions. It is of course impossible in one book to account for more than a small fraction of religious experiences with nature, so I select paradigmatic examples to serve as representative case treatments, with each religious world contributing a distinctive model of human relationship with nature, such as enlightened limited partnership, mother and child, or tempered human dominion.

No religion in this study—or, presumably, anywhere—presents us with one, simple way of experiencing the natural world. The anthropologist Brian Morris claims that "all human societies have diverse, multifaceted, and often contradictory attitudes toward the natural world"; and religions are no different in their assorted and sometimes conflicting experiences with nature. In their attitudes toward nature, religious worlds are like stained-glass windows, as they consist of separate pieces embodying many disparate hues, yet expressive patterns still may be discerned. Because of this, all the models that I explore are inherently tensive and ambiguous, such as animals are worthy of love but not of a meaningful place in religion, humans are separate from but deeply interwoven with nature, or humans favor themselves but remain peer friends with natural beings.[27]

For example, chapter 1, "All the Christian Birds Chanted," visits an innovative Christian pet blessing ceremony in order to go beyond the marginal heterodoxy of John Muir and more fully explore religious experiences with nature in the Christian tradition. Looked at historically, Christians have long loved animals, as the church portrays some animals as friends of saints, frowns upon the practice of animal sacrifice, and documents sporadic occasions when animals practice religion. But it is also generally true that in Christianity animals, like all other natural beings, stand inferior to humans, who alone have salvific souls and exercise dominion over the natural world. In the end we discover that Christianity, while embodying many different outlooks, provides a model in which animals have been worthy of sometimes-lavish love but not worthy of salvation or an authentic place at the communion table. However, pet blessing ceremonies like those described provide a contemporary grassroots challenge to this historical legacy.

In chapter 2, "The Donkey Who Communed with Allah," I probe experiences with nature in the Islamic world. Historically Islam inherited strong attitudes of human superiority to the natural world from Judaism, Christianity, and Greek philosophy. Nonetheless, Islam's approaches to the natural world differ from those of its Abrahamic cousin religions, as many animals fare better under Islam due to Quranic injunctions, theological innovations, and cultural traditions. Islam inspires a measure of spiritual respect for natural beings, because they form communities as do human beings, sometimes possess souls, may rarely serve as religious guides, and even more rarely have mystical experiences of their own. At the same time, humans remain firmly superior to the rest of the natural world. Islam thus leaves us with noblesse oblige as our primary model of relationship with the natural world, wherein superior humans must care gently and well for inferior animals.

In an alternative to this Abrahamic religious situation, chapter 3, "Hindu Trees Tremble with Ecstasy," ethnographically explores the roles of sacred rivers, plants, and cows in Gaudiya Vaishnavism, one sect of the Hindu tradition. Fieldwork at a Hindu ashram reveals devotees who spiritually reverence cattle as holy mothers through rituals, dietary practices, and the establishment and operation of a large no-kill cattle sanctuary. These Hindus also reverence Tulsi, the holy basil plant, as a mother goddess in both belief and ritual. India's sacred rivers enhance this sense of the Divine Mother, as they are thought to be living, watery incarnations of benevolent mother goddesses. Therefore in this chapter we find powerful mother-child images of human relationship with sacred nature. But we also find limits to the veneration of nature as our mother, such as the need to control dangerous snakes.

In chapter 4, "Sharing Mayan Natural Souls," we investigate the traditional world of the contemporary Maya of Central America. From ancient times Mayan religions have insisted on a religious obligation of reciprocal sacred action among humans, many natural beings, and gods. Through this ethic, the Maya live within a deep network of interrelationships with sacred nature yet remain distinctly human. In a variety of ways, including the sharing of souls with animals, shamanic transformations into jaguar form, and agricultural nature mysticism in the cornfield, the Maya world leaves us with a model of relationship in which humans remain discrete from but closely interwoven with the nonhuman natural world, and human fulfillment occurs in terms not of overcoming nature as an individual but of entering nature more deeply.

Chapter 5, "Friendly Yetis," presents a picture of a sacred human-animal hybrid in the form of the legendary yeti. Setting aside questions regarding the material existence of yetis, in examining Tibetan folk beliefs we find that yetis are thought to exist in a vaguely defined realm between human and animal and thus have simultaneous human and animal characteristics. When yetis are at their most human, they are gentle beings who may practice religion or pose as nice friends. When they are mostly animal, it is because they are holy incarnations of local mountain gods, charged with keeping order by enforcing the mountain gods' will. Yeti folklore thus imparts to us experiences in which sacredness appears as both human and animal at once, with varying results, thus highlighting the essential ambivalence with which humans approach natural forms.

In chapter 6, "Enlightened Buddhist Stones," we return to the expansive vision of John Muir but in a dramatically different package. Intensive fieldwork at a Vietnamese Buddhist monastery uncovers doctrines in which humans recognize their deep interconnections with the natural world, broadly conceived, as part of the path to the goal of nirvana. Living among stones considered to be Buddhas, the monks and nuns adopt nonviolent and environmentally friendly lifestyles and forms of practice. They learn spiritual lessons from trees, tigers, snakes, storms, and a variety of other natural entities. While some other chapters in this book focus by necessity mainly on animals, this chapter teaches us that stones and water can be enlightened, too. But with the help of practices from the Cheyenne First Nations group, we also learn about some of the limitations of such a broad spiritual regard for the natural world.

As we travel through two Abrahamic religions, two Asian high religions, and two geographically disparate folk traditions, we will find experiences with nature that may be unfamiliar to Westerners, who are not used to worshipping lakes or receiving spiritual teachings from trees. For instance, in the Christian Acts of Peter, a dog raises its front paws in the air and uses human speech to preach. But such experiences, which exhibit a sense of partnership with nature, are valuable for their unfamiliarity, because they teach us new ways of looking at the world. These varying and interesting experiences often show genuine concern for natural beings who are considered companions, gurus, or divinities and reveal a touching sense of human partnership not just with animals but also with flowers, lakes, and mountains. Also, since many of these stories really are more about humans than about natural beings, they betray operative human attitudes toward the natural world, and we can learn much by studying these attitudes. As the historian Keith Thomas has said: "For all the defects of imaginative literature as a historical source, there is nothing to surpass it as a guide to the thoughts and feelings of at least the more articulate sections of the population." Thus, if we look behind the foreign or magical elements of some stories, we just may find some useful hardheaded advice. Indeed, we will find that in some of these stories elements emerge that accord with contemporary scientific research. Or, as the Chinese classic *The Journey to the West* puts it: "When creatures can speak human language, they generally tell the truth."[28]

Along with these moments of genuine partnership with nature, in each religion we also will find attitudes of human superiority of some type, since religion frequently aids and abets the myth of human superiority. Among the many variable religious forms that we will study, human-centered attitudes appear constantly, although they are manifested in varying ways. This seems unsurprising, since members of many species show favoritism to their own kind. But along with the universality of human-centeredness, we will see that each religious form distinctively includes alternative animal- or environment-friendly elements, just as a quilt blends individual patches. In the milieu of Abrahamic religions anthropocentrism predominates, but in other religious worlds sometimes biocentric and ecocentric perspectives occupy center stage, with anthropocentrism somewhat marginalized, as we have already seen with the eccentric Muir and will see again among Hindus, Maya, Buddhists, and Himalayan residents.

Because the religions in this study all embrace in some way the myth of human superiority, we discover a grim conclusion: just as humans frequently treat their conspecifics with selfishness and arrogance and even feel noble in doing so, so do we often treat animals and other natural beings with selfishness and arrogance, especially since they cannot complain in a language that we understand well. Since we have not yet extinguished human-on-human slavery, we may be saddened but not surprised when humans treat natural ones like slaves as well.

Senses of human superiority may lead us to do terrible things to natural beings even when we claim to love them. Pet-parrot caregivers often love their birds, but parrots are now endangered in their home jungles, not just because of habitat loss but also because of the trade in pet birds. Cases of animal hoarding are familiar, where an attitude of the animals' needing human care leads people to adopt more pets than they can properly nurture. Exotic animals like tigers are collected because we need to save tigers, only to have caregivers discover that managing a tiger in the back yard is more difficult than they expected. Further, numerous studies have shown that we often approach pets as substitutes for other humans, leading us to psychologically exploit animals while we claim to be loving them. From this, we often treat pet animals as humans, when instead animal experts tell us we should respect them as dogs, cats, or other creatures with their own species-specific existential affairs and concerns. Moreover, to preserve our treasured pets and livestock we fence our homes and roads, thus inhibiting members of many different species from freely seeking food, water, and mates as they organically would. Personally, as a so-called animal lover I have two pet dogs in my back yard, but they kill every rabbit, squirrel, gopher, and gecko that enters the yard; the rabbits involved may not consider my pet keeping fully to reflect love of animals—should rabbits, in their own ways, actually ponder such things. Thus there seems to be substance to the groan of George Bernard Shaw that precious animals sometimes "bear more than their natural burden of human love." As it is with love toward our fellow humans, perhaps we would do better if we were to pay more attention to developing unselfishness in our love toward others and spend less time insisting on how much we love.[29]

The philosopher Mary Midgley claims that a sense of superiority to other species is normal for all beings. The cat that enjoys slowly taunting its prey before killing it appears to be expressing an experience of dominance, for just one example. But this provokes questions: Can cats, or any other species, really claim to be superior? Just as humans consider themselves superior for their intelligence, may not eagles be considered the superior species because humans cannot match their ability to fly? May dolphins be considered superior beings for the way that they swim? In the end, are not all standards of superiority simply in the eye of the beholder? The philosopher Montaigne posed the issue this way: "When I play with my cat, how do I know that she is not passing time with me rather than I with her?" Or, as Xenophanes put it in the sixth century B.C.E.:[30]

> But if cattle (or horses) or lions had hands,
> And were able to draw with their hands and do works as humans do,
> Horses would draw the forms of gods like horses,
> And cows like cows, and figure their bodies
> The same as they themselves have.

Therefore we may do well to reconsider the myth of human superiority, which portrays humanity as qualitatively better than all nonhuman natural beings. Throughout history many reasons have been put forward for humanity's superiority: intellect, possession of emotions, ability to make tools, ability to reason, ability to create art, ability to suffer, possession of organized social groups, possession of culture, language ability, ability to think for the future, and ability to act morally, among others. All these standards have been debunked in their qualitative formulations in recent years by scientists who study animal behavior, thus scientifically eliminating many arguments in favor of the myth of human superiority. Previously perceived barriers between humans and nonhuman nature have been shown to be differences of degree, not of kind, or not to exist at all. Instead, animal-behavior specialists such as Donald Griffin, Franz de Waal, and Marc Bekoff increasingly stress the continuity with rather than the divergence of humans and other animals in terms of reason, emotion, and behavior. In this book we study these perspectives from religious points of view and question the myth of human superiority in terms of another marker of supposed human superiority: the ability to practice religion. This study presents numerous stories in which animals are said to engage in religion, and especially in the epilogue I explore the question of how we may understand such tales.

Whether humans are superior to natural beings or not, it remains true that only if we understand both experienced human superiority to nature and partnership with nature can we understand who we are, where we have been, and where we are going if we wish to positively, beneficially, and authentically experience the natural world. Examining religious experiences with nature highlights how we may have gotten ourselves in trouble with the natural world but also how we may get out of trouble. Learning more about the natural world aids our understanding of other beings in our environment on their own terms, and this knowledge can then be parlayed into relationships with our neighbors in the nonhuman universe that are mutually constructive to a greater degree.

I

All the Christian Birds Chanted

The weather reports predicted a dire tropical storm for the first Sunday in October, the day of the Blessing of the Pets at All Saints Episcopal Church in the southeastern United States, but I was not going to miss the opportunity. Since it is one of the most popular church days of the year, other folks were not going to miss it either, and I arrived to find a church room filled with twenty-four dogs, two cats, their caregivers, and other congregants. An image of Francis of Assisi, the Christian patron saint of animals, adorned the cover of the day's program, and the service praised Francis many times. The atmosphere was both solemn and lighthearted, engendering jokes along with serious religion. When the chief pastor, Reverend John, entreated the congregation *Let us pray,* a wolfhound who had otherwise been silent began to bark, eliciting peals of good-natured laughter. After this prayer, instead of the traditional request to the congregation, *Please be seated,* Reverend John insisted, *Sit!* as one would command a dog, again prompting happy guffaws from the group. During quiet moments in the service, congregants and pets noiselessly socialized freely and for the most part amiably, although the cats remained quite concerned about the canine gathering that surrounded them.

An assistant pastor started the service with a reading from Genesis 1:20–31, a passage to which I will return:[1]

And God said, "Let the waters bring forth swarms of living creatures, and let birds fly above the earth across the firmament of the heavens." So God created the great sea monsters and every living creature that moves, with which the waters swarm, according to their kinds, and every winged bird according to its kind. And God saw that it was good. And God blessed them, saying, "Be fruitful and multiply and fill the waters in the seas, and let birds multiply on the earth."

And there was evening and there was morning, a fifth day.

And God said, "Let the earth bring forth living creatures according to their kinds: cattle and creeping things and beasts of the earth according to their kinds." And it was so. And God made the beasts of the earth according to their kinds and the cattle according to their kinds, and everything that creeps upon the ground according to its kind. And God saw that it was good. Then God said, "Let us make humanity in our image, after our likeness; and let them have dominion over the fish of the sea, and over the birds of the air, and over the cattle, and over all the earth, and over every creeping thing that creeps upon the earth." So God created humanity in his own image, in the image of God he created him; male and female he created them.

And God blessed them, and God said to them, "Be fruitful and multiply, and fill the earth and subdue it; and have dominion over the fish of the sea and over the birds of the air and over every living thing that moves upon the earth." And God said, "Behold, I have given you every plant yielding seed which is upon the face of all the earth, and every tree with seed in its fruit; you shall have them for food. And to every beast of the earth, and to every bird of the air, and to everything that creeps on the earth, everything that has the breath of life, I have given every green plant for food." And it was so. And God saw everything that he had made, and behold, it was very good. And there was evening and there was morning, a sixth day.

After this, a reading of Psalm 148 encouraged the congregation to praise God and to recognize nature's praise of God. Then Reverend John delivered the sermon. Claiming that humans are not the only species on earth whom God loves, Reverend John implored us to thank pets for the good things they bring to us and mentioned his own experience with Stripes, his rescue kitten. Stripes, he told us, is a good teacher, because like Francis of Assisi he practices what he preaches and so has helped to lead Reverend John to God's teachings about love, compassion, and trust. After this sermon, congregants silently joined Reverend John in the Blessing of the Animals prayer:

> Most high, almighty Lord, our Creator, yours are the praise, the glory, the honor and all blessings! To you alone do all things belong. Be praised for giving us the animals, birds and fish which fill your world. May we think of you and thank you when we play with and care for our pets. Be praised for making us so happy to have our pets and to have them to play with. We ask you, Lord, that we may be good to our pets always, so that they may be happy also. Help us always to take care of them so that they will be healthy. O God, your world is wonderful. May we all come into your even greater world of the kingdom of heaven, where we shall see even more wonderful things, and where we shall live and love for ever. This we ask to your eternal praise, and to our blessing. Amen.

As is standard Episcopal Church practice, an assistant pastor sanctified the service with sweet incense from the smoking censer he waved while walking through the sanctuary. Then he walked through the sanctuary again and, using a long-handled spoon, sent sprinkles of holy water throughout the church, these drops landing on humans and pets alike. In this way the pets in attendance were blessed.

When it came time for the Eucharist, the offering of bread and wine, leashed pets and their humans approached the altar in a line. First came Dale, smartly dressed in a white shirt and tie, with his schnauzer projecting an attitude every bit as regal as Dale's. A poor young lady in an African-print skirt followed, struggling with one Labrador retriever who could not wait to get to the altar and another Lab, who pulled in the opposite direction to play with dogs in the back of the church. Then Cora, in a blue flower-print dress, was led by her energetic husky dog Skipper to the altar.

Following the others, Skipper and Cora went first to the right of the altar, where an attendant gave Skipper a smile, a pat on the head, and an ordinary dog biscuit (cats got fish-flavored treats). Then Skipper and

Cora moved to their left, where the chief pastor offered a smile to Skipper and consecrated bread and wine to Cora. Then Skipper and Cora returned to their seats. In this way all twenty-six pets and their humans made it through the Communion ritual in surprisingly good order. The service ended after the Eucharist, and Skipper and Cora went home. Cora was satisfied that she had fulfilled her religious obligations to herself and was happy to have included Skipper in the religion of Jesus. Skipper seemed glad to have enjoyed a snack and lots of friendly pats from strangers.

Such events with animals in the church are exceptional, as they would not have happened even a few years ago. Christianity has a long history of blessing working farm animals on the feast day of St. Anthony Abbot in January, and globally there still are working-animal blessing rituals done in connection with Anthony. But it is only since the 1980s that we find an explosion of blessing ceremonies specifically for pets rather than for working animals, like the one that Skipper attended. Most of these new rituals appeal to St. Francis of Assisi rather than St. Anthony, and they are timed for Francis's feast day, October 4. The scholar of Christianity and animals Laura Hobgood-Oster traces this pet blessing movement to the Cathedral of St. John the Divine in New York City in the 1980s, followed by emulators then spreading rapidly to virtually every state in the United States. This reorientation of the ritual of the blessing of farm animals derives from many Christian pet keepers who want their beloved pets to participate in their religion, as they participate in other family activities, and this expansive movement spawns numerous Internet sites such as blessingoftheanimals. com. Some commentators cite influence from New Age sources in energizing this movement, and others mention the movement's interfaith character. The adoption of this ritual, often in an ad-hoc form, changes the Christian world in practice, if not yet in theory, as animals come to church now far more than ever before in Christianity's two-thousand-year history. This situation begs the following questions: Why is this unprecedented, historic movement happening now and taking the forms that it does? What may be the positive effects of this innovation? How should its practitioners, and their animal friends, understand their places in Christian history?[2]

Answering these questions highlights two principal approaches to nature in the Christian world. On one hand, Christians have deeply loved animals, as the church has understood animals as friends of saints, who have prayed for and protected a variety of species. The church also self-consciously did away with the practice of animal sacrifice that was so widespread in the ancient Mediterranean world. At times animals even practice religion like humans, as a donkey shows spiritual insight, birds pray and prophesy, a variety of animals venerate saints, crickets celebrate the Mass, and in apocryphal texts lions receive baptism. Christians also express love for animals through the recent creative expansion of pet blessing ceremonies like Skipper's.

But it is also generally true that in Christianity animals, like all other natural beings, stand inferior to humans, who exercise dominion over them. Normally animals are thought to lack souls and therefore relevance in the quest for salvation, usually resulting in the extreme marginalization of animals within Christianity, as we have already seen in Muir's childhood brand of it. Across the three branches of Roman Catholicism, Orthodoxy, and Protestantism, major Christian thinkers consistently have allotted high places to humans and low places to animals—if they have even thought about animals at all. Because of this relative lack of regard for natural entities, Laura Hobgood-Oster, who works as hard as anyone to make Christianity more animal-friendly, nonetheless morosely laments that animals have "no input whatsoever with respect to theology and practices.... Christianity seems to embody the pinnacle of the religion of 'the human.' ... Christianity generates a gulf between human animals and all other animals that might be impossible to bridge." So what we find in this chapter is that Christianity, although embodying many different outlooks, historically considers animals worthy of sometimes lavish love but not worthy of salvation, equality with humans, or a true place in religion. The new blessing-of-the-pets movement arises as something of a challenge to this legacy.[3]

To understand properly how these attitudes of love for and superiority over animals coexist, we need to survey some Christian theological history, beginning with Egypt in antiquity. Around the time of Jesus's birth, Greeks, Romans, and Jews remarked, sometimes derisively, about the intensity with which ancient Egyptians reverenced animals. Egyptians regarded animals such as falcons, ibises, rams, gazelles, baboons, dogs, cats, mongooses, shrews, crocodiles, snakes, scorpions, and scarab beetles as sacred through their intimate associations with various gods, so they were protected by royal decrees. Egyptian temples typically enshrined live animals as objects of veneration, the most famous of these temple animals being the Apis Bull of Memphis, who symbolized the nation as the presence on earth of the creator deity, Ptah. When one Apis Bull died, the nation both mourned the dead bull and celebrated as another bull was anointed. After death, such temple animals received very elaborate funerals, which included full-scale mummification. These mummies might later be used for divination by priests, who would, through a ritual called incubation, sleep in the temple and wait for the animal's spirit to send a prophetic dream.[4]

Such animal veneration dismayed Greeks and Romans, who preferred anthropomorphic gods; likewise dismayed were the great Christian evangelist Paul, who counseled against animal worship in Romans 1:22–23, and the early Christian leader Clement of Alexandria (ca. 150–215 C.E.), who in his *Paedagogus* wrote of Egyptian temples:[5]

The temples sparkle with gold, silver and mat gold and flash with coloured stones from India and Ethiopia. The sanctuaries are overshadowed by cloths studded with gold. If, however, you enter the interior of the enclosure, hastening towards the sight of the almighty and look for the statue residing in the temple and if a *pastophoros* [shrine priest] or another celebrant, after having solemnly looked round the sanctuary, singing a song in the language of the Egyptians, draws back the curtain a little to show the god, he will make us laugh about the object of worship. For we shall not find the god for whom we have been looking inside, the god towards whom we have hastened, but a cat or a crocodile, or a native snake or a similar animal, which should not be in a temple, but in a cleft or a den or on a dung heap. The god of the Egyptians appears on a purple couch as a wallowing animal.

Clement's disdain for "wallowing" animals exemplifies a primary Christian approach to the natural world, which begins with the biblical passage from Genesis 1:20–31 that we saw previously, and passages like this from Psalms 8:3–8:

> When I look at thy heavens, the work of thy fingers,
> the moon and the stars which thou hast established;
> what is man that thou art mindful of him,
> and the son of man that thou dost care for him?
> Yet thou hast made him little less than God,
> and dost crown him with glory and honor.
> Thou hast given him dominion over the works of thy hands;
> thou hast put all things under his feet,
> all sheep and oxen,
> and also the beasts of the field,
> the birds of the air, and the fish of the sea,
> whatever passes along the paths of the sea.

These biblical passages from Genesis and Psalms clarify several things regarding human relationships with natural beings. First, humans, and only humans, are made in God's image. Waterfalls may thrill, and hawks amaze, but only humans rejoice in the divine imprint. This instantly elevates humans above all other natural beings, as a human is worth more than "many sparrows" (Luke 12:7). But there is more. Genesis 1, Psalms 8, and other biblical passages explicitly enjoin humans to enjoy "dominion" over nature and be managers, as it were, of the natural world. The earth, in fact, should be "subdued." What this means has been debated often, of course. Descriptions for "dominion" have included "to shepherd," "to lead about," "to govern," "to dominate despotically," or "to tame." Some contemporary Christians use the word "stewardship" rather than "dominion," emphasizing that God is the owner and humans manage nature simply on loan. But whether it is the word "dominion" or "stewardship" that one chooses to use, in the Christian universe humans generally are empowered managers of the natural world and have significant discretion in how they manage things. This sense of superior human command of inferior nature historically has permeated all three Abrahamic religions, Judaism, Christianity, and Islam.[6]

These biblical notions of human superiority are central in Christianity, having been bolstered with such elements of Greek philosophy as the Great Chain of Being. This concept, described by Arthur O. Lovejoy as "one of the half-dozen most potent and persistent presuppositions in Western thought," has dominated Christian cultures for so long that Christian and post-Christian Euro-Americans fairly may be suspected to embrace it unconsciously. In a tour de force the ancient Greek philosopher Aristotle set about the task, later embraced by Linnaeus, of classifying all natural beings. Grouping and subgrouping entities through their noteworthy characteristics, Aristotle wrote of a continuum from minerals to plants to animals to humans to the Unmoved Mover. In the *History of Animals* and *On the Soul* (*De Anima*), Aristotle stressed that these realms were not separate classes but blended into each other, much as the colors of the spectrum of light gently transition from one hue to another. Thus, in its purest Aristotelian form, the Great Chain of Being includes the idea of continuity rather than separation between species, and Aristotle himself resisted thinking in terms of a hierarchy. Nonetheless he wrote of the "perfections" of various types, thus opening the door to hierarchical thinking. Several philosophers then barged through this door, reifying Aristotle's types into exclusively classed levels. From this reification, Jews, Christians, and Muslims adopted a ladderlike Great Chain of Being, integrating angels as a class ranked above humans but below God. Over time the Great Chain of Being solidified within Western cultures as a ranked ordering of the universe, with minerals at the forgotten bottom of the chain, having only existence; above minerals are plants, which possess existence and life; animals, which add motion and appetite to the qualities of plants; humans, having a rational, spiritual soul not found in supposedly lower forms; angels, which are pure spirit; and finally God, absolute perfection, above everything else.[7]

Because of their places below animals at the bottom of the Great Chain of Being, minerals, water, and plants enjoy almost no religious regard in Christianity. People in church call God their "rock"; Jesus walked on water, and Moses parted the Red Sea; and the Psalms praise the cedars of Lebanon. But aside from relatively undeveloped, trivial appearances like these, Christian regard for the universes of minerals, water, and plants pales in comparison with some other religious forms that we will see in this book. For one example: holy water is not sacred in itself but is made sacred only by human blessing rituals. In the end animals alone exist near enough to humans in the Great Chain of Being to make a dent in the Christian religion. For this reason, as in all Abrahamic religions the Christian story of religion and nature predominantly involves only animals, since minerals, water, and plants have virtually no religious relevance in themselves, although they may be tools for human religious ends.

However, Christianity is no one thing. Ethiopia provides a fascinating exception to this last principle, since the Ethiopian Orthodox Church, the largest of the so-called Oriental Orthodox churches, partly embraces ecocentric sacred regard for minerals, water, and plants—on church properties. This church split with the rest of the Western Christian world at the Council of Chalcedon, in 451 C.E., the Ethiopian church preferring to retain its miaphysite understanding of Jesus's having just one nature. Because it did not conceptually split Jesus's human and divine natures, as did the Western churches, the Ethiopian church better retained an ethos wherein the natural world is not separate from the sacred. As well, because of its relative geographic isolation, the Ethiopian church developed somewhat independently of Europe, along a trajectory that included elements from indigenous Ethiopian culture.

Reflecting beliefs found in Ethiopian folk religions, saints are thought to physically reside in natural beings on church properties, so that diverse natural forms appear more like the god-animals of the ancient Egyptians than they do like Clement's "wallowing" animals. For instance, Mary, Mother of God, may be found in a sycamore, as she prefers residing in the "tree of life" that has been reverenced in the region since antiquity. In practical reality this means that current-day Ethiopian churches function as sacred nature sanctuaries, with churches typically maintaining large forests on their premises despite the rampant and problematic deforestation in the rest of the country. On church land digging the earth is forbidden; one may not cut plants, regardless of economic impact; nor may one hunt animals that seek refuge, as all natural beings, including the earth, enjoy a sense of divinity. This sense of a sacred nature preserve appears in John Binns's description of the Abo church in Gondar: "It is a tranquil spot. There are many trees with an abundance of birds with brightly coloured plumage and a continual singing. From the edge of the ridge are glorious views over the valley of the Angareb River below." Bodies of water such as Lake Tana also may contain divinity, at least at times. Although outside of church lands an ethic of dominion resembling that of the rest of the Christian world applies, Ethiopian church grounds nonetheless inject an ecocentric sense of spiritual respect for minerals, water, and plants that is largely out of step with the rest of Christendom.[8]

But natural beings in the churches of Ethiopia are not sacred in themselves. Instead, they are sacred because they provide homes for the saints and God. Sycamores enjoy holiness only because Mary, Mother of God, cavorts in them, not because sycamores possess intrinsic divine energy. Even the sun is not divine, as according to the Ethiopian holy book *Kebra Negast,* Ethiopians of old were cured of their misguided solar veneration when Makeda, queen of Sheba, learned from Solomon to revere the otherworldly, invisible deity of the Bible instead.

Thus Ethiopia, despite its ecocentric church sanctuaries, joins the rest of the Christian world in teaching, following the Great Chain of Being, that nonhuman natural beings have no souls. It was a constant of ancient Greek philosophers, apart from the Pythagoreans, to affirm that humans have souls—typically, rational souls, based on language use—which animals do not have. Moreover, we know that the human incarnation is different from others from 1 Corinthians 15:39: "For not all flesh is alike, but there is one kind for men, another for animals, another for birds, and another for fish."

Influenced by this environment, the monumental Christian figure Augustine (354–430 C.E.) taught that the rational souls of humans go to an afterlife but animals are soulless. For him, irrational animals by constitution can seek only physical bodily peace, not a spot in heaven. Unlike animals, a human possesses a rational soul, which subordinates "all that part of his nature which he shares with the beasts." Humans, and humans alone, may seek the "peace of the rational soul," which requires divine guidance to realize a seat in heaven. Augustine's voice in denying rational souls, and hence heaven, to animals became and remains the theological standard everywhere but at the farthest fringes of the Christian world. As the saying has it, "All dogs go to heaven"; but they do so within folk belief outside Christianity, not in the official doctrines of mainline churches. Revelation 22:25 specifically denies dogs entry into the heavenly New Jerusalem. This is why, to my knowledge, there are many church-oriented programs to save animals from mistreatment but there are no mainline church missions to save the souls of animals.[9]

Humans thus have dominion over nature, reside at a higher level in the Great Chain of Being, solely retain God's image, and alone possess salvific souls. Christianity uniquely adds one more human-superior claim to this mix: from a Christian point of view it is indisputable that if God incarnates in creation, God does so not as a turtle or a cucumber vine but specifically as Jesus, a human being. As we read in Genesis, humans, and only humans, are Godlike. For these reasons many scholars have described Christianity as possibly the most anthropocentric of all religions. In general Christianity supports an entirely human-centered vision, and animals appear only on the periphery.

Animals have almost never been able to join the church, although, paradoxically, animals have been excommunicated from the church at times. St. Guinefort offers an interesting example of this last point. In Lyons in the twelfth century there lived a lord, lady, and newborn child, and their treasured pet greyhound, Guinefort. One day when the child was left alone, a large snake approached its crib. Protecting the child, Guinefort attacked the snake, killing it but receiving wounds in the process. The father came home to find a bloody child and a dog with a bloody mouth. Rashly suspecting the dog of attacking the child, he proceeded to kill the dog. However, closer inspection later revealed the true story, and the father was filled with regret for killing Guinefort. He put the dog's corpse in a well, covered it with stones, and planted trees as a memorial to the brave greyhound. Villagers then came to regard the dog as a martyred saint and made pilgrimages to the place for healing and intercession. But this practice horrified the Christian inquisitor Étienne de Bourbon, who ordered the shrine taken down and the dog disinterred, and then declared Guinefort, the unfortunate greyhound, a heretic. Here we see the ambivalence that marks human relationships with the natural world bearing a Christian flavor, as Guinefort could be an unofficial holy saint or an official heretic, depending on whom one asked.[10]

Further, if nature mysticism is the direct experience of sacredness in and through nature (rather than just appreciation for nature), then Christianity almost totally lacks nature mysticism. As in the other Abrahamic religions, God should be experienced invisibly, transcendent beyond creation, not as a willow tree. Nature mystical experience represents a heresy that distracts one from proper worship of the invisible God, who exists beyond nature. We see the difference between mere appreciation for nature and nature mysticism in the life of the eccentric John Muir. Muir's Transcendentalist writer friends such as Emerson and Thoreau, who are sometimes incorrectly referred to as nature mystics, actually hewed closer to orthodoxy in experiencing nature not as a deity in itself but as a sacrament that leads beyond itself to an invisible, transcendent divine. For instance, in *Nature* Emerson wrote of "the reverential withdrawing of nature before its God," indicating a separation between divinity and the natural world. Contrarily, in Muir's more heretical nature mysticism, nature could not withdraw "before its God," because nature *was* God, as we have seen.[11]

Some may object to my characterization of animals as tangential to the Christian world, calling attention to reverence for nature through symbols such as the Lamb of God or the presence of animals in Christian art. In this vein, the great American theologian Jonathan Edwards (1703–58) experienced nature as an expression of God's positive qualities, writing that "God's excellency, his wisdom, his purity and love, seemed to appear in every thing; in the sun, moon, and stars; in the clouds, and blue sky; in the grass, flowers, trees; in the water; and all nature."[12]

Such indeed are natural appearances, but usually as mere symbols, not necessarily as real beings, following a long Christian tradition. For example, in Job 38 God appeals to sublime manifestations of nature in order to teach Job about inscrutable divine power. Augustine described the (soulless) natural world as a book to be read in order to discern revelation for human benefit. The medieval Christian leader Bonaventure said: "Whoever is not enlightened by the splendor of created things is blind; whoever is not aroused by the sound of their voice is deaf; whoever does not praise God for all these creatures is mute; and whoever after so much evidence does not recognize the First Principle is an idiot." And Job 12:7–10 counsels us:[13]

> But ask the beasts, and they will teach you;
> the birds of the air, and they will tell you;
> or the plants of the earth, and they will teach you;
> and the fish of the sea will declare to you.
> Who among all these does not know
> that the hand of the Lord has done this?
> In his hand is the life of every living thing
> and the breath of all mankind.

Certainly such symbolic thinking has a place in Christianity, just as in all religions, and Christianity rightly may be commended for being somewhat nature-friendly with this. These symbolic approaches, recognizing divinity through nature, utilize beautiful images to evoke spiritual concord between natural beings, humans, and God. Symbolic approaches further provide some place in Christianity for natural beings, as apart from the new pet blessing rituals the tradition mostly excludes nonsymbolic, real animals. Moreover, such symbolic approaches may be the first step in developing nature mystical tendencies.

But problems with this approach arise when we consider that symbols, as human imaginative constructs, enjoy a sense of freedom from material reality and that real natural beings may pay the price for this freedom. Animals have no control over how they are symbolized, since "we are free to imagine them as we like," as the philosopher Montaigne said. Because humans choose what symbols mean, throughout history natural symbols have been used to justify not just racism, sexism, social oppression, and war but also derogatory attitudes toward animals. The philosopher Mary Midgley tells us: "Many animals quite harmless to humans and even useful, such as toads, spiders, and grass-snakes, have suffered a great deal from being draped with unsuitable symbolic values. Carnivores like wolves and lions have been viewed quite unrealistically as deliberate criminals, murdering wildly for the fun of it."[14]

This principle of symbolic misuse of animals is manifest, ironically, in the Church of Satan, which intentionally uses animal imagery reflective of historical Christian depictions of the devil as a debased animal, with the head of a ram, goat, or bull. Such pejorative uses of natural beings emerge especially when animals are approached only symbolically, without any accompaniment from real animals, because then human expression loses a considerable anchor in reality. Every religion employs natural beings as symbols, but some religions find ways to include real natural beings, too, and thus mitigate this problem somewhat. This is one reason why the current pet blessing movement, in which real animals attend church, may be capable of bringing significant historic changes to Christianity.

When real animals become divorced from religion and we approach nature in a symbol-only way, we tend to treat animals unfairly. I may be saved by contemplating God in an eagle, but the eagle gets no religious reward for being my inspiration. In this mode natural beings appear to generously give spiritually, yet they receive nothing in return, because they stand outside heaven. This attitude is not one of mutuality. When we embrace natural beings only as symbols, we necessarily relate to them as if they exist purely for our sake.

Additionally, when we regard natural beings solely as symbols, there remain few obstacles to the exploitation of real natural entities. In an important essay Lynn White demonstrated that the reading of nature to discover God in the natural theology of the Middle Ages transformed, over time, into the scientific and technological practice of reading nature in such a way that nature may be dominated. We see this process with one of the most revered figures in Christianity, Thomas Aquinas, who encouraged us to ponder nature as a religious symbol yet still argued that cruelty to animals is not a sin in itself. Aquinas said that we should all appreciate the greatness of God in the wonder and majesty of creation, writing:[15]

> For he produced things into being in order that His goodness might be communicated to them; and because his goodness could not be adequately represented by one creature alone, he produced many and diverse creatures, that what was wanting to one representation of the Divine goodness might be supplied by another. For goodness, which in God is simple and uniform, in creatures is manifold and divided; and hence the whole universe together participates in the Divine Goodness more perfectly, and represents it better than any single creature whatever.

But Aquinas also followed Augustine and the Great Chain of Being in teaching that animals lack rational souls, and from this claimed that "All animals are naturally subject to humans." Moreover, Aquinas argued that because animals lack souls, not only do they have no hope of reaching heaven; they "have no moral status in themselves," and so cruelty to animals is not a sin in itself, as "charity does not extend to irrational creatures." In this light, Aquinas taught that cruelty to animals should be avoided, but only because it may lead to cruelty to humans. Aquinas thus instructs us that even for a great doctor of the church, reverence for nature as a symbol for the divine does not inhibit attitudes that can lead to the maltreatment of natural beings. Regarding nature as just a marvelous symbol for God's greatness provides few resources for developing genuine and wholesome relationships with real natural beings. To be fair, later Cardinal John Henry Newman would provide a Roman Catholic counter to Aquinas's views on animal cruelty when he wrote, "Cruelty to animals is as if humanity did not love God."[16]

So far I have explored some attitudes of human superiority in Christianity, but of course these attitudes do not exist by themselves. Amid attitudes of human superiority, Christianity embraces more zoacentric (human-and-animal-centered) flavors. For instance, Christianity's almost total lack of rituals of animal sacrifice makes the tradition stand out when compared with the other Abrahamic religions. Although there have been and continue to be animal sacrifices on the margins of Christianity, from the beginning of the religion church leaders sought to make the new faith distinctive from other Mediterranean religions by forbidding animal sacrifice. But excepting the voice of Arnobius of Sicca, petitions against sacrifice for the animal's benefit were rare, and arguments against animal sacrifice mostly were directed against the worship of false gods, as we see in Acts 14:14–18. It was claimed that Jesus, the Lamb of God, was *the* sacrifice for the whole world. In this perspective, no other physical sacrifice matters; any further attempt at sacrifice could be considered sacrilege; and unless the sacrificer were Jewish, animal sacrifice meant worship of false gods, as 1 Corinthians 10:18–20 portrays it.[17]

Interestingly, it fairly may be argued that this elimination of animal sacrifice helped animals who otherwise would be victims but overall actually lowered the place of animals in Christianity, given that real animals no longer had any role in religion. As the church strengthened, it specifically targeted the issue of nature religion in indigenous localities and tried to wipe out all forms of nature worship, whether they included sacrifices or not. This battle often pitted urban Christians against country-dwelling *pagani*, who practiced indigenous nature worship instead of or along with Christianity, giving us our words "pagan" and "heathen" as well (those who worship on the heath). Thus part of the battle against animal sacrifice involved banning animals from any kind of church participation, diminishing animals' status. On this Lynn White said: "By destroying pagan animism, Christianity made it possible to exploit nature in a mood of indifference to the feelings of natural objects." The historian Keith Thomas claimed: "The pagan divinities of grove, stream, and mountain had been expelled, leaving behind them a disenchanted world, to be shaped, moulded, and dominated."[18]

Still, Christianity shows animal-friendliness in a variety of stories, beginning with the most provocative and unusual animal in the Bible, Balaam's ass. In a story from Numbers 22:21–31, one day Balaam rode his donkey along with the princes of Moab. Balaam's donkey, spotting an angel of God with a sword drawn in the road, swerved to avoid the angel. But Balaam did not see the angel, so he cursed and beat the donkey for insubordination. Later the angel appeared again, forcing the donkey to push Balaam against a wall, and again the donkey was beaten by the spiritually blind Balaam. On a third encounter with the angel, the donkey simply lay down and was again beaten. At this the donkey complained to Balaam in a human voice, and Balaam awoke to the presence of the angel. The angel then chastised Balaam: "Why have you struck your ass these three times? Behold, I have come forth to withstand you, because your way is perverse before me; and the ass saw me, and turned aside before me these three times. If she had not turned aside from me, surely just now I would have slain you and let her live." Because the donkey recognized and responded to an angel that Balaam did not see, she exhibited spiritual insight superior to Balaam's. His donkey peered into the spiritual world in a way unlike humans, as supposedly do the many animal oracles who inevitably emerge to predict matches with every World Cup international football tournament. If respectful spiritual perceptiveness is a religious practice, this donkey practiced religion.

Amid the early Christian battles against nature worship, there were many texts that vied for canonization in the Bible, which was not assembled before 325 C.E. Apocryphal texts—books that were very popular but did not eventually find a place in the Bible—sometimes sipped lightly at the fountain of animal worship, which they otherwise fought. This inclusion of nonhumans made them much livelier and open in their attitudes toward animals than are the canonical texts, and so they offer rich windows, as the biblical texts do not, on the attitudes toward nature in Christianity's formative years. Two apocryphal extensions of the biblical Acts of the Apostles—the Acts of Paul and the Acts of Paul and Thecla—contain perhaps the most surprising story about religion and nature in the Christian world. As the story goes, one time the evangelist Paul walked the road to Jericho with a widow, Lemma, and her daughter Ammia. While they prayed at a rest stop, a "great and terrible" lion approached. The lion threw himself at Paul's feet and, in his own words, Paul inquired:[19]

"Lion, what wilt thou?"
But the lion said: "I wish to be baptized."
I glorified God, who had given speech to the beast and salvation to his servants. Now there was a great river in that place; I went down into it and he followed me.... I myself was in fear and wonderment, in that I was on the point of leading the lion like an ox and baptizing him in the water.
I took the lion by his mane and in the name of Jesus Christ immersed him three times. But when he came up out of the water, he shook out his mane and said to me: "Grace be with thee!" And I said to him: "And likewise with thee." The lion ran off to the country rejoicing.

Later in the Acts of Paul, the Ephesians arrest Paul, and a crowd clamors for his execution as a sorcerer. In Roman custom for the punishment of heinous crimes like sorcery, many ferocious animals were made ready to kill Paul in a stadium spectacle. In the execution ring one of these animals, a lion, approached Paul. But this was not just any lion, as it was the feline from the baptism, and the two recognized each other immediately. Just then a hailstorm erupted that was so violent, all the other animals were killed and the human crowd ran away, leaving Paul and the baptized lion untouched. The lion then disappeared into the wilderness, and Paul escaped on a ship sailing for Macedonia.[20]

This distinctive, fantastical, and vivid tale pushes the boundaries of acceptable Christian belief. There remains no reason for animal baptism such as the lion received if animals cannot reach heaven or join the church. Nonetheless, around the year 200 the controversial Hippolytus accepted the story as authoritative on the grounds of its resemblance with the lion taming of the Bible's Book of Daniel. The church patriarch Jerome (d. 420 C.E.), whom we will see the Maya call "Father Jaguar" later in this book, could have been sympathetic with this argument, as Jerome himself was said to heal an injured lion who later tamely served Jerome's monastery and mourned Jerome's death. Instead, Jerome silenced Hippolytus by declaring the Acts of Paul inauthentic precisely because of the lion baptism, and his voice became the church standard. Over time Jerome's position against animal baptism became so taken for granted that some enemies of the church performed satirical baptisms of animals in order to mock Christianity.[21]

Another apocryphal text, the Acts of Philip, contains a possibly eliminated animal baptism. At the urging of Jesus, the disciples Philip and Bartholomew, along with Philip's sister Mariamne, traveled on foot to Opheorymos, where they hoped to convert snake worshippers as part of the church's campaign against nature veneration. In Act 8 of the Acts of Philip the group was startled in some woods to meet a leopard and a goat's kid, who used human language to request prayers and religious instruction. Philip and Bartholomew then prayed:[22]

No one surpasses your compassion, O benevolent Jesus. For you precede us and correct and instruct us through these animals, so that we might believe still more and complete with zeal that which was entrusted to us. Now then, Lord Jesus Christ, come and grant life and breath and a firm constitution to these animals, that they might forsake their savage and beastly nature.... Let a human heart be born in them.

And at that moment the animals rose up, both the leopard and the kid, lifted up their forefeet and glorified God, and said with human voices: "We glorify and bless you, you who have visited us and remembered us in this wilderness, you who have transformed our savage and wild nature into tameness, and freely given us the divine word and placed in us a tongue and a mind so that we might speak and confess your name, because your glory is great."

Later, after Act 10 appears to have been removed intentionally from the manuscript, in Act 12 the humans practice the Eucharist, and the animals vociferously beg to join, too. The animals argue that "God considered us worthy to participate in all of these marvels; why now do you not consider us worthy to receive communion?" The animals say that they have "become like human beings, and truly God lives in us." But in the end the leopard and kid are denied the Eucharist, as instead Philip only sprinkles the animals with water, just as the pastor did the pets in the All Saints Episcopal Church pet blessing ceremony. In this story, the curious way that the animals argue for their participation in Communion has led to suspicion among scholars such as François Bovon that the animals were baptized in the missing Act 10 and that that is, in fact, why Act 10 is missing.[23]

Getting away from marginal texts and entering more into the mainstream of the Christian tradition, Athanasius's *Life of Antony* includes an interesting story about an Egyptian monk named Paul the Hermit. Pioneering a desert-retreat lifestyle for more than sixty years, Paul did not have to leave his hermitage for food, as a devoted crow brought him bread, just as a raven fed bread to Elijah in the Bible (1 Kings 17:6). Paul's hermitage was a hangout for various undomesticated animals who were tamed by the saint's spirituality. When Paul the Hermit died, two lions came to dig his grave. The crow and the lions in this story aid a saint and thereby perform acts that, in humans, are acts of religious devotion. These animals practiced Christianity, in a fashion.

We also find an animal who appears to practice religion in the story of Eustace and the stag from *The Golden Legend*.[24]

While hunting one day, a Roman soldier, Placidus, came upon a herd of deer. One of these, a large stag, impressed the soldier with his incredible size and beauty. As the stag ran into the dense woods, the soldier followed, pondering how to capture this animal. Suddenly he noticed a cross with the image of Jesus between the antlers of the deer. The voice of the divine came from the stag's mouth and said, "O Placidus, why are you pursuing me? For your sake I have appeared to you in this animal. I am the Christ, whom you worship without knowing it. Your alms have risen before me, and for this purpose I have come, that through this deer which you hunted, I myself might hunt you." The next morning, the vision appeared to him again, with the stag as the vehicle for revelation. The soldier changes his name to Eustace and becomes a Christian.

If converting others to Christianity is a religious practice, this stag practiced religion.

Sometimes animals appear to practice religion but on closer inspection do not, as we see with St. Ciaran. Like other saints, he wished to live in the wilderness, and so he began a monastery in "a vast solitude ... thick with forest." There under a tree he encountered a wild boar. Ciaran calmed the boar, who came to Ciaran "as though to be his serving man," and the boar became his first disciple, as if a monk. The boar helped Ciaran build his cell by bringing twigs and grass. Then a fox, badger, wolf, and deer joined the community, each a model of gentleness and obedience to "the saint's words in all things, as if they had been his monks." The animals all lived there, for the rest of their lives, completely tame. But of course, when this story speaks of animals becoming monks, it cannot mean this literally, as in the Christian world only humans may be consecrated as monastics.[25]

Ciaran was an Irishman; and perhaps more than anyone else in Western Christianity, medieval Irish and English saints, coming from a Celtic nature-worshipping heritage, exhibited fascinating and rich religious experiences with nature. Take, for example, St. Brendan in his *Voyage.* Every year of his seven-year sea travels to find the Promised Land of the Saints, Brendan and his monastic brothers spent the Easter feasts on the "island of the birds." Perhaps reflecting pre-Christian Neolithic and Celtic traditions in which divinity appears in avian form, the birds there prayed incessantly with notable piety, and for Brendan's men, wearied by their long and dangerous journey, "the chanting of the birds revived their spirits":[26]

> As Brendan's company came near the landing place they had chosen on that island, all the birds chanted as if with one voice, saying, "Salvation belongs to our God who sits upon the throne, and to the Lamb!"
>
> And again: "The Lord God has given us light. Appoint a holy day, with festal branches up to the horn of the altar." Thus they chanted and beat their wings for a long time—for about half an hour.

Imagine being lost at sea and arriving on an island of gleefully praying birds! But in these vivid stories the devout birds did more than this, since they also kept the monastic hours and joined Mass:[27]

> When the hour of vespers had come all the birds in the tree chanted, as it were with one voice, beating their wings on their sides: "A hymn is due to thee, O God, in Zion, and a vow shall be paid to you in Jerusalem." They kept repeating this versicle for about the space of an hour. To the man of God and his companions, the chant and the sound of their wings seemed in its sweetness like a rhythmical song.

One perceptive bird in particular prophesied where Brendan would spend his holidays during the seven-year journey—stops that included resting on the back of the tame whale Jasconius—and prophesied that Brendan would eventually reach his goal, the Promised Land of the Saints. If prophesying represents religion, this clairvoyant bird practiced religion also.

But it is not just birds who practice religion in the *Voyage of Brendan*, since fish do as well. It happened that Brendan's group found itself in very clear water, making it easy to see the fish. On the boat Brendan began celebrating the Mass. A giant throng of fish, of every species and color, arrived from many directions. The fish joyfully swam around the boat in a wide arc as Brendan undertook his priestly function. When the Mass was done, the fish dispersed. Venerating a saint during Mass as the fish did Brendan in this terrific story indicates a humanlike religious practice.[28]

These stories of Brendan may be the most interesting and poignant in this chapter, as they contain tales of animals who buck the norm and practice religion, thus significantly leveling possible differences between animals and humans. Even more, unlike apocryphal lions and leopards who practice religion, Brendan's tales belong to the mainstream of the Roman Catholic tradition. Finally, overt human agendas are lacking in Brendan's stories, leaving them with a more innocent quality. Brendan's adventures indicate a deep sense of Christian intimacy and friendship with the natural world, so that while Francis of Assisi rightly enjoys fame as a nature-friendly saint, Brendan also deserves a significant measure of respect on this count.

As we can appreciate from these stories, Christian saints seem to manifest power over nature through their saintly charisma and especially the ability to tame dangerous natural beings. This theme appears in the New Testament when Paul shows his power over nature by remaining unhurt by a viper bite in Acts 28:2–6. Stories about a post-Celtic saint named Cuthbert also exhibit this dynamic. On one occasion Cuthbert spent the night waist-deep in the chilly sea, praying and keeping vigil. When he arrived back on shore very cold, two otters respectfully approached him and then warmed and dried Cuthbert with their bodies. Another time Cuthbert was out with a companion, and the two were hungry. An eagle came, dropping a fish as a gift. Before the men ate, however, out of fairness the ever-considerate Cuthbert made sure that the eagle received half of the fish. Cuthbert also calmed a violent storm, and on another occasion the sea miraculously produced a wooden board for construction that perfectly fit Cuthbert's specifications. Cuthbert thus wielded spiritual power over nature, and the natural entities who tended to him performed acts of devotion. But the stories themselves openly tell us that this power should remind us of "what obedience is due to saints," and so in a sense the stories are less about otters or eagles and more about the greatness of Cuthbert.[29]

A number of stories mark this theme of spiritual power over nature as relatively common among Christian saints because such stories help to establish credentials as a saint or encourage belief in the human-only church. We detect ambivalent attitudes toward nature in some of these stories of animal devotion to saints, since on one hand animals engage in religion like humans by aiding or venerating a saint, whereas on the other hand the human saint clearly inhabits a superior position in relation to the natural world.

In the stories about the twelfth-century British saint Godric we find a more physical sense of human power over nature. Godric showed extreme kindness to animals, taking them into his clothes for warmth on a cold winter day and offering lodging to animals in need. Furthermore, he had a cow who needed daily pasturing, but Godric did not want to break from his prayers for cow-herding duties, and his assistant, being very young, kept falling asleep on the job. So one day Godric spoke to the cow with gentleness and reason, commanding it to take care of its own pasturing. This the cow did for years afterwards.

Godric further showed his kindness to animals in a famous hunting story. Godric lived in quiet solitude in a forest hermitage when one day a stag, chased in the hunt, appeared at his door shivering, exhausted, and crying in terror. Counseling the stag to hush, Godric invited the animal into his hut and closed the door. Soon barking dogs and hunters arrived, and the hunters asked Godric if he had seen their quarry. He replied, "God knows where he may be." At this, the hunters left. Godric kept the stag in his hut until nightfall, when the hunters would surely be gone from the forest. For years afterwards the stag would visit the saint, lying at his feet in gratitude for saving his life.[30]

But Godric was no pushover. He planted some fruit trees to provide food for human visitors and tolerated no incursion on them from deer or other animals. When he could, he would verbally encourage animals to quit the fruit trees, but if they failed to get the message, he would not hesitate to beat them with his rod to drive his message home.[31]

Godric defended his fruit even from birds, despite the fact that from the earliest days of the Christian tradition birds have been positive symbols, as they reach heavenward in flight and have wings like angels.

In folklore birds perform many beneficial functions, like the crow who provided food for Paul the Hermit or the praying, prophesying birds that Brendan encountered. The renowned and influential Christian patron saint of nature, Francis of Assisi (1181–1226 C.E.), also favored birds, because to him they exemplified the Christian virtues of gentleness and simple living. So when he saw a boy carrying a small flock of doves caught in a snare, Francis successfully implored the boy to give him the birds. Francis chastised the doves for allowing themselves to be caught and then made nests in the monastery for the birds, who stayed at the cloister like pets until Francis allowed them to leave. As described within *The Little Flowers of Saint Francis,* an authoritative collection of stories from his life, another time Francis rested under a tree when a large number of birds of many types settled down on his head, shoulders, and limbs, all singing lovely songs in happiness at Francis's presence. Feeling invited by the birds, Francis decided to make that very spot the place of his hermitage on Mt. Alverna. These stories offer uncommonly vibrant versions of a common theme: the ability of saints to tame wild nature.[32]

In another story, Francis walked with his colleagues until they came upon trees covered with an innumerable variety of birds, with a similar massed congregation of birds on the ground. Francis bade his friends wait for him and began to preach to the avian multitude. He delivered a kind but clear message about the need to be grateful for God's gifts, during which not a single bird made a motion or sound. When he finished, the birds opened their mouths, stretched their wings, and bowed their heads in joyful acknowledgment of his message. Francis then made the sign of the cross over the birds and bade them to leave, at which point the birds took flight in four groups, choreographed a sign of the cross in the sky, and then disappeared to the four cardinal directions. *The Little Flowers* tells us that this event of deep communion with pious avians happened to show "that the preaching of the Cross of Christ, which had been renewed by St. Francis, was to be carried throughout the world by him and his friars."[33]

Figure 2. Francis of Assisi preaches to birds. (©iStock.com/
Number: 16979276, 2011, Artist: duncan1890.)

Thus Francis invited wild birds to practice religion by listening to a
sermon. Another bird helped Francis himself practice religion, thus
exhibiting devotion to the saint. For a period of time a falcon lodged
with Francis, and this bird woke Francis in time for morning prayers
each day by calling and beating its wings. If Francis was infirm, the falcon would with seeming compassion let him sleep later. The falcon also
acted as a nice daytime companion, and Francis thus appreciated and
felt affectionate toward the animal.[34]

But Francis's lore concerns more than just birds. There was one cold
winter morning on which none of the monastery brothers but the

indomitable Francis attended the early service. However, Francis was not alone at Mass, because a cricket joined him, as brothers who arrived late discovered. Further, in some of Francis's iconography he is depicted with a wolf, the wolf of Gubbio. As the story goes, this wolf preyed on townsfolk, and the people were terrified. Francis intervened, approached the wolf, and the wolf attacked him. But Francis made the sign of the cross and commanded the wolf to be calm, calling him "Friar Wolf," and because of Francis's powerful charisma the wolf ceased its aggression. Francis then preached to the wolf that it should adopt the Christian values of love and mercy and attack the townspeople no more. He offered the wolf a deal: the animal would agree to kill no more, and the townspeople would agree to feed him. The wolf accepted this proposal. According to the story, for years after that day the wolf peacefully roamed the village as a welcome member of the community.[35]

Stories like these, in which leopards seek Communion or crickets perform Mass, highlight a more animal-friendly dimension for Christianity than its usual human-centered orientation. From angel-spotting donkeys to birds attending sermons, we learn animals may be spiritually sensitive creatures. Animals even practice religion through baptism, prayer, prophecy, devotion to saints, and performing church services, thus challenging, at least in folktales, the common notion that only humans practice religion. These stories teach us that humans may wish to relate to animals in ways acknowledging that animals have their own religious lives and spiritual agendas, therefore making Christianity more zoacentric, or religiously embracing both humans and animals.

But even in some of these stories, there lurk anthropocentric attitudes. The story of Paul's baptized lion appears to have been rejected from the Bible perhaps for being overly generous to animals. Philip's pious leopard and goat kid, so eager to take Communion, could not practice Christianity unless they became more humanlike. Godric is kind to animals but does not spare the rod when protecting human food. In addition, one of Francis's early disciples, Salimbene, called it a "foul blemish" that members of the Franciscan Order "play with a cat or a whelp or some small fowl"; and the keeping of pets, as Francis did his falcon, was banned by his own order in 1260 C.E. Further, Cuthbert's stories explicitly tell us that lively tales regarding saints and animals are not really about nature; they are about increasing faith in the saints and the church.[36]

But even with human-centered clothing like this, such animal-friendly stories represent a previous high point for animals in Christian experience. As Europe entered the Reformation period, the outlook for animals in the church became bleaker, as we see with René Descartes, often thought of as the father of modern philosophy. Like Augustine and Aquinas, Descartes argued that animals have no heaven-going souls, stating, "The souls of animals are nothing but their blood" and decrying it as error "to imagine that the soul of the brute is of the same nature as our own." Because they have no rational souls, Cartesian animals are "automata which move without thought," and Descartes famously compared animals to mechanical clocks. Since animals are just machines, Descartes proposed, as did Aquinas, that cruelty to animals is not a sin in itself and that animals are religiously irrelevant. Because of the deep and widespread influence of Descartes's philosophy, his views regarding human superiority to soulless animals remains a standard perspective in Christian cultures.[37]

Aquinas's and Descartes's teachings then mingled with intellectual elements from the Reformation, the scientific revolution, and the Enlightenment to banish animals even further from the churchyard. All these movements celebrated the human being as paramount in importance, thus diminishing the role of nature in religion. The Reformation also chased the saints, and their animal friends whom we have met, from the congregation. Modern science, begun as a quest to understand God's majesty in nature, transformed with the aid of technology into a quest to conquer nature, following Francis Bacon's well-known charge to humans to approach nature scientifically and "bind her to your service and make her your slave." To those in the pews, animals became reduced to just quaint symbolic images and cute decorations for church windows; and the natural world became a universe of soulless objects, even in the secular humanism outside religion proper in Christian cultural areas.[38]

The late twentieth and the early twenty-first century appear to mark the first significant change in fundamental Christian attitudes toward nature since Descartes, as a more animal-aware sensibility emerges in various Christian worlds. This shift includes altered attitudes toward animals arising from the contemporary practice of intensive pet keeping. Human relationships with companion animals are ancient and commonplace; for example, at the time of European contact, Native Americans kept pet raccoons, moose, bison, wolves, and bears, and generally were especially fond of dogs. But the contemporary practice of intensive pet keeping, together with related billion-dollar industries such as professional breeding, pet shops, rescue shelters, puppy mills, and kennels, has appeared only since the Victorian age: a relatively recent phenomenon. The American Society for the Prevention of Cruelty to Animals (ASPCA) was not formed until 1866, and animal cruelty was not legally condemned in the United Kingdom until 1876. Now pets are most popular in the relatively wealthy and developed areas of North America, Europe, and Japan, and more than half the households in both the United States and the European Union extend care to pets. We see how recent this movement really is when we consider that most of the numerous dog breeds recognized today have developed only over the last 150 years, not over millennia.[39]

Undoubtedly the keeping of pets has beneficial effects, as the huge sums of money spent on otherwise economically unproductive animals attest. Many people genuinely enjoy relationships with companion animals, some of whom are stray at some point and are seemingly grateful to dwell in caring homes, so that keeping pets has led to myriad genuine friendships across species boundaries. Moreover, numerous studies describe the positive health benefits of keeping pets, from quicker healing to prolonged lifespan, and dogs and cats have proved themselves helpful partners in some forms of psychotherapy. The therapists Aaron

Katcher and Alan Beck tell us: "Once pet keeping is seen as an extension of human nurturing, its value becomes more obvious." Seeing-eye and search-and-rescue dogs obviously accentuate this sense of health from a companion animal. And, if increasing population is a species good, some animals benefit, as domesticated dogs and cats now far outnumber members of their original wild species.[40]

Personally I have been a caregiver for quite a few beloved pet dogs, cats, turtles, horses, cattle, donkeys, rabbits, spiders, fish, hamsters, and caterpillars who have made me happy, as I hope that they have been happy with me. But it is precisely out of love for such animals that we should recognize that contemporary intensive pet-keeping practices are not without potentially problematic elements of human superiority. While keeping pets often is a profound expression of love for animals, this does not prevent mixing in a strong dose of human self-love, as we can see from Descartes's affection for his dog Monsieur Grat or Hitler's well-documented fawning over his dog Blondi. Or consider loving pet keepers in ancient Egypt, some of whom could not bear the thought of the afterlife without the company of a favorite pet. As part of their funerals their living pets were mummified and buried with the caregivers so that pets, too, could join Osiris in the afterlife, ensuring that that these pets were literally loved to death by their humans. Further, although keeping pets may help to solve the problem of stray animals, it also contributes to it, since if none of us kept dogs, cats, or Burmese pythons, none of these creatures could go astray. Again, I raise these issues as a pet caregiver myself, not in order to insult pet keepers but to highlight potentially troublesome human-centered approaches when it comes to our roommates with tails, as these bear on religious aspects of pet-keeping practices. After all, humans strongly influenced the evolution of pet animals in making them, as much as possible, just what we wanted them to be.

The human-animal interaction specialist James Serpell tells us that human vanity and self-indulgence more than concern for the animals themselves prompts many pet-keeping relationships. Pets may be approached not as animals with lives of their own but as surrogates for missing or dysfunctional human relationships, such as when they serve as erstwhile children. Moreover, out of our fancied love for pets, we create and then cling to so-called pure breeds, which notoriously suffer numerous health problems because of their unnatural selection. To the scholar Yi Fu-Tuan, pet keeping arises from fundamental human insecurity, which is expressed through playful dominance over nature. Alternatively, the environmental scientist Paul Shepard tells us that because humans evolved within a rich natural environment, we have an innate, genomic desire to consort with natural beings. But through misguided selfishness, Shepard tells us, we drove natural beings out of our lives, as for dinner we now hunt for pizzas on the Internet rather than nuts and berries in the forest. Therefore we keep pets as a small shred of our lost natural paradise and in so doing utilize them as our "biological slaves."[41]

Shepard is not alone in equating pet keeping with slavery. One may describe both intensive pet keeping and slavery as institutions where one person, the master, claims ownership of a living biological being. The master controls the life, death, living conditions, health care, reproductive opportunities, and movement of the owned. Markets thrive in which these owned beings are bought and sold. Further, a slave master may try to do his captives what he supposes is a favor by making them more like him, such as converting them to his religion, whereas a dog master may treat a canine as if it were human supposedly out of love, even though animal experts unanimously preach that it is better to treat a dog or a cat as such, not as human. Because of these social resemblances between pet keeping and slavery, I personally speak of pet "caregivers," not pet "owners," under the theological justification that only God can own a living being.

But whatever the role of human-centeredness in pet keeping, it is undeniable that intensive pet keeping has brought animals closer to the center of human life through their coming to occupy a more prominent place in the home rather than the barn, unlike traditional farm animals.

Because of this proximity, pets, living in human habitats, inspire the integration of animals into religion, as pet keeping raises crucial religious questions regarding both the religious lives of pets and the religious dimension of their deaths. This dynamic then changes the Christian world.

When one develops a close relationship with an animal, as is typical in intensive pet keeping, the death of a pet can be very traumatic for the caregiver, who may struggle with the idea that a beloved friend is gone forever. Perhaps for this reason, it is not uncommon for pets' caregivers to wish to see their furry friends in the afterlife, and thus folk beliefs in a pet heaven appear to be growing throughout the core areas of intensive pet keeping: North America, Europe, and Japan. These beliefs spread through such media as the anonymous international Internet-sensation poem "Rainbow Bridge." Since appearing in the 1990s, "Rainbow Bridge" has offered hope to those with recently deceased pets:

> Just this side of heaven is a place called Rainbow Bridge.
>
> When an animal dies that has been especially close to someone here, that pet goes to Rainbow Bridge. There are meadows and hills for all of our special friends so they can run and play together. There is plenty of food, water and sunshine, and our friends are warm and comfortable.
>
> All the animals who had been ill and old are restored to health and vigor. Those who were hurt or maimed are made whole and strong again, just as we remember them in our dreams of days and times gone by. The animals are happy and content, except for one small thing: they each miss someone very special to them, who had to be left behind.
>
> They all run and play together, but the day comes when one suddenly stops and looks into the distance. His bright eyes are intent. His eager body quivers. Suddenly he begins to run from the group, flying over the green grass, his legs carrying him faster and faster.
>
> You have been spotted, and when you and your special friend finally meet, you cling together in joyous reunion, never to be parted again. The happy kisses rain upon your face; your hands again caress the beloved head, and you look once more into the trusting eyes of your pet, so long gone from your life but never absent from your heart. Then you cross Rainbow Bridge together.

The Rainbow Bridge and similar beliefs may offer Christians conso-
lation in the face of the loss of a pet, which often is distressing. However, belief in the Rainbow Bridge is a folk tradition, not a Christian
one. As we have seen, in Christianity animals generally cannot go to
heaven, because they lack the equipment—a rational soul—to get
there. Thus the belief that pets go to heaven definitely appears in the
Christian universe but is not in itself a Christian belief. The growth of
this extra-Christian belief may be traced, at least in part, to a human
need to retain a spiritual relationship with a lost, beloved nonhuman
friend.

Human need looms as well in the pet blessing movement, as we find
in the blessing ceremony I recounted at the beginning of the chapter.
Caregivers sincerely wanted their beloved pets to receive the blessings
of their treasured church, and so it is no wonder that pet lovers like
Cora, whom we saw previously, were so heartened by the experience.
Few animals had the opportunity to receive this blessing, and so it was
a meaningful event. But however warm, moving, and enjoyable the
experience of this ceremony was, something remained amiss. At this
ceremony Cora, just like all the human attendants, received the consecrated bread and wine of the Eucharist; but Skipper, her husky dog, like
all the pets, received only ordinary treats. Although *The Book of Common
Prayer* of the Episcopal Church describes partaking of the wine and
bread in the Eucharist as "the principal act of Christian worship," the
pets were denied this. Even on the animals' big day in church, the
humans, not the pets, received the consecrated substances, and it was
humans alone who therefore received the salvific blessing. The animals
were blessed, but with the same nonsalvific, worldly blessing that might
be used for golf clubs or a car. Leaving the wine aside, Skipper could
have been fed consecrated bread (and certainly would have savored it)
but was not. Skipper got a dog biscuit for the stomach and seemed
happy for it, but no real food for the soul. Skipper's spiritual status was,
for the most part, unchanged by the ceremony, which therefore is not
very animal-centered, despite appearances to the contrary.[42]

Skipper did not get the Eucharist because dogs remain unworthy of the important ritual of Communion. Jesus said in Matthew 7:6, "Do not give dogs what is holy," and the church follows suit. As we have seen everywhere in Christianity but at its furthest margins, to offer the Eucharist to animals is pointless, as animals lack souls and hence cannot be saved, and perhaps also sacrilegious, profaning God's saving gift through misuse. Therefore Skipper's species identity denied him an important approach to God, just as it did the leopard and the goat kid who unsuccessfully pleaded to take Communion in the Acts of Philip. For this reason, pets now attend church in unprecedented numbers but are second-class citizens when they do so, being still forbidden to join the church in fact.

This sense of ambivalence regarding Skipper's attendance at church also appeared in the sermon, in which Reverend John said that he learned religious lessons with the help of his rescue kitten, Stripes. Reverend John crafted his sermon very cleverly, as it was in order to please the congregation, which wanted animal-friendly inspiration, that he left the impression of Stripes's offering him spiritual teachings. But through twists of wordplay, Reverend John followed orthodoxy in never crediting Stripes as a spiritual teacher of humans. He would say, "Stripes is so full of love" and then say, "if only we could love as God loves us," rhetorically removing Stripes from the equation and focusing solely on human relationships with God. Reverend John followed the same strategy with such qualities as being in the moment, not holding grudges, and trusting instincts and emotions, as well. In a sermon ostensibly celebrating the spiritual life of Stripes the cat, Reverend John actually argued through skillful use of language that God is the only spiritual teacher, thus avoiding the heresy of ascribing religious agency and ascendance to animals. In the end, therefore, the church service did not go far toward recognizing sacredness in pets. This pet blessing ceremony included real animals in an innovative way, but in its construction it aimed more toward pleasing human pet keepers than toward raising the religious status of animals. Given the historical roots of the ritual, we should not be surprised to find such limits.

Reverend John's rhetorical juggling prompts questions regarding the meaning of rituals wherein animals are minimally but not transcendentally blessed. Some church leaders claim that the sanctuary is never so full as on the day of the blessing of animals, making the ceremony an important recruitment tool, and clergy who otherwise oppose the rite may perform it anyway for this reason, highlighting the grassroots power for potential change inherent in the pet blessing movement. Sociological trends may indicate a human-centered pastoral function, too: the unparalleled expansion of pet keeping has created a unique new spiritual demand among human churchgoers, and church leaders must adapt to meet this demand, inventing new theology and—especially—new ritual along the way. Maybe most important of all, both clergy and congregants at All Saints Episcopal Church said that they participated in the ritual to honor the important roles of animals in our lives. These participants in the pet blessing ceremony emphasized how moving and valuable the ritual was for them, and many other Christians say the same. We get a sense of the sincerity of these people when we consider that some who are involved are not aware that church doctrine generally prevents the true blessing or entry into heaven of their pets, and sometimes these people become quite dismayed when they discover this. Some of them then have responded by calling for a greater place for animals in the church.[43]

This contemporary pew-power movement carries the potential to change Christian history, as few things that are this positive for animals have happened for some time in Christianity. Within the Christian universe there exists a growing awareness of our more troublesome relations with the natural world: the scholar of Christianity Elizabeth A. Johnson tells us that "an increasing number of superb theologians and ethicists have taken up the challenge to consider the natural world as a proper subject of attention." Pet blessing rituals, with their inspiration from the bird-loving and cricket-befriending Francis, appear to represent a lay, grassroots, practical outcome of this shift, as real animals are in the sanctuary in previously inconceivable numbers. Pet blessing participants typically believe that their pets have spiritual needs and, responding from the ground up, are insisting on greater participation in the church for their animal friends. This sensibility would have pleased Basil, the fourth-century saintly bishop from Caesarea, who prayed:[44]

> Oh God, enlarge within us the sense of fellowship with all living things, our brothers the animals to whom Thou gavest the earth in common with us. We remember with shame that in the past we have exercised the high dominion of humanity with ruthless cruelty so that the voice of the earth, which should have gone up to Thee in song, has been a groan of travail.

Other Christian movements beyond the United States also work to create a more significant place for natural beings in the tradition. For instance, among the African Independent Churches of Zimbabwe one finds the Association of African Earthkeeping Churches, composed of more than two million Christians in more than 150 churches. These nature-loving churches innovatively combine the Eucharist with tree-blessing and tree-planting ceremonies. Teaching that the healing ministry of Jesus included healing the earth, so that green living is part of what it means to be Christian, they reverence trees and other natural beings as part of the body of Jesus, whom they understand as a guardian spirit of the land. In this movement sin includes activities that lead to soil erosion, squandering of water resources, pollution, and the unnecessary felling of trees. Although some question the orthodoxy of this movement, there is no doubt that these Earthkeeping churches inject a potent ecocentric voice into ongoing dialogues among today's Christians.[45]

From tree planting in Zimbabwe to pet blessings in the United States and beyond, some current Christians seek to adapt the tradition to more nature-friendly realities. We can witness other moments of religious change if we return to the world of ancient Egypt and its worship and mummification of temple animals. Animal mummification in Egypt appears to have been extremely popular until the end of the first millennium B.C.E. Although the practice may have declined during the first few centuries after Jesus, it was after Christianity became much more vigorous in the Nile Valley, in the fourth century C.E., that animal mummification came to an end. This shift reflects the divergent cultural values we have examined. Then, in the seventh century, a new religion, Islam, entered Egypt from Arabia. While building on attitudes developed by its Abrahamic cousin Christianity, Islam also retained some older ideas, like Egyptian reverence toward cats, as well as adding fresh approaches of its own, as we will see in the next chapter.

2

The Donkey Who Communed
with Allah

Judaism contains numerous tales regarding the need to treat animals with kindness. One of these stories from the Babylonian Talmud concerns the third-century-C.E. rabbinic scholar Judah the Prince, who succeeded the luminary Rabbi Akiva and served as the primary redactor of the important Mishnah. One day a calf was being led to kosher slaughter when it broke free and hid under the robes of Judah the Prince, crying in fear. Unmoved, Judah coldly said to the calf, "Go, you were created for this purpose." For his lack of sympathy with the calf, Heaven then punished Judah with a variety of painful and embarrassing stomach problems that lasted for thirteen years. Over these years he often prayed for relief from his poor health, but Heaven did not listen, just as Judah had failed to listen to the calf. Then one day Judah spied his maid in the act of killing a couple of small weasels in the house and restrained her, citing Psalm 145, "The Lord is good to all, and his compassion is over all that he has made." In response to this benevolence toward the weasels, Heaven withdrew Judah's punishment, and his stomach problems disappeared.

Another Jewish story comes from a Midrashic commentary that describes a post-flood conversation between Shem son of Noah and his descendant Abraham, the great prophet revered by Judaism, Christianity, and Islam alike:[1]

Shem and his family were in the ark during the great flood, and Abraham asked: "By what merit were you able to leave the ark and begin a new life?"

Shem responded: "Through the merit of acts of *tzedakah* [the obligation to give charity] that we performed in the ark."

Abraham then asked, "To whom did you give *tzedakah?* There were no poor people in the ark; there was only you and your family."

Shem replied: "All night, we were busy feeding the livestock, wild creatures, and birds; in fact, we were too busy to sleep!"

Abraham said to himself: "If they were able to leave the ark because of the *tzedakah* which they gave to livestock, wild creatures, and birds, then how much more would I accomplish if I performed acts of *tzedakah* for human beings who are created in the Divine image!" He then opened an inn for needy travelers, and he provided them with food, drink, and escort.

A couple of elements of these stories invite our consideration, one being the obvious theme of kindness to animals. Because Judah the Prince showed no sympathy for the escaped calf, the Divine taught him about the value of kindness by scourging him until his attitude had become more compassionate. Likewise, the prophet Abraham learned from Shem and the rest of Noah's family to be benevolent toward animals. As we see, Judaism encourages its followers to treat animals gently and has transmitted such ideals to other religions.

However, notions of human superiority hover implicit in the story of Judah the Prince and explicit in the story of Abraham. Judah is chastised by Heaven not for supporting animal slaughter but for not having sympathy with the sacrificed, thus maintaining a sense of human priority in the food chain. And Abraham's words "How much more would I accomplish if I performed acts of *tzedakah* for human beings who are created in the Divine image!" exhibit a clear sense of human supremacy. As we saw in the last chapter with Christianity, we find in these stories the common Abrahamic religious thread of human superiority to natural beings.

These two attitudes of kindness on the one hand and superiority on the other sometimes combine into an outlook demanding that humans care for natural beings precisely because they are less than human. As the argument goes, just as human infants require caring approaches because they do not yet manifest all the qualities that reputedly make humans superior, so we must nurture animals, who also lack these qualities. Or, just as the ideal powerful feudal lord tended to his power-less serfs through an attitude of noblesse oblige, so in this perspective humans, as the dominant actors, are obligated to care for animals. This attitude of noblesse oblige typifies Islam, the next religion under our microscope, although like all religions Islam retains a number of differ-ent, and sometimes conflicting, perspectives under this purview.

Historically Islam developed an attitude of noblesse oblige toward the natural world in part because of influences from Judaism and Chris-tianity. Additionally, because for the most part Muslim scholars studied and commented on many Greek philosophical classics before Chris-tians did, ideas of human superiority from the Great Chain of Being and other Hellenic sources thrive in the Islamic world every bit as much as in the Christian. Nonetheless, Islam's approaches to the natu-ral world differ somewhat from those of its Abrahamic cousin religions. Whereas under Islam plants, water, and minerals remain essentially irrelevant for religious consideration, animals in many ways (but not always) fare better in the Islamic world than they do in other Abra-hamic locales because of Quranic injunctions, theological innovations, and cultural traditions. Following the saying of the prophet Muham-mad "It behooves you to treat the animals gently," Islam retains a more zoacentric (human-and-animal-centered) character than Christianity. As we have seen, Christianity has struggled to stigmatize cruelty to animals, whereas Islamic ethics clearly prohibits animal cruelty for the animals' sake. Thus the legal scholar Kristen Stilt tells us: "The rules of Islamic law on animal welfare, established in the seventh century, do more to protect animals than the laws of any country today."[2]

One way in which Islam diverges from Christianity is its generally greater respect for the spiritual essences of animals. In Islam all nonhu-man natural beings, including animals, are thought to be intrinsically *muslim* (surrendered to God), which condition is the goal of Islam. Each blade of grass, each zebra, each rock formation, effortlessly obeys the commands of God in a pose of submission. As we read in Quran 22:18: "Do you not see how to God bows down all who are in the heavens and on earth, and the sun and moon, the stars, the mountains, the trees and animals, and many people too?"[3]

This Islamic perspective differs from other Abrahamic views in that nature is not simply a sign of divinity; nature is sacralized as a creation of God. In the Bukhari hadith collection (an authoritative set of teachings beyond the Quran), Muhammad says, "The earth has been created for me as a mosque and as a means of purification," making the planet itself a holy place. Even more, all natural beings not only are *muslim;* they actively honor God constantly, as we see in Quran 17:44: "The seven heavens and the earth sing His praises, and all who are therein. There is nothing that does not sing His praise, but you do not understand their songs of praise." In popular literature, *The Thousand and One Nights* (incorrectly known as *The Arabian Nights*) describes choirs of birds who sing hymns to Allah. On this basis the ecologically minded Muslim scholar Seyyed Hossein Nasr wrote, "In destroying a species, we are in reality silencing a whole class of God's worshippers."[4]

Because natural beings are fundamentally *muslim* and eternally praise God without breaking a sweat, there is a sense of admiration for natural beings. As Quran 40:57 states, "The creation of the heavens and earth is far greater than the creation of humanity." Humans must work hard to realize deeply the goal of being surrendered to God, yet an apple tree does just this unceasingly, without special toil. This is why the great Islamic mystic Rumi portrayed some animals as superior to humans in love by saying, "Wolf and bear and lion know what love is: he that is blind to love is inferior to a dog!"[5]

Humans and natural beings share the same goal of submission to God and share other characteristics besides. The Quran (6:38) tells us that animals have communities, just as do humans: "There is no creature that crawls on the face of the earth, no bird on the wing, but they are nations like you." This understanding provides a strong foundation for an ethic of care for animals, as for some commentators they are perceived on this basis to possess moral rights. Indeed, nothing in Islam restricts the concept of rights to humans only. Ahmad ibn Habit, a jurist from the Abbasid period, even proposed that animals have their own prophets, although his proposal did not take root. But just like human prophets, Quran 16:68 tells us that bees may receive revelation: "Your Lord inspired the bees: 'Take the mountains for your habitation, as also the trees and what they erect on a trellis. Then eat of all fruits and follow the paths of your Lord, made easy for you.' "[6]

Like human prophets, animals also can pray. Muhammad said that a rooster's morning crowing was his prayer, and he valued roosters for waking everyone up for the first prayer of the day. In the Shii tradition of extracanonical hadith sayings, a pregnant lion asked Imam Musa al-Kazim to pray for her trouble-free delivery, and in turn the lion prayed for the health of the imam, his family, and his compatriots. A provision of Shii Islamic law bans branding or hitting animals in the face, because animals pray. The Turkish shaykh (mystical master) Nursi spoke to cats and discovered that they pray to Allah, and it is not only Nursi who could converse with animals. In Quran 27:16–18, ants and birds engage in verbal communication with humans. In a Shii hadith, the lark is described as an informer to God about the enemies of the Prophet's family. The saints Zayn al-Abidin and Ibrahim ibn Adham both spoke to deer. A lizard greeted Muhammad by saying, "Peace be upon you, Prophet Muhammad, messenger of God!" and Muhammad communicated with a camel, as we see in this instructive story:[7]

> One day the Prophet entered a grove and there he saw a camel. When the camel saw the Prophet, he moved toward him. Tears were flowing out of its eyes. The Prophet approached him, rubbed his head, and the camel calmed down. The Prophet asked, "Who is the caregiver of this camel?" A young man said, "He is mine, oh Messenger of Allah!" The Prophet said, "Don't you fear Allah, who handed you the care of this beast? He complained to me that you do not feed him and you overwork him." The Prophet then bought the camel and sent him to graze with other free camels until he died naturally.

Although the camel in this tale benefited from Muhammad's treatment, perhaps no other beings have prospered from positive Islamic attitudes toward animals more than cats, as a saying attributed to Muhammad tells us "Love of cats is part of the faith." Muhammad, a cat person, famously cut off his sleeve because he had to go to prayer but did not want to disturb the cat sleeping on his garment. One of Muhammad's companions often carried a kitten in his sleeve and thus received the nickname Abu Hurayra, "Father of the Little Kitten," and the thirteenth-century Mamluk sultan al-Zahir Baybars endowed a cat's garden at the High Court of Cairo so that cats could receive loving care, perhaps reflecting an Arab folk saying, "The tyranny of cats is better than the justice of mice." Cats even have prompted spiritual renunciation:[8]

> The grammarian Ibn Babshad was sitting and eating with friends on the roof of a mosque. During the meal, a cat kept coming up, begging a morsel, and leaving, only to return again shortly. Ibn Babshad and his friends eventually followed the cat to the roof of the adjacent building, where the cat was carefully feeding a blind feline colleague. Ibn Babshad was so moved that he took a vow of poverty for the rest of his life, trusting in God alone to provide.[9]

As one can see, cats and other animals are sacralized in Islam in ways that they usually are not in the last chapter's Christian tradition, leading to some interesting Islamic outcomes. Cruelty is explicitly forbidden, following the example of a woman who went to hell for starving a cat. One may not kill frogs, magpies, ants, bees, hoopoes, swallows, or bats. Killing another type of animal without good reason is tantamount in heinousness to killing a human being. Even when pests are killed, there is a religious reward for killing them humanely. Hunting for food is allowed, but hunting for sport is not (despite the activities of emperors like Akbar), and carnivores are forbidden as food sources, thus pleasing lions, tigers, and the like, who may be killed only in self-defense, and taking whose hides is by extension forbidden. Further, all hunting is forbidden in the *Hima* (sanctuary) holy cities of Mecca and

Medina and during pilgrimage. Islamic law also forbids the caging of birds for pets, as birds should fly freely. Fancy dogs cannot be kept merely as status symbols. According to the thirteenth-century legal scholar Izz al-Din ibn Abd al-Salam, animals, even if they are useless to humans because of illness or age, maintain rights to food, water, mates, safe and reasonable working conditions, and comfortable lodging. Following this ethic of compassionate care for animals, the influential contemporary Muslim ecologist B. A. Masri opposes factory farms, vivisection of animals for scientific experiments, fur use, and animal abuse as un-Islamic.[10]

Teachings on the soul provide another difference between Islam and Christianity. In contrast to Christianity, in Islam one cannot argue that animals lack souls. Following Neoplatonic influences and the Quran, Islam teaches that all breathing beings, animal and human alike, have an animal soul, *nafs al-ammara,* a base soul that pursues needs, wants, and survival. It is this animal soul that guides all creatures as they eat, drink, sleep, reproduce, and so on; and within humans the animal soul also channels greed, jealousy, and the like. Because they possess this soul, animals enjoy a measure of intrinsic value.

But this difference between Christianity and Islam in teaching about souls is not so great as it may seem at first blush. Although the issue has been debated, in consonance with later Neoplatonism the dominant Islamic tradition avers that humans, and only humans, possess a second, rational soul, a *nafs al-lawwama* (in another tradition, *al-ruh*), which provides conscience and the ability to choose between right and wrong. This soul, not the animal soul, is the soul that ultimately goes to heaven. The rational souls that only humans possess allow them to make moral choices and therefore earn a heavenly reward, and because of this, humans remain spiritually superior to animals and all other natural beings. In other words, the ability of humans to choose to be *muslim,* owing to their sole possession of a heavenly, rational soul, makes them superior. Animals may be effortlessly *muslim,* but lacking the ability to choose of a rational soul, they may not be saved to Paradise. Instead, on

the Day of Judgment, humans will be rewarded with heaven or punished with hell, but animals simply will turn to dust and disappear.
Nature thus is sacred, because it reflects the divine creative act; but it is
not fully divine in itself.

Alternatively, some Muslims—for example, the previously mentioned Shaykh Nursi, the Arab poet al-Maari, and the Shii theologian
Mulla Sadra—have taught that animals may go to heaven. Belief in a
heavenly destiny for animals was standard among the Mutazilites, philosophical theologians connected with Shiism who lived in southern
Iraq in the eighth, ninth, and tenth centuries, as evidenced by the
thinkers al-Jabbar and al-Hadathi. But their views are not typical. For
instance, when one Mutazilite, al-Nazzam, taught that animals go to
heaven, the jurist al-Baghdadi uttered a more mainstream voice in
rejection, laconically saying that al-Nazzam was welcome to his heaven
of pigs, dogs, and snakes.[11]

Because for most Muslims only humans go to heaven, they enjoy a
superior cosmic position vis-à-vis animals, resulting in the dominion
or stewardship over nature that we have seen in Christianity. Humans
act as God's *khalifa,* his specially appointed managers of the natural
world, as the Quran tells us that "It is God who placed the sea at your
service" (45:13) and "He it was Who made the earth subservient to you.
So roam its byways and eat of His provisions" (67:15). Camels, horses,
mules, and donkeys are created specifically for humans (Quran 16:5–8),
and so are sea creatures (Quran 16:4). Quran 33:72 avers that God first
offered this trust (*al-amana*) or dominion to the heavens, the earth, and
the mountains, but they declined to accept the heavy responsibility.
Humans accepted the responsibility but ever since have been unjust
and intemperate in their stewardship. Nonetheless, humans are God's
best creation, as they were created in "fairest proportion" (Quran 95:4)
and receive admiration even from angels, and so they are a good choice
for this duty of dominion. God retains ownership (Quran 4:126), but
nature is at the service of humans as an "inheritance" (Quran 7:129).
Modernists and fundamentalists often understand this stewardship to

mean relatively free dominance over nature, but more environmentally conscious Muslims will argue that we should be thrifty and smart in our uses of nature in order to minimize our debt for God's generosity. Either way, although Islamic managers of nature may have less discretion in their stewardship of animals than Christians do, nonetheless Islam resembles Judaism and Christianity in providing superior human stewards with the services of inferior natural beings.

As we see in the other Abrahamic religions, this human stewardship at times works to the disadvantage of various natural entities, the first disadvantage involving the relegation of minerals, water, and plants to religious obscurity. For instance, in Islam minerals generally lack almost any sense of spiritual relevance. To be sure, there are some positive passages about mountains in the Quran, such as their being offered dominion over nature before humans were. And the Black Stone of Mecca experiences spiritual action daily, standing as it does at the eastern corner of the Kaaba, the rectangular stone building at the center of Mecca's great mosque. As part of the pilgrimage to Mecca, pilgrims circumambulate the Kaaba seven times counterclockwise. Lucky pilgrims infiltrate the large crowds to physically touch the Kaaba or, best of all, the Black Stone, with their hands. The stone itself is not monolithic but consists of eight parts pieced together. These parts are said to float on water. Lacking a direct scientific test, theories about the stone's material include basalt, agate, meteorite, and desert glass formed from a meteorite impact. But whatever the Black Stone may be, it is not an object of worship in itself. Although there are stories of its miraculous powers, the common Islamic understanding is that it is a symbol of God only, not an embodied divine appearance. Other mineral incarnations are no more sacred.[12]

Water is seen as a chief sign of God in nature. Muhammad advised water conservation and, echoing this, the contemporary Muslim environmentalist Ibrahim Adbul-Matin, interestingly, encourages colleagues in the faith to know and limit their "wudu number," or water consumption for the required ritual ablutions. But water is not divine, not even the water of Zamzam in Mecca, which enjoys a reputation for having healing qualities. To worship natural beings like water is illicit in Quranic Islam for, as Nomanul Haq put it: "Given the uncompromising and radical monotheism of Islam, nature can never acquire divine status. Any idea of nature worship would crack the very core of Islam." Thus Islamic thinkers generally pay little theological attention to water, just as with minerals, as instead they direct worship to a fully invisible God. This makes true nature mysticism, the direct experience of sacredness in and through nature rather than just nature appreciation, largely as absent in Islam as it is in the Christian world.[13]

Plants, well below humans in the Great Chain which influences Islam, are sacralized as God's creations. Both the Quran and various hadiths speak against the useless cutting of plants, Muhammad encouraged the planting of trees even on the day before the Day of Judgment, and the afterlife Paradise consists of heavenly plants. But there is no question of earthly plants' having souls or going to heaven, and so in many Islamic writings, even those regarding ecology, they are overlooked. We see the relative lack of spiritual respect for plants clearly, if with irony, in their frequent employment as patterns in Islamic art. Islamic aesthetics forbids representing Muhammad, other humans, or animals in works of art, for fear that their appearance may distract worship from God alone. But plants are perfectly fine as subjects for Islamic art and sometimes are considered ideal, the implication being that they may be used because no one would ever be so foolish as to worship a plant. Therefore we encounter many beautiful pieces of Islamic art with floral themes, like the superb semiprecious stone inlays at the Taj Mahal, which paradoxically highlight the relatively low spiritual esteem for plants.

For these reasons I describe Islamic approaches to the natural world as anthropocentrism mixed with zoacentrism, or human-and-animal-centeredness. Humans are favored; animals have some intrinsic value and rights, and almost no religious value or rights pertain to the other natural-world constituents of minerals, water, and plants. Moreover, this zoacentrism has a human-centered edge, as animals are valued, at least in part, because of their similarities with humans.

But it is not just minerals, water, and plants who suffer low spiritual favor, as previously we saw al-Baghdadi scoff at al-Nazzam's concept of heaven for including pigs and dogs. Pigs suffer ill regard, as eating swine is forbidden as impure by the Quran, just as in Judaism, and pigs are thought to be unclean for their eating feces. From this, few Muslims raise pigs, and they are absent from many regions of the Islamic world. The keeping of pigs, thus, can demark hogless Muslim communities from pork-eating non-Muslim communities, with negative Islamic connotations, and Muslims may express hatred or racism toward non-Muslim neighbors by describing them pejoratively as pigs, or as related to pigs.[14]

Despite the low status of pigs, perhaps no animal has a harder time in the Islamic world than the dog. The Islamicist scholar Richard Foltz tells us that an ancient, foundational Semitic hostility toward dogs pre-dates Islam. References to dogs in the Bible, Jewish rabbinic tradition, and Christian patristic tradition are overwhelmingly disapproving. Muslim hadith traditions regard them quite negatively overall, including tales in which black dogs are described as evil or Muhammad ordered that some dogs be killed.[15]

From this, dogs in many Muslim lands have been kept for guarding, hunting, or shepherding, but they have not often been family-member pets as found in contemporary Europe, Japan, or the United States. All schools of Muslim law except the Maliki consider dogs to be fundamentally unclean, and after touching a dog one may not pray before washing oneself and changing clothes. The great Sufi mystic Attar unfavorably compared the *nafs*, the soul that must be tamed and subdued on the spiritual path, with dogs. In many places in the Islamic world, when dogs are kept as pets, they are perceived by others as symptomatic of a problematic Westernization among the caregivers. For this reason, in 2002 the Iranian leader Khamenei banned both the sale of dogs and public dog walking. Foltz tells us, "Most dogs in the

Muslim world are mangy, desperate strays, shunned and feared by almost everyone." Even *The Case of the Animals versus Humans*, to be discussed more extensively later, attacks dogs as greedy, selfish, and beggarly traitors to their fellow animal colleagues. One of the worst Arabic and Persian put-downs is calling someone a son of a dog.[16]

Foltz further tells us that the treatment of dogs provides a primary identity marker in places like Iran, where Muslims live alongside Zoroastrians. Zoroastrianism teaches that all animals have souls, but following the prophet Zarathustra's famous dualism, animals are categorized as good or bad. Good animals, which should be protected, include dogs. A dog may substitute for a human in two-person rituals; a dog is a required part of many rituals, such as funeral ceremonies; and dogs have been given funerals much like those of humans. Cats, on the other hand, belong in the category of bad animals in Zoroastrianism. This situation reverses the Islamic regard for cats and disdain for dogs, providing a behavioral identity marker between the two communities that has led, in times of strife, to Muslims' antagonizing their Zoroastrian neighbors by outlawing or even torturing dogs.[17]

Like all religions, Islam arises as a patchwork of attitudes, and not all Muslims dislike dogs. For example, a famous saying describes a prostitute who took pains to make sure that a dog got a drink at a well and had her sins forgiven by this action. It appears that Muhammad permitted dogs in mosques. And there also exists a curious short text from the tenth century, *The Book of the Superiority of Dogs over Many of Those Who Wear Clothes* by Ibn al-Marzuban, which favorably compares dogs against humans. Al-Marzuban retells a story, originally from the *Panchatantra* and similar to that of the Christian St. Guinefort, in which a father must temporarily leave his infant son alone with the family dog. Upon returning, the father does not see his child but he sees that the dog has blood all over its face. Certain that the dog has eaten the baby, the rash father then kills the dog. But later the father finds his baby safely sleeping, along with the dog-wounded corpse of a snake that had threatened the child. The man then is filled with remorse for falsely accusing and then killing the innocent dog. As retold in *The Book of the Superiority of Dogs,* this story glorifies the protective dog and vilifies the father as both stupid and vindictive.

Further, although al-Marzuban describes humans as primarily dishonest, dogs are authentic: "If your dog wags his tail at you, then you can be sure that his tail-wagging is genuine. But do not trust the tail-wagging of people! Many's the tail-wagger who is treacherous!" Dogs are reliable, trustworthy, helpful, protective, and grateful, whereas humans are not.

However, when all is said, rather than offering true praise of dogs, al-Marzuban appears rhetorically to embrace simple disgust with humans rather than any admiration of canines. He does not thereby rehabilitate the Islamic canine image. For instance, al-Marzuban says,[18]

> Gone are the real people and the reign of glory is over;
> All but a few are dogs!
> He who is not a wolf in his dealings with people
> Will these days be eaten up by wolves.

Therefore, despite its provocative title, *The Book of the Superiority of Dogs* leaves the low regard for dogs in the Muslim world essentially unchanged.

The dominion of humans, besides being troublesome for dogs, also strongly impacts other critters through the practice of animal sacrifice that Islam prescribes. But before I enter a specific discussion of Islamic animal sacrifice, I should introduce some general issues. Many Euro-Americans immediately respond to the idea of animal sacrifice in a visceral, horrified way. They think that animal sacrifice is not part of their culture. They assume that animal sacrifice is necessarily cruel. And they wonder why someone would waste perfectly good food in a religious ritual. Although I in no way advocate religious animal sacrifice, I suggest that such Euro-American responses are, in context, off the mark.

First, the assumption that Euro-Americans do not practice animal sacrifice is problematic. In 2012 American factory farms sacrificed, or slaughtered, 33.9 million cattle, 113.3 million pigs, 8.6 billion chickens, and 250.2 million turkeys, or in total 24 million animals daily. The demise of millions of turkeys for the Thanksgiving holiday in the United States alone far outstrips in blood any of the gory animal-sacrifice festivals sponsored by Roman emperors of old. Although one may rightly claim that these are commercial rather than religious killings, this actually makes the situation worse, for reasons I will mention shortly; and we still are left with the reality that animals have sacrificed their lives. But the daily factory-farm mass animal sacrifices are kept out of sight and thus out of mind for most people. As Lisa Kemmerer put it: "Compassion is a central teaching of every major religion, but most people are unaware of how animal industries operate, of how our economic choices either do or do not contribute to intense suffering and uncounted premature deaths."[19]

As for the supposed cruelty of religious animal sacrifice, the American factory-farm system actually fares poorly by comparison in terms of living conditions. As is typical with animal sacrifice globally, and true to the Islamic tradition, animals designated for religious sacrifice are treated with loving care before their demise. They are a special gift to the sacred, so the sacrificer will pamper the animal to make it as healthy and happy as possible—the best gift. Islamic animals for private sacrifice typically are fed and watered quite well, get treated like animal royalty over their shortened lives, and are thought to be blessed by their participation in the sacrificial ritual. Personally, the healthiest animals that I have seen in many trips to Muslim parts of India are those designated for sacrifice.

Compare this with the American factory-farm lives of animals such as chickens. Birds are unnaturally confined in overcrowded cages, where they cannot spread their wings, and their beaks and tails are removed to create space and limit injury. Food may be withheld from egg layers for up to two weeks to force molting and thus hurry a new cycle of fertility. Broiler chickens may have more freedom of movement but still spend their lives in huge, crowded, filthy warehouses where the

Figure 3. Goat decorated for its sacrifice. (©iStock.com/ Number: 28711914, 2013, Artist: ertyo5.)

floor material consists of wood chips soaked through with chicken excrement. Like many animal species, chickens have societies organized around a hierarchical order, but factory life creates social frustration for birds since cramming thousands of them into one expansive space inhibits their abilities to negotiate social status. Further, factory chickens may be pumped full of antibiotics, which ironically over time may make them sicker, and growth drugs, leaving them exposed to unnatural body chemistry and toxins. For these reasons, most of us would prefer to be an animal designated for private religious sacrifice than an animal in an American commercial factory farm. And factory-farm animals receive no religious blessings for their sacrifices, for whatever this may be worth.[20]

Some folks will object that the method of killing, especially the use of stunning to render the animal unconscious, is more humane in factory farms than in religious sacrifices. While stunning before sacrificing has become a commercial standard for large animals because it is perceived as relatively painless, it is not without problems. Sometimes stunning does not work. Sometimes stunning done wrong kills the animal with great pain. And there is evidence that bleeding, and hence the time window of possible pain, takes longer with a stunned animal. At any rate, although there remains some traditionalist Muslim opposition to the use of stunning in the sacrifice, there are no insurmountable obstacles in Islamic law to adding stunning to the ritual practice. In 1982 Shaykh Muhammad al-Najjar of Al-Azhar University issued a *fatwa* to this effect, arguing that stunning in itself is not illicit in Islam but only stunning to death is.[21]

As for the objection that animal sacrifice wastes food: globally, animals sacrificed in religious rituals commonly are eaten. In many contexts the sacrificed animals, considered sacred manifestations of divinity, *must* be eaten, on the premise that if, as the saying has it, you are what you eat, then the eater becomes blessed from the inside out. This situation does not pertain to Islam, because sacrificial animals are not divine. But still, food is not wasted, as Islam encourages followers to eat one-third of the sacrifice themselves, give one-third to neighbors, and offer one-third as charity to the poor. The hide, or its monetary equivalent, should be given to the poor. Not often does an American factory farm freely give away two-thirds of its meat to battle poverty.

As I said, I do not intend these remarks to promote animal sacrifice, given that animals fight for survival much more often than they voluntarily terminate their lives, making obvious the extreme human-centeredness in killing animals for the religious sake of humans. But this understanding allows us to explore the Islamic sacrifice more fruitfully. On the tenth day of the month of Dhu'l-Hijja, Muslims should sacrifice an animal on the Id al-Adha holiday, which is part of the period of the Hajj (pilgrimage to Mecca). Muslims should perform the sacrifice whether they are on the Hajj or not, although the sacrifice is not required of the poor or non-Hajj travelers. In enacting this sacrifice Muslims feel that they are following the *sunnah* or example of the prophet Ibrahim

(Abraham), who in Genesis 22:1–14 nearly sacrificed his son Ismail (Isaac in the Judeo-Christian tradition) in divine obedience before God mercifully substituted a ram for sacrifice instead, although the ram sacrifice is implicit in the Islamic rendering of the story in Quran 37:100–110 rather than explicit as it is in the Genesis version. Accordingly, most Muslims consider physical animal sacrifice to be required, and one may not substitute something else, such as money.

Understood correctly, the sacrifice requires inner devotion to God, not the shedding of blood, just as with Jewish animal sacrifice. The sacrifice symbolizes the sacrificer's inner state, a "practical proof of one's devotion to one's Creator." It does not atone for sins or work magically, and only one's inner purity makes it acceptable. Of this inner emphasis, Quran 22:36–37 says:

> We have assigned livestock for you to be part of the rituals of God. In them there is good for you. So mention the name of God upon them as they are tied up for sacrifice. When fallen upon their sides, eat thereof and feed the beggar, humble or importunate. Thus did We create them to serve you, that you might give thanks. Their flesh and blood shall not reach up to God; rather, it is your piety that will reach Him.

Reflecting this inner understanding of the sacrifice, it is inadvisable or forbidden, depending on whom you ask, for the sacrificer to trim nails or hair during the month of Dhu'l-Hijja until the sacrifice is finished. This allows the sacrificer to enter a ritually pure state of *ihram,* as do participants during the Hajj (pilgrimage to Mecca) also.[22]

Muslims follow the example of Muhammad in their choice of animal: sheep, goat, buffalo, cow, or best of all, camel. The acceptability of cows for food and sacrifice in Islam reverses a pre-Islamic Arab taboo against beef, but the preeminence of camels in the sacrifice continues a pre-Islamic Arabian tradition. One family sacrifices a goat or sheep, but seven families may join together for a camel, cow, or buffalo. Following the principle of offering the best to God, Islamic law bans blemished animals, those who are blind, lame, lean, or mauled in some way. Camels must be at least five years old; cows or buffaloes, two years old; and one year of life is required of sheep and goats. Camels are sacrificed standing up, whereas the other animals are sacrificed lying down.[23]

For humane reasons, the sacrificial knife must be as sharp as possible but must not be sharpened in front of the animal. The sacrificer must do the cut or at least be physically present while another person cuts. Pronouncing the name of Allah over the animal, the sacrificer places the knife's blade between the throat and the breastbone and kills with one swift and, ideally, painless motion. Following Quranic regulations, the whole experience should be as comfortable and free of suffering for the animal as possible. The carcass then is bled completely, although the blood may not be consumed. This method of slaughtering animals must also be used in the factory farms that multiply each year in the Muslim world if everyday meat is to be *halal*, acceptable according to Islamic law.[24]

Because the sacrifice may result in a heavenly reward for humans but not for the sacrificed animals, consideration of the sacrifice reminds us that in Islam humans, who alone may enter heaven, can use natural beings much as they wish, as in the practical proof of devotion in the sacrifice, provided that they do so responsibly. Animals have rights but otherwise may be put to human use both literally and figuratively. Given this ethos, animals often are utilized to symbolize the greatness of God for human benefit, a metaphorical sacrifice, and many pieces of Islamic literature call attention to natural forms as wonders that should inspire human holy awe for God. Quran 3:190 provides an example:

> In the creation of the heavens and the earth,
> In the rotation of night and day,
> Are sure signs for people possessed of minds;
> They who make mention of God, standing, sitting, or reclining,
> Who reflect upon the creation of the heavens and the earth:
> "Our Lord, You did not create all this in vain, glory be to you!"

But, as we saw in the Christian world, the position of revering nature as a beautiful symbol of God's greatness has limits, as by itself it says more about humans than it does about nature. Nature's purpose anthropocentrically leads to salvation for humans and no one else, with the result that the natural world paradoxically becomes devalued. We see this in a story told by the mystic Rumi:[25]

> A Sufi [Muslim mystic] came to a beautiful orchard and, instead of enjoying the beauty of nature, sat on the ground and laid his head upon his knees. His friend was bewildered: "Why doest thou sleep? Nay, look at the vines, behold these trees ... and green plants.... Turn thy face toward these marks of Divine Mercy!" He replied, "The marks of the Divine are within the heart. That which is without is only the mark of the marks."

Regardless of the final merit of regarding nature as a sign for God, what this reverence for nature as a symbol for God's greatness has meant for Islamic cultural forms such as philosophy, art, and literature is that usually animals and other natural entities serve purely as inspirations or stand-ins for humans. There exists little concern for animals themselves, with the focus remaining on what animals can do for people. As Foltz put it, animal figures are "employed as symbols for particular human traits, or ... entirely anthropomorphized actors in human-type dramas. In other words, even where nonhuman animals appear, the real message is about humans. This holds true in the realms of philosophy and mysticism as well as in popular literature and the arts."[26]

But among Muslims, the Sufis, who are the mystics of Islam, have been more likely to emphasize the intrinsically sacred status of nature than more legalistic Muslims, in parallel to some of the Christian saints we saw previously. To Sufis, submission to God means the experience of *tauhid,* the oneness of divine reality, with the understanding that the worshipper and everything around her are facets of omnipresent divine oneness. Sufis believe that their true selves, like the selves of everything, are God, and they seek to experience reality in this way. Sufis therefore pursue a rich, living, and direct encounter with divine unity in a powerful mystical experience. As one hadith states, "One who knows himself knows his Lord." Accordingly, a traditional formulation of the Sufi spiritual path prescribes the introspective experience of *fana,* annihilation of the individual human self, through ascetic and meditative practices designed to quiet individual appetites and develop humility. With this annihilation, one realizes *baqa,* remaining in the true, divine Self. Exhibiting this, when the Sufi Ibrahim ibn Adham was asked why he was unmarried, he said, "If I only could, I would divorce myself," so that there would be nothing left but the experience of Allah.[27]

Because Sufis often have more expansive understandings of nature as sacred, in their training and lore they tend to integrate natural forms in lively ways. The mystic seeks to be engulfed in the fire of God like a moth in a flame; the Sufi longs for God like the nightingale longs for the rose, or the seeker pursues an experience of unity as a drop of water merges with the ocean of God. But perhaps the most visible example of this use of natural beings is the mystical novel *The Conference of the Birds* by the great Sufi Farid al-Din Attar, who employs magnificent natural imagery to offer profound mystical teachings for human use. In *The Conference of the Birds,* a group of birds seeks its king and asks a hoopoe for advice. The hoopoe tells them that after an arduous journey across five valleys and two deserts, they will reach Mt. Kaf and their king, the Simurgh, the benevolent giant bird of Persian legend, whose name has been taken to mean "thirty birds." The different birds in the group of seekers serve as allegories for different human personality types. Because of their personality foibles, on the long journey many birds die, get lost, fatigue, and so on, leaving only thirty birds to arrive at the king's palace. In the palace the birds at first are puzzled, finding no king, until they realize that they have found the *Si murgh,* "thirty birds," in themselves. That is, throughout their long journey divine truth lurked within them, although they did not recognize it. *The Conference of the Birds* thus teaches that the mystical path is filled with troubles until the mystic finds her true self, which is God, within.

In his *Memorial of the Saints* (*Tadhkirat al-Auliya*), Attar offers more tales for mystical instruction. Sufis use meditation as one of pathways for seeking God and as mentioned previously, cats commonly hold a special place in Islamic hearts. Thus a cat once acted as a mentor for two Sufis: Shebli, a revered Sufi master, visited his friend Nuri, an accomplished mystic in his own right, and found him absolutely motionless in meditation. Shebli asked, "How did you learn to remain so still in meditation?" Nuri replied, "From a cat crouching over a mouse-hole. He was much stiller than I was."[28]

Sufis attract controversy in the Muslim world because, even if true Sufis practice the letter of the Quran by fulfilling the Five Pillars of Islamic life, they also explore the spirit of the Quran in ways that may be perceived by non-Sufis as pushing the envelope of orthodoxy. We catch a hint of this subversiveness in this story, in which a dog—otherwise despised in the Islamic world—teaches spiritual renunciation and humility to the great mystic Bistami:[29]

> One day Abu Yazid al-Bistami was walking down the road when a dog came to his side. Abu Yazid drew in his clothes [so as not to be polluted].
>
> The dog said, "If I am dry, no damage is done. If I am wet, seven waters and earths will make peace between us. But if you draw in your clothes like a Pharisee, you will not become clean, not though you bathe in seven oceans."
>
> "You are outwardly unclean," commented Abu Yazid; "I am inwardly unclean. Come, let us work together, that through our united efforts we both become clean."
>
> "You are not fit to travel with me and be my partner," said the dog. "For I am rejected by all humans but you are accepted by them. Whoever encounters me throws a stone at me, yet whoever encounters you treats you like King of the Gnostics. I never store up a bone for the morrow, but you have a barrel of wheat stored up for it."
>
> "I am not fit to travel with a dog!" exclaimed Abu Yazid. "How then will I travel along with the Eternal and Everlasting One? Glory be to that God, who educates the best of creatures with the least of creatures."

But these tales question more than just notions of dogs. Although the Quran condones the eating of meat and vegetarian perspectives remain relatively uncommon in Islam, one tale about the pioneering Sufi Rabia supports vegetarianism while highlighting the theme that saints can tame animals (as we saw in the chapter on Christianity) through their *baraka,* their spiritual charisma:[30]

One day Rabia had gone to the mountains. She was soon surrounded by a flock of deer and mountain goats, ibexes and wild donkeys which stared at her and came to approach her. Suddenly her friend Hasan of Basra came on the scene and moved toward Rabia. As soon as the animals spotted Hasan, they fled, leaving only Rabia. This dismayed Hasan.

"Why did they run away from me and associate so tamely with you?" he asked Rabia.

Rabia countered, "What have you eaten today?"

"A little onion pulp," Hasan replied.

"You eat their fat," Rabia remarked. "Why should they not flee from you?"

On the path to entertaining sacred experiences Sufis try to develop *tawakkul*, trust in God. For Sufis, God in the end is the only actor, and so the mystic should cultivate as deep a sense as possible of trusting God to provide, as we saw earlier, when Ibn Babshad embraced a vow of poverty after witnessing cat-on-cat generosity. For example, animals assisted Rabia in showing us what trust in God is all about. Once Rabia was boiling some food and needed but lacked an onion. Just then, a bird appeared with a wild onion in its beak and gave the onion to her. Another time, Rabia had just sown her grain field with seed when hungry locusts arrived, threatening to eat her crop before it could even start to grow. Rabia prayed to Allah "If You will it, I will give my food to Your enemies or Your friends," and the locusts disappeared.[31]

Tawakkul includes the idea of trusting God to protect one from dangerous animals. On this account, both in legend and in reality Sufis enjoy fame for seeking out mystical encounters with lions to develop this trust. Nuri, whom previously we saw learning meditation from a house cat, himself courted lions:[32]

One night a report came to the people of Qadesiya that a saint needed rescue from the Valley of Lions. All of the people then went to the Valley of Lions. There they found that Nuri had dug a grave and was sitting there, surrounded by crouching lions. The people interceded and took Nuri back to Qadesiya, asking him his story.

"For a while I had eaten nothing," he told them. "I was traversing the desert when I espied a date tree. I had a longing for fresh dates. Then I said,

'There is still room left for desire. I will go down into this valley, that the lions may rend you, my appetite; then you will no longer desire dates.'"

As we saw with Rabia, the spiritual charisma of the *waliya* (saint) who has cultivated trust in God may tame wild animals. Many lions and other wild beasts frequented the house of the saint Sahl al-Tostari, who fed and cared for them, and another Sufi, Abu Said, tamed a dangerous serpent while teaching a disciple:[33]

> On an outing one day, Abu Said and one of his disciples passed through a region infested with poisonous snakes. As they were walking, a snake slithered close to Abu Said and began to wrap itself around him. The disciple, struck with fear and wonder, stood motionless. Upon seeing the condition of his disciple, the shaykh said, "Do not be frightened. This snake has come to pay his respect and will not harm me. Do you wish him to say hello to you as well?"
>
> "I certainly do!" replied the disciple eagerly.
>
> Abu Said responded, "That, my friend, will never happen so long as it is your ego that desires it!"

As we saw in the Christian world, animals who are tamed by saints practice religion through their devotion to the holy figures. Once pacified, these animals, even lions, may become helpful friends, as the Sufi Ibrahim al-Khauwas learned in a twist on the old tale of Androcles and the lion:

> One day in the desert I came upon a tree where there was water. I beheld a huge lion making for me and committed myself to God. When he came near I noticed he was limping. He lay down before me and groaned. I saw that his paw was swollen and gangrenous. So I took a stick and cut open the paw, till all the pus was drained, and then I bandaged the paw with a rag. The lion arose and went away. Presently the lion returned, bringing his cub. They circled around me wagging their tails, and brought a round bread and laid it before me.

Interestingly, Rabia did not just tame animals; she resurrected them. The Sufi writer al-Munawi relates that once Rabia was on a pilgrimage when her transport, her camel, died. She prayed to Allah to restore life to the camel, and God did. The camel survived until it had taken Rabia all the way home. Another saint, the Egyptian Nafisa, even exhibited power over water. It seems that one year the Nile River did not give its annual life-enabling floods, and frightened farmers came to Nafisa, claiming that their crops would fail because there would result a lack of irrigation water. She gave them her veil to cast upon the river, which immediately rose to fill irrigation canals and end the danger.[34]

These stories of cats who model meditation, dogs who teach humility, and lions who repay health-care favors are fascinating tales that employ natural beings to teach human mystical lessons. But perhaps the most interesting story in Attar's *Memorial of the Saints* involves an animal who appears to practice mystical religion like a human:[35]

> It seems that one day a Sufi named Abu Othman al-Hiri was walking to school. On his way he passed an ancient caravanserai [a kind of truck stop for pack animals]. He peered in to find a donkey with large sores on its back and too little strength to repel the raven which was pecking away at the sores. Abu Othman was filled with compassion for the donkey. Dressed opulently, Abu Othman nonetheless took off his silk robe and covered the donkey, using his unwrapped turban as a bandage. With mute elegance the donkey at once communed with God Almighty.

Animals in Islam should just be signs of the wondrousness of God, not receptors of mystical experiences! The donkey's mystical experience of communion with God, if we take it at face value, embodies an alternative face of Islam, one in which animals, like Paul's baptized lion, practice religion. Although uncommon, there are other, similar examples, such as the bees who receive revelation in Quran 16:68 and the animals who are tamed through their devotion to a Sufi saint. Muhammad's inspired camel also founded a mosque:[36]

> When the Prophet Muhammad migrated to Medina, he rode a she-camel named al-Qaswa. As she strode through town many friends and relatives of Muhammad tried to grab her halter in order to make her stop, so that they might have the honor of hosting Muhammad. But each time Muhammad ordered her release, saying that she "was under the command of God."

With loose reins she eventually made her way to an informal place of prayer which had been set up by Assad Ibn Zurarah and knelt at the entrance. She paused for a moment, then arose and walked away. But the camel had not gotten far before she turned, returned to the prayer plot, and knelt in the same spot as before, this time flattening her stomach to the ground. Muhammad alighted, bought the plot of land, and commenced construction of a mosque on that very spot.

Animals are not supposed to practice religion in Islam, but this camel did, helping with the devotional task of founding a mosque. In another tale, which resembles the Christian story of Eustace and the stag, a deer likewise practices religion by converting Ibrahim ibn Adham to a deeper form of Islam. As the story goes, one day Ibrahim was hunting in the wilds on horseback. He had recently experienced some shocking things and was in a state of confusion, and so he hoped that a hunt would clear his mind. But as he rode, he heard a voice call *Awake!* four times. Just then he encountered a deer and prepared to give chase. The deer spoke to him, saying, "I have been sent to hunt you. You cannot catch me. Was it for this that you were created, or is this what you were commanded?" Ibrahim responded to the deer with a powerful mystical experience, transforming him and changing his life forever by causing him to embrace his mystical calling. Sure faith was now established in him.[37]

Lest we think that such experiences are simply products of the desert or relics from a lost past, we should consider a 1990s example of animal spiritual practice from a Sufi center in Birmingham, England, affiliated with the shaykh Sufi Abdullah. Mystics at this center primarily practice *zikr,* or rhythmic chanting of the glorified names of God in concentrated mystical meditation. One day a human disciple was cleaning one room at the center when he heard the sound of *zikr* coming from another room. The disciple recounted, "When I looked into that room, there was no one there. But I kept hearing the *zikr.* Then I looked up and saw there was a pigeon sitting on the edge of the roof doing the *zikr.*" This unexpected meditating bird reflects a tradition in which pigeons are thought to have spiritual longings, as their cooing resembles the sound of Persian *Ku ku?* "Where is He? Where is He?"[38]

These stories of animals with spiritual capabilities alert us to animal-affirming perspectives nestled within Islam's overarching human superiority. Also, as with all religious forms, we discover further animal-friendly perspectives if we explore the interfaces between high religion and local folk religions. When we look at how Islam has mixed with various indigenous traditions, what we find are syncretic blends in which pre- or non-Islamic nature religions dissolve into Islamic realities. Take, for instance, the case of the Islam of the Tsakhur people of Dagestan. Indigenous religions of Dagestan project a belief in the Master of Animals, a spirit found in many indigenous religions who serves as the spiritual leader of all animals and therefore strongly controls hunting. Not unlike the Greek Artemis or the Roman Diana, a pleased Master of Animals brings game to the hunter, whereas an offended Master of Animals withholds game. In the case of the Tsakhur people, this means that hunters have little incentive to cease worship of this nature spirit. However, as we have seen, Quranic Islam leaves no room for the worship of spirits of nature rather than an intangible God. The Tsakhurs resolve this dilemma in part by Islamizing their Master of Animals. Called Abdal, a variant of the traditional Muslim name Abdallah ("Servant of God"), he remains the patron of animals, living in the mountains, where he nurtures, herds, and milks wild animals. Alternatively appearing as a white beast or a white man, as the patron spirit of the hunt he allows hunters success, but only insofar as necessary to fulfill *zakat*, the charitable giving that Islam requires. In this way Abdal shows us that, in everyday practice, Islam may absorb elements of nature religion by giving them an Islamic veneer.[39]

Another example of this principle comes to us from the Ivory Coast. The West African Islamic world, as frequently is the case in Islam, engages in the veneration of Sufi saints. These "friends of God," spiritually powerful while living, gain perhaps even more spiritual potency after death. Because of this potency, they often act as intercessors with

God, and prayers are addressed to them. Such worship among the Jula people on the Ivory Coast enables a syncretism in which Islam blends with traditional local beliefs in another Master of Animals, the spirit Manimory. One day long ago the anthropomorphic Manimory disappeared into the forest, became one with it, and gained the ability to protect hunters within it. Thus any successful hunt relies on the blessings of the forest spirit Manimory, adding a biocentric dimension to Ivorian Islam. As part of their initiation into Manimory's mysteries, hunters sacrifice kola nuts and chickens. Then they invoke blessings to increase game, such as "May Allah grant Manimory's blessing" or "May Allah make the fields sweet by the intercession of Manimory," chants that at once straddle the boundaries between Quranic Islam, Sufi saint veneration, and Ivorian folk traditions. Hunters also call on Manimory, whom we may even call a Sufi Saint Master of Animals, to gain the power to shape-shift during the hunt, increasing their prowess by making them invisible to prey. To this end Jula hunters chant to Allah and to Manimory to enable chameleon power:[40]

> To whom did Allah give the power to change shape?
> The chameleon says something:
> The chameleon becomes it.
> That which the chameleon sees,
> The chameleon becomes it.

This privileging of Manimory for worship provides an exception to the mainstream Islamic tradition, which as we have seen primarily describes human-animal relationships in terms of an attitude of noblesse oblige whereby humans, as the superior creatures, care for inferior, natural beings. We also have found some other ad-hoc exceptions, such as a donkey with mystical experience and a camel who determines the location of a mosque. Similar exceptions arise in a more cogent way in a fascinating work, *The Case of the Animals versus Humans before the King of the Jinn*. Written by the anonymous Brethren of Purity group (Ikhwan al-Safa), who lived in the Iraqi city of Basra in the late tenth century, *The Case of the Animals versus Humans* asks fundamental questions regarding human-animal relationships and succeeds in lending an animal-friendly sense that animals are subjective agents in themselves, with thoughts, feelings, and agendas of their own. Although the book remains authoritative only among Ismaili Muslims, it explores a vast array of human-animal topics in ways that clearly reflect many shared Islamic perspectives.

The story begins when a ship full of humans wrecks on the remote island of Saun, whose king is the jinn (supernatural spirit) Biwarasp the Wise. Myriads of animals populate the island, which until the shipwreck lacked humans, all living in peace and harmony with one another, secure and unafraid. But quickly the shipwrecked humans take to hunting animals or putting them to work, as if the animals are their runaway and rebellious slaves. Dismayed by this turn of events, the animals then air their grievances before King Biwarasp, who convenes a court and invites the humans and the animals to state their respective cases. At the court the humans argue, following many different criteria, that animals are their slaves because of human superiority. Conversely, the animals demand freedom by indicating how the humans' claims are founded on suppositions that are arbitrary at best and untrue at worst. For example, the human side claims superiority over animals because of humanity's superior intellect. To this the animals respond:[41]

> As for your supposedly superior minds—we find not the least trace or sign of that. If you had such powerful intellects you would not have boasted over us about things which are not your own doing or won by your own efforts but which are among God's manifold gifts, to be recognized and acknowledged as acts of grace. The intelligent take pride only in things of their own doing—wholesome arts, sound views, true sciences, upright conduct, just practices, ways pleasing to God. As far as we can see, you have no advantage to boast of but only groundless claims, baseless allegations, and bootless choler.

When the humans claim superiority because of their possession of organized social groups, the bee likewise hammers at humanity: "So, were this human to study the life of the ants and consider their ways, he would find that they have science, understanding, discernment, awareness, knowledge, governance, and an ordered polity, just as humans do, and he would not boast of superiority on that score." By the way, this understanding that ants possess organized social groups mirrors that of contemporary zoology.[42]

The Case of the Animals versus Humans proposes an interesting answer to the question of animal religions. When humans claim that they are superior because they practice religion, they are immediately rebuked by the nightingale:[43]

> Said the delegate of the birds, "Had you reflected on the matter, O human, and given it serious thought, you'd have realized that all these things count against you, not in your favor.
>
> "Because all these [religions] are penalties, chastisements to expiate sin and atone for wrong-doing, or to restrain you from foul, shameful doings ... we are free of sin and evil, indecency and disgrace. We don't need the rituals you boast of.
>
> "God sent his prophets and messengers only to miscreant peoples.... But we are clear of all these things. We submit to our Lord, acknowledge Him and humbly believe in Him, proclaiming his oneness without cavil or doubt."

Thus *The Case of the Animals versus Humans* tells us that animals do not have religions because, unlike morally problematic humans, animals do not need them.

During the debate both sides hurl insults, but otherwise behavior speaks as much as the arguments themselves. The animals appear orderly, cooperative with each other, and polite. The animals also are openly and intrinsically *muslim,* or submitted to God, a fact that the nightingale uses to rhetorical advantage in claiming, "All these ills beset you humans because you rebelled against your Lord, spurned the obedience due Him, and ignored His charge. We're far above all this." Humans, on the other hand, act as disorganized, confused, and arrogant liars and hypocrites. So, whereas a cricket delivers a moving song in praise of God, the humans conspire to win the debate through cheating or bribery.[44]

In these ways, the course of the debate deals blow after blow to the myth of human superiority over animals, making the end of the tale more jarring. Finally the humans argue that they are superior, and hence worthy of taking animals as slaves, because they go to heaven but animals do not. When the nightingale objects that animals can't go to hell, either, the human argument shifts to claim that only humanity produces saved saints: "We have among us prophets and their devisees, imams, sages, poets and paragons of goodness and virtue, saints and their seconds, ascetics, pure and righteous figures, persons of piety, insight, understanding, awareness, and vision, who are like the angels on high!" The jinn king and the animals immediately accept this argument without question or assessment—in a work that otherwise is thorough in assessment—and, strangely, the humans win the debate. Perhaps the authors of *The Case of the Animals versus Humans* feared charges of heresy for subverting the myth of human superiority and thus limply bowed to orthodoxy in the end. Regardless, despite this odd finish, *The Case of the Animals versus Humans* exhibits many of the multivalent concepts of religious relationship with natural beings, particularly animals, in the world of Islam. The text discloses a fundamental tension in Islam between, on one side, humanity's superiority and the rights and obligations that this superiority entails, and on the other side, perceived conceptual limits both to human supremacy and to corresponding human privileges.[45]

These tensions have shaped Islam as it has spread and adapted to local cultures. An extreme example of this mixing with local cultures involves Islam's blending with Hinduism in India to form the separate religion of Sikhism, which was first taught by Guru Nanak (1469–1539 C.E.). As a spiritual leader, Nanak enjoyed a variety of remarkable encounters with nature. One such event from his youth happened on a day when Nanak herded the family cattle in the forest. Nanak's cattle slipped away from him, entered the property of a neighbor, and devastated the crops, leaving the neighbor enraged by Nanak's apparently having fallen asleep on the job. A member of the community then went to investigate. He found Nanak under a tree, deep in a meditative trance rather than sleeping. Above his head hovered the hood of a cobra, who used its body to protect Nanak from the hot noonday sun. Because of Nanak's saintliness, miraculously the field that had been ravaged by Nanak's cows returned to normal, with not a blade out of place.

This story reflects a theme that we have seen in the Islamic world: the ability of saints to tame otherwise dangerous animals and control natural forces. But this story also calls our attention to the profession of cow herding in India, which over time has been so esteemed as a calling that it has deeply influenced Hinduism as well as Sikhism. We now turn to this world of Indian pastoralism.

3

Hindu Trees Tremble with Ecstasy

Four millennia ago *The Epic of Gilgamesh* offered us a wonderful example of tragic dalliance with a divine animal. The brash Gilgamesh, king of Uruk in Mesopotamia, had just ignored counsel and, with the help of the Sun god, Shamash, defeated Humbaba, the ogre of the Cedar Forest. Returning to Uruk, Gilgamesh cleaned himself after the battle to resume his regal appearance. But as self-adoring as the proud Gilgamesh may have been at that moment, the goddess Ishtar was even more smitten with him. Daughter of the preeminent sky god Anu and symbolized by the planet Venus, Ishtar was the Mesopotamian goddess of love, sexuality, and war, and was closely identified with lions, sometimes being called the divine lioness.

As the goddess of sexuality Ishtar was insatiable, and she looked upon the handsome and successful Gilgamesh with great longing. She proposed marriage, promising Gilgamesh both power and riches. Gilgamesh refused, citing the lineage of previous mates whom Ishtar had destroyed: a bird, lion, horse, shepherd, and the harvest god, Tammuz. Enraged that Gilgamesh had spurned her, Ishtar returned to heaven and demanded that her father, Anu, give her the Bull of Heaven (the constellation Taurus) in order to exact her revenge. At first Anu refused, chastising his daughter, but after she threatened to open the gates of hell and unleash the dead to feast on the living, Anu finally relented, releasing the Bull of Heaven upon Uruk to kill three hundred people. Eventually Enkidu, Gilgamesh's colleague, was able to grab and hold the Bull by its tail while Gilgamesh slaughtered the holy beast, and the two then offered the Bull's heart to the Sun god, Shamash. Ishtar's revenge plot thus ended: she mourned the loss of the Bull of Heaven, but Gilgamesh remained happy to have avoided marriage with the leonine goddess.[1]

Gilgamesh's near-marriage to a deity who could take animal form is not the only example of such matches. Speaking more broadly, there are many other examples of religious experiences with nature that assume the form of various familial relationships, not just spousal ones. Some of these relationships, such as the near-union of Gilgamesh and the holy lioness Ishtar, take the form of *kin biocentrism,* in which humans are thought to relate to nonhuman living beings in terms of fictive or real family dynamics. Bears are our siblings, our cousins, our grandparents, or something similar. Likewise, *kin ecocentrism* reflects family dynamics, but of course more broadly includes stones, bodies of water, and so on.

We discover both these concepts at New Talavana Dham, a Hindu center in the southeastern United States, where devotees approach cattle, the holy basil plant, and rivers as sacred natural mothers. New Talavana highlights the idea of considering at least some natural beings as persons in their own right, having their own feelings, concerns, and agendas. Religiously interacting with natural beings who are persons, especially mothers, New Talavana devotees relate to them with attitudes of gratitude, respect, intimacy, and reverence, much as one may approach one's human mother.

New Talavana, resting firmly in the Christian Bible Belt of the United States, embraces the natural world in a way quite different from many of its Bible Belt religious neighbors. This difference arises in part because of the adopted Indian origins, and hence the fundamental presuppositions, of New Talavana Hinduism. Since Indian thought largely lacks influence from the Greek Great Chain of Being, the scholar of Indian religions Harold Coward tells us: "In contrast to the Western traditions where humans are frequently described as being separate from nature over which they have dominion, Indian thought has seen humans (in their embodied lives) as an intimately interconnected part of nature." Whereas the Abrahamic religions have waged battle against nature religions, Indian traditions more often have instead creatively fused strains of nature religion into major religious forms such as Hinduism, Buddhism, Jainism, and Sikhism. This is why the Hinduism scholar David Haberman says: "One need only travel about India to observe reverence toward natural forms: the worship of mountains, forests, animals, trees, ponds, rocks, plants, and rivers as natural forms of divinity." He further tells us that many Indian Hindus regard plants like trees as holy persons with their own sacred inner lives.[2]

Because of this notion that natural beings are holy persons, New Talavana's theology and philosophy embrace a greater role for nature than that typically appearing in Christianity. A number of Indian sacred texts serve as New Talavana scriptures, but the most important of these are the *Caitanya Caritamrta*, the *Isopanisad*, the *Bhagavad Gita* (and the larger *Mahabharata*, of which it is a section), and what many people know as the *Bhagavata Purana*, which New Talavana reverentially calls *Srimad Bhagavatam* because of its importance. Although there exist a number of fine translations of these texts, I will use the same paper and electronic translations of them that local devotees use in order for us to enjoy the most authentic *rasa* ("flavor") of New Talavana spirituality.

These texts describe the greatness, centrality, and exploits of the central deity, Krishna, "the Supreme Personality of the Godhead." Both fully transcendent and fully immanent, the monotheistic Krishna alone is the creator, maintainer, and destroyer of the universe, with all other divine powers serving him. The god Vishnu appears as an expansion of Krishna, not vice versa as one often finds. *Bhagavata Purana* 1.3.28 declares: "Lord Shri [Honored] Krishna is the original Personality of Godhead," and the *Isopanisad* tells us:[3]

The Personality of Godhead is perfect and complete, and because He is completely perfect, all emanations from Him, such as this phenomenal world, are perfectly equipped as complete wholes. Whatever is produced of the Complete Whole is also complete in itself. Because He is the Complete Whole, even though so many complete units emanate from Him, He remains the complete balance.

The powerful demigods cannot approach Him. Although in one place, He controls those who supply the air and rain.... He is within everything, and yet He is outside of everything.

In both the *Bhagavad Gita* and the *Bhagavata Purana,* Krishna, the Absolute, appears on earth in India in human form. This Krishna is not really human or material, but he creates the *avatar* (illusory appearance) that he is human for our benefit, in order that we may understand him more clearly. In this appearance he is joined by his elder brother, Balarama, who himself represents a divine appearance of the powerful serpent deity Sheshanaga, the multiheaded cobra who provides a canopy for the deity Vishnu in Hindu art and myth.

Exhibiting a face that Abraham's God never shows, several times Krishna appeared on earth intentionally in animal forms: as a fish, tortoise, boar, and the lion-human hybrid Narasimha. This led the Madhva Gaudiya Vaishnava tradition, the lineage of Indian religion to which New Talavana belongs, to include natural beings in vibrant ways from its inception, this vividness beginning with the tradition's founder, Shri Chaitanya Mahaprabhu. The charismatic Chaitanya (1486–1534 C.E.) led an important revival of *bhakti* (devotional) Hinduism in the eastern Indian states of Bengal, Odisha, and Jharkhand. Considered by devotees to be Krishna himself, he possessed a spiritual genius that inflamed passion for Krishna in whomever he met. Following *Bhagavata Purana* 11.5.32, Chaitanya taught that the most essential and effective spiritual practice for our current *Kali Yuga* (dark age) is *sankirtan,* the chanting and singing of Krishna's name. Inspiring huge crowds to ecstatically chant the name of Krishna, Chaitanya turned entire cities upside down: "Thousands of people were following him. Some were crying and some were laughing,

Figure 4. Poster of Chaitanya at the Festival of the Cow.
(Photo: Author.)

some were dancing and some were singing, and some were falling on
the ground, offering obeisances to the Lord. And all of them were roar-
ing the holy name: 'Krishna! Krishna!'"[4]

But it was not just humans who burned in the inferno of love for
Krishna while in Chaitanya's presence. In a truly rich story from the
Caitanya Caritamrta we find that Chaitanya not only tamed animals, as
we saw with Abrahamic saints; he even inspired tigers and deer to cud-
dle, like the wolf peacefully lying with the lamb in Isaiah 11:6:[5]

When the Lord [Chaitanya] passed through the solitary forest chanting the holy name of Krishna, the tigers and elephants, seeing Him, gave way. When the Lord passed through the jungle in great ecstasy, packs of tigers, elephants, rhinoceros, and boars came, and the Lord passed right through them. Balabhadra Bhattacarya [Chaitanya's companion] was very much afraid to see them, but by Shri Chaitanya Mahaprabhu's influence, all the animals stood to one side.

While Shri Chaitanya Mahaprabhu was bathing in a river, a herd of maddened elephants came there to drink water. While the Lord was bathing and murmuring the *Gayatri* mantra, the elephants came before Him. The Lord immediately splashed some water on the elephants and asked them to chant the name of Krishna. The elephants whose bodies were touched by the water splashed by the Lord began to chant "Krishna! Krishna!" and dance and sing in ecstasy. Some of the elephants fell to the ground, and some screamed in ecstasy.

Sometimes Shri Chaitanya Mahaprabhu chanted very loudly while passing through the jungle. Hearing His sweet voice, all the does came near Him.... While Shri Chaitanya Mahaprabhu was passing through the jungle, five or seven tigers came. Joining the deer, the tigers began to follow the Lord. Seeing the tigers and deer following Him, Shri Chaitanya Mahaprabhu immediately remembered the land of Vrindavana [the ideal religious place]. He then began to recite a verse describing the transcendental quality of Vrindavana. "Vrindavana is the transcendental abode of the Lord. There is no hunger, anger or thirst there. Though naturally inimical, human beings and fierce animals live together there in transcendental friendship." When Shri Chaitanya Mahaprabhu said, "Chant Krishna! Krishna!," the tigers and deer began to chant "Krishna!" and dance.... Indeed, the tigers and deer began to embrace one another, and touching mouths, they began to kiss. When Shri Chaitanya Mahaprabhu saw all this fun, He began to smile. Finally He left the animals and continued on His way.

Needless to say, in this dynamic story the elephants who scream in ecstasy, as well as the tigers and deer who embrace in spiritual love, appear to practice religion.

As Chaitanya's teachings passed through later generations in eastern India, they entered the hands of A. C. Bhaktivedanta Swami Prabhupada, known to his disciples as Shrila Prabhupada, who was tasked by his guru Bhaktisiddhanta Saraswati to spread Chaitanya's message to the English-speaking world. Responding to his teacher's charge, in 1965 Prabhupada arrived in New York City at the age of 70, penniless, homeless, and armed only with some of his own scriptural translations and the hope of igniting Chaitanya's devotional fire in Manhattan. Exhibiting as much willpower, energy, and organizational ability as any religious leader of the twentieth century, it was not long before Prabhupada gathered a circle of disciples who became known as Hare Krishnas, as they praised Krishna like Chaitanya while chanting the *Maha-mantra* taught to them by Prabhupada:

> *Hare Krishna, Hare Krishna, Krishna Krishna, Hare Hare*
> *Hare Rama, Hare Rama, Rama Rama, Hare Hare.*

According to a pamphlet from Prabhupada's movement, this sacred chant means, "O all-attractive, all-pleasing Lord, O energy of the Lord, please engage me in Your devotional service."[6]

Prabhupada legally incorporated his movement in 1966 as the International Society for Krishna Consciousness, or ISKCON. Then, in a remarkable explosion of growth, within a matter of just a few years there were ISKCON outposts in many different cities and countries around the world, resulting currently in more than four hundred temples speaking more than thirty different languages and having spread to every continent but Antarctica. Before he died in 1977, Prabhupada personally initiated more than five thousand disciples. At first largely a movement of Western converts, since the 1990s many people of Indian descent have joined, making ISKCON a multicultural and multiethnic community.[7]

ISKCON everywhere is known for its charitable food programs. In a practice initiated by Prabhupada, every Sunday ISKCON centers host "love feasts," which include chanting, spiritual instruction, and the "honoring," or eating, of *prashadam*, food blessed by being first ritually offered to Krishna. As *Bhagavad Gita* 3.13 says, "The devotees of the Lord are released from all kinds of sins because they eat food which is offered first for sacrifice." Krishna himself eats the *prashadam* blessed food with his glance, leaving plenty for everyone else. Honoring *prashadam,* "grace in an edible form," is not just eating delicious food; it is a fundamental way that one can serve Krishna, earning ISKCON the nickname "the kitchen religion." Always vegetarian, *prashadam* consists of wholesome ingredients, making it nutritionally as well as spiritually healthy. Anyone who eats *prashadam,* even an animal, receives at least a human rebirth in the next life, so ISKCON happily distributes food compassionately, including through its noteworthy international Food for Life charity, which New Talavana supports through proceeds from its Good Karma Café restaurants.[8]

Part of the early expansion of ISKCON included establishing farm communities to teach and live its motto, Simple Living and High Thinking, emphasizing the protection of cows, sustainable organic production, and back-to-nature lifestyles. New Vrindavan, established by Prabhupada in West Virginia in 1968, arose first. Now sixty ISKCON farms exist across the globe, including five others in addition to New Talavana in the United States.

The seed for New Talavana within the ISKCON empire emerged from the founding of a temple in New Orleans in 1971. Some of the members there wished to leave their urban environs and protect cows in the countryside, as Krishna did, and so they bought a two-hundred-acre rural property in 1974. In 1975 Shrila Prabhupada visited the community and charged it with becoming an embodiment of ISKCON principles. Over the next few years devotees bought more adjacent property, so that by 1981 New Talavana reached its current size, approximately 1,200 acres, making it the second largest ISKCON farm community. Of this land, about four hundred acres consists of tall longleaf-pine timberland, typical of the region, and sometimes timber is sold. Wetlands occupy about two hundred acres. Cow pasture makes up 367 acres, and about another two hundred acres embraces residential, orchard, and garden locations. Twenty ISKCON families live near the farm, with another five families residing on the farm itself, along with eight single men. Most

of these people provide sometimes-substantial service to New Talavana without receiving a wage, although they get plenty of physically
and spiritually healthy *prashadam* blessed food. Besides these people on
or near the farm, there are several hundred more community members
more or less within driving distance.

Religious teachings at New Talavana derive primarily from Shrila
Prabhupada, who personally initiated some of the longtime devotees.
Prabhupada emphasized that now we are in the degenerate age of our
universe's life, the *Kali Yuga,* during which time religious practices that
may have worked in the past no longer are effective. Instead, to combat
the *Kali Yuga* Krishna specifically left us practices that are so easy to
follow, they'll even work at this dark time. As described in *Bhagavad
Gita* 11.54, these practices begin with surrender to Krishna's grace.
Through a grace that is so powerful it saves even demons, Krishna
wants us to return to him in *vaikuntha,* the nonmaterial spiritual sky,
and will make this possible if we do our part. This occurs through loving service to Krishna, this service taking many different forms.

It is difficult to overstate the importance of this idea of service in ISK-
CON; for just one example, Sanskrit names for devotees always affix Dasi
or Dasa, female and male, respectively, for "servant." Prabhupada wrote,
"There is no difference between the kingdom of God and the devotional service of the Lord." Through passionate service one comes to
understand Krishna and one's relationship to him, one's "Krishna consciousness," more clearly. As the scriptural *Isopanisad* puts it:[9]

> One should know perfectly the Personality of Godhead Shri Krishna and
> His transcendental name, form, qualities and pastimes, as well as the tem-
> porary material creation with its temporary demigods, men and animals.
> When one knows these, he surpasses death and the ephemeral cosmic
> manifestation with it, and in the eternal kingdom of God he enjoys his
> eternal life of bliss and knowledge.

The "eternal kingdom of God" and the "pastimes" of Krishna stand out
in this passage. Full realization of *buddhi-yoga,* or Krishna consciousness,
provides one at death with an eternal place with Krishna in *Goloka-*

Vrindavan, the highest and purest cosmic realm of the spiritual sky. The first part of this name, *Goloka,* translates as "Heaven of Cows," and *Vrindavan* denotes a holy place in India's Yamuna River Valley where Krishna spent his boyhood, simultaneously existing both on earth and in the Heaven of Cows. Unlike other spiritual domains, there is no rebirth out of the Heaven of Cows, so arriving in this blessed realm breaks the cycle of reincarnation that Hinduism asserts.

Set against the background of a timeless agrarian, rural north India, in the Heaven of Cows the youthful Krishna eternally herds cattle, accompanied by his brother, other male cowherd friends, and adoring *gopis,* female cowherds, who serve as models for emulation because of their devotion to Krishna. The cattle of the Heaven of Cows are not ordinary earthly cattle but *surabhis,* cows who grant wishes, and Krishna communicates with them by lowing. Wish-granting trees grow there as well. Krishna also cavorts with peacocks, his *vahana* or spiritual animal companions, and of course his loving devotees. In the Heaven of Cows devotees do not become one with Krishna, nor do they imitate him, as may happen in other forms of Hinduism. Instead, devotees seek peaceful, joyful service to their deity in imitation of the cowherdesses who spiritually swoon for Krishna.

In this wonderful Heaven of Cows, Krishna; Balarama; Radha, a cowherdess who represents the greatest embodiment of *prema,* or selfless spiritual love; other cowherdesses; and many other characters enjoy pastimes, or spiritual-play events. In their youth Krishna and Balarama act as cowherds, and accordingly many of these pastime stories involve Krishna's treasured cattle or the cowherdesses who were driven to spiritual ecstasy by the sound of Krishna's playing the flute. Of course, just as Chaitanya inspired tigers and deer to embrace, so in his flute-playing pastimes in *Bhagavata Purana* 10.21.9–19 Krishna causes even clouds to swell out of love, rivers to feel jubilation, and plants to tremble with spiritual joy:[10]

My dear *gopis,* what auspicious activities must the flute have performed to enjoy the nectar of Krishna's lips independently and leave only a taste for us *gopis*, for whom that nectar is actually meant! The forefathers of the flute, the bamboo trees, shed tears of pleasure. His mother, the river on whose bank the bamboo was born, feels jubilation, and therefore her blooming lotus flowers are standing like hair on her body.

Using their upraised ears as vessels, the cows are drinking the nectar of the flute-song flowing out of Krishna's mouth. The calves, their mouths full of milk from their mothers' moist nipples, stand still as they take Govinda [Krishna as a cowherd] within themselves through their tear-filled eyes and embrace Him within their hearts.

In the company of Balarama and the cowherd boys, Lord Krishna is continually vibrating His flute as He herds all the animals of Vraja [the area around Vrindavan], even under the full heat of the summer sun. Seeing this, the cloud in the sky has expanded himself out of love. He is rising high and constructing out of his own body, with its multitude of flower-like droplets of water, an umbrella for the sake of his friend.

When Lord Krishna plays on His flute, the sweet music causes the moving living entities to become stunned and the nonmoving trees to tremble with ecstasy. These things are certainly very wonderful.

But just as these ecstatic trees admire Krishna, in turn he admires them, saying to his cowherd friends:[11]

> Just see these greatly fortunate trees, whose lives are completely dedicated to the benefit of others. Even while tolerating the wind, rain, heat and snow, they protect us from these elements. Just see how these trees are maintaining every living entity! Their birth is successful. Their behavior is just like that of great personalities, for anyone who asks anything from a tree never goes away disappointed. These trees fulfill one's desires with their leaves, flowers and fruits, their shade, roots, bark and wood, and also with their fragrance, sap, ashes, pulp and shoots.

However, despite these prominent roles for heavenly natural beings in the highest realm, earthly animals and plants cannot find their way there. In material reality all living beings, including plants, have souls, but devotional practices can be properly done only by humans. Despite spurious stories about Chaitanya's liberating a dog or the deity Vishnu's sending the elephant Gajendra to the Heaven of Cows, generally animals (and, in this school of Hinduism, plants) must wait to be reincarnated as humans before they may find spiritual release. Thus humans remain spiritually superior to animals and plants.

In this vein Prabhupada said: "The human being is the elder brother of all other living beings. He is endowed with intelligence more powerful than animals for realizing the course of nature and the indications of the almighty father." Prabhupada also maintained that humans without Krishna consciousness live "just like a tree, eating just like a camel and having sex just like the dogs and hogs," because animals, plants, and all other nonhuman natural beings have completely forgotten the preexistent Krishna consciousness, which is in all of us. It is of interest that Prabhupada also said that humans are superior to animals in the matter of wearing clothes, a notion that we saw humorously challenged in the Islamic world.[12]

Reflecting his teacher Prabhupada's comments, temple President Yogindra Vandana Das Adhikari told me:

> Each species has some unique characteristic; our unique characteristic comes from our brains, our rational minds. Humans alone have the capacity to think philosophically and seek to end suffering. Although human lives are diverse, generally humans are above animals because of our ability to think. Only humans understand how to become liberated from suffering. Animals cannot do so because they eat, sleep, and so on, without a deeper understanding.

To highlight differences between humans and animals, Yogindra told me the story of Bharata from the *Bhagavata Purana*. At one time Bharata, a man of great devotion and spiritual power, lived in forest solitude. One day, out of compassion, he adopted an orphaned baby deer. But rather than merely caring for the deer, Bharata became obsessed with her—so much so, that he forgot his religious practice and began to spiritually wither. His religious downfall became complete when Bharata died while searching for the doe after she became lost one day. Following *Bhagavad Gita* 8.6, your thought at death determines your next rebirth, so the deer-fixated Bharata was reborn as a deer. Yet Bharata still had enough insight to understand what had happened and lamented his descent from excellent practitioner to an animal form, which cannot practice religion.

From this, New Talavana maintains an ideology of superior human stewardship over nature that is not entirely unlike the Christian notion. Humans remain ascendant over natural forms and may use them in the service of Krishna. In addition, there remains a minimal resemblance between Aristotle's Great Chain of Being and New Talavana's reincarnation system, which from the bottom up ranks the universe into rebirth realms of hellish beings, ghosts, animals, humans, and demigods. However, the New Talavana ethic instructively differs from Christian notions of stewardship in at least two ways. First, in other places there are gods and other magical beings who are more powerful than or otherwise are superior to humans. Thus, although humans occupy a higher level than animals and plants, there exists no claim that humans are the *ultimate* creation and are entitled to the privileges that this lofty position is thought to confer. Also, within New Talavana notions of stewardship, uses of nature are limited to only what will serve Krishna. In *Bhagavad Gita* 9:27 Krishna says, "Whatever you do, do that as an offering to me." This ethic approves using natural beings to serve human needs but not to fulfill excessive or selfish desires. Yogindra told me,

> Humans have stewardship over nature, but not dominion. Dominion is the exploitation of nature, whether it be by killing cows or killing elephants just for the ivory. Exploitation is mindless greed, not just fair use. Dominion does not mean that we can do anything we want. The natural world is owned by Krishna, not us, and we must treat it the way that Krishna wishes it to be treated.

Despite the fact that souls in a material, earthly cow form cannot transmigrate to the Heaven of Cows, cattle, like all natural beings, retain a sense of sacredness, because Krishna is in all things or, better said, all things are in Krishna. Krishna tells us in *Bhagavad Gita* 7.12, "I am, in one sense, everything, but I am independent. I am not under the modes of material nature, for they, on the contrary, are within me," creating a sense of panentheism, an ecocentric linking of the sacred and the natural worlds not entirely unlike that of the American naturalist John Muir. But cattle don't just possess souls like other animals; they are supreme animals, as Krishna's special companions. The *Mahabharata* tells us that cattle, "guileless in their behavior," are superior even to gods like Brahma, make the best gift, cleanse one of sin, and are "the foremost of all things." Moreover, although Hindus vary in perspective, in this school of Hinduism the highest animal rebirth is as a cow or bull, with big cats and primates just below.

Krishna, through his joyful cowherd pastimes as well as his protection of bovines, taught us that to serve him is to serve cattle. He instructed us to make use of and be grateful for the five helpful products of the cow: milk, cheese, curd (yoghurt), urine (which has medicinal properties), and dung (for medicine, fuel, and many other uses). So, as longtime devotee Mayapur Dham Dasa plainly put it, "To put Krishna at the center of your life is to put cows at the center of your life, since Krishna loved cows so." This caring service to cattle is a primary reason for New Talavana's existence. This would have pleased Gandhi, who said: "Cow protection to me is one of the most wonderful phenomena in human evolution. It takes the human beyond his species.... Humanity through the cow is enjoined to realize his identity with all that lives."[13]

Before describing New Talavana cow protection, let me first clarify what this service to the cow does not mean. Cattle have played roles in religion as long as any domesticated animal, as we can trace cattle veneration back to ancient central Asia and Africa and perhaps back to prehistoric Paleolithic reverence for the aurochs, the wild ancestor from whom domesticated cattle descended. Archaeological evidence indicates a cult of bull worship in southern Turkey at least by 7,700 B.C.E., and cattle were specifically worshipped in ancient Egyptian, Babylonian, Minoan, Hittite, Canaanite, Celtic, Mesolithic European, and Indo-European religions, as we have already seen with the Apis Bull and the Bull of Heaven. Cattle display their considerable power to instigate religious forms even in the negative: for example, the Shin Dard people of Gilgit abhor cattle and cow's milk as religiously impure. But perhaps nowhere is religious fervor for cattle stronger than among the Maasai of Kenya and Tanzania. Being seminomadic cattle herders, like Hindus in India the Maasai are utterly dependent on their cattle to provide staple foods like milk, yoghurt, and butter, as well as urine and dung for medications, home construction, cleansers, and other needs. Further, the Maasai divide their society into Red and Black Cow totem groups, thus regarding their cattle as living ancestral deities. Because of this, the Maasai spare no effort in pampering what are to them, in a sense, manifest family gods with hooves.[14]

But in contrast to the Maasai deification of the cow as well as common Western misconceptions, Hindus generally do not worship cattle as gods. There is a goddess of the cow, Kamadhenu, who is a wish-fulfilling cow like the *surabhi*s of the Heaven of Cows, but she lacks a cultus or temples of her own and often remains buried within the myriad symbols of Indian religions. Within their bodies cattle may contain deities such as Lakshmi but remain just animals, not deities in themselves. More than as a god in his own right, the holy bull Nandi is reverenced with images and flower offerings as a symbol for the awesome power of the Hindu deity Shiva, for whom Nandi is a spiritual animal companion. Likewise, images of cows appear on New Talavana's altar, and urban ISKCON members are encouraged to keep photos of cows in their homes, but these images serve to remind one of Krishna and his protection of cows, not to provide objects of worship.

Rather than worshipping cattle as gods, New Talavana devotees cherish them as one of our holy Seven Mothers, the other six being our birth mother, the wife of the spiritual teacher, the wife of a king, the wife of a priest, a nurse, and Mother Earth. *Go Mata,* Mother Cow, provides us with staple foods and medicines, just like a good mother. Even when dead, her body can provide us with medicines and leather. Moreover, cows act as malarial shields for humans, protecting us from disease like a good mother. As such, we owe Mother Cow our holy reverence, respect, and gratitude. Further, Krishna loves, protects, and herds cattle, and accordingly we should follow his wishes and do so as well. Finally, a January 1985 ISKCON *Back to Godhead* article mixes humor and insight in describing cattle not as gods but as "ruminating mystics," who miraculously create milk from grass: "The soul embodied as a cow can turn grass into milk. And the soul embodied as a human being can turn his consciousness toward God." The article argues that such alchemical bovine "sages" deserve a good cow-protection program.[15]

An underlying assumption of New Talavana's cow protection involves the pan-Indian ethical value of *ahimsa,* nonharm. Made famous in the modern age by Mahatma Gandhi, *ahimsa* has deep historical roots in Indian culture. Shrila Prabhupada defined *ahimsa* as not doing "anything which will put others into misery or confusion" and exhibited this value in several ways, including in his oft-repeated phrase "Real philosophy is nothing more than this: 'friendliness to all living entities.'" He was known, for instance, to be careful in walking around rather than on ant hills. Also, the experienced devotee Mahindranath told me that on one occasion ISKCON members at another center cut down a tree to make a path. Prabhupada chastised them, describing the incident as the pointless loss of a tree, since the path could have been rerouted. This showed Mahindranath that Prabhupada possessed a "total concern for nature." Applying this nonharm concern to cattle, Shrila Prabhupada repeatedly said that killing a cow is the greatest sin.[16]

The New Talavana devotee Mayapur Dham Dasa offered an example of *ahimsa.* In his cabin on the farm, Mayapur found a dead bug that was being eaten by ants. Whereas others might have killed the ants immediately and then cleaned the area of insect corpses, Mayapur allowed the ants to feast for a couple of days. He did this because ants "are civilized…. Ants are incredible: I could never communicate through chemicals like they do." A young devotee named Sanjaya, a social worker, expressed a similar attitude of *ahimsa* in saying: "Just because something is not useful to us does not mean that we can kill it. We don't kill elderly people who are past their productive usefulness, after all. But we still kill useless animals as part of contemporary practice. This is not compassionate and provides a challenge to the larger society."

At New Talavana *ahimsa* in practice results in not only cow protection but also thoroughgoing vegetarianism. Indeed, to be a devotee is to be vegetarian, as all one's food should be *prashadam* blessed food, and *Bhagavad Gita* 9.26 tells us that *prashadam* is always meat-free. In the *Mahabharata* we find, "The one who, desiring pleasure of the self, abstains from killing helpless animals with a stick, would attain happiness." Prabhupada taught: "Human beings are meant to eat vegetarian food. The tiger does not come to eat your fruits. His prescribed food is animal flesh. But humanity's food is vegetables, fruits, grains, and milk products. So how can you say that animal killing is not a sin?" Prabhupada also wrote that, "Those who eat meat and fish generally are called demons [and] cannot understand God."[17]

Following his guru Prabhupada, temple president Yogindra Vandana Das argued strenuously for a vegetarian diet. Yogindra told me from a New Talavana perspective that if Krishna asked for meat as *prashadam,* they would give it to him, but that is not what he asked for. Then speaking more generally, Yogindra said that we have teeth like herbivores, not carnivores, showing that we are natural vegetarians. He related that we sweat like herbivores but unlike carnivores such as dogs or tigers, showing our natural place among the herbivores. Also, humans should serve Krishna, and we must eat to survive to do this; and in human survival vegetables are required but meat is not. Moreover, he said, you have to kill an animal in order to eat it, but the same is not true for a plant, so eating plants is more compassionate. For instance, you can eat a cucumber, but the plant lives on. As for root vegetables, Yogindra said that foods like potatoes will die with the onset of cold weather anyway, so harvesting them right before winter does not change their fate. "And you can cut the top off of a carrot and plant it," he related, "and it will grow again." This philosophy of not having to kill the plant to eat it is the official ISKCON position, he finished.

In their book *Divine Nature* the ISKCON authors Michael A. Cremo and Mukunda Goswami additionally propose an ecological argument for a vegetarian lifestyle, claiming that vegetarianism, by causing us to eat lower on the food chain, is more environmentally friendly. They say that the eating of meat and its related industries result in deforestation, as land must be cleared to graze beef cattle. Meat eating introduces agricultural inefficiencies, because plant foods go much farther when eaten directly instead of being fed first to meat animals. Overgrazing and grain production contribute to the erosion of valuable topsoils. Further, they state, the meat industry adds greenhouse gases both from burning fossil fuels and from animal emissions while it simultaneously creates water depletion and pollution. Cremo and Goswami thereby assert that "reducing or eliminating meat consumption would have substantial positive effects on the environment."[18]

Exhibiting this attitude, the New Talavana devotee Mayapur Dham Dasa said to me:

> All over the world people are relishing the flesh of the cow. But she's so sweet and loving and innocent, with big lotus eyes. And they say that you can pet a cat or a dog and your blood pressure immediately goes down, but I like to pet cows. The cows—they're completely on another level. If we could be as humble as a cow, that would be amazing.
>
> The cow is one of our Seven Mothers who nurture us. Who gives milk to all humankind? Who is so generous and loving? Especially dairy cows—they have those big, beautiful eyes ... they are persons [rather than things]. Demigods are present in the body of a cow. Shrila Prabhupada says that everything about the cow is valuable, since in India even when dead, cobblers come and take the skin of the cow to make shoes.
>
> We just want people to understand, they don't have to eat the cow. There are other ways to eat and still get more protein than you need. Shrila Prabhupada encourages protein consumption through eating cheese and milk and yoghurt. The same flavor is there, but then you are not eating blood. Eating a cow is as bad as you can be; it is the most sinful thing that you can do.

On her lovely houseboat, another decades-long devotee, Mohanasini, told me:

Cows are so sweet! You know, people have dogs and cats, and they never think of slaughtering them. But cows—they are so sweet and precious, and they are sent to the slaughterhouse regardless, without any thought given to their feelings or their right to live. All beings have a right to live, not just us.

You lose your quality of mercy by killing and eating animals. We have dominion over animals, but this doesn't mean that we can slaughter them. We should take care of them. What do cattle give us? The cow gives us milk, butter, cheese, *ghee* [clarified butter] for cooking, and even the dung can be made into flat patties for cooking fuel, as they do in India. And the ox tills the field. So they give us so much more alive than you get by killing them. We don't need to do that. This is why we have so much war in the world, and so much difficulty, because of karma. If you kill, you will be killed.

Supplementing Mohanasini's karmic kill-and-be-killed outlook, her husband, Mahindranath, added: "As long as you have these slaughter-houses, you're going to have people flying planes into buildings. There's going to be violence. We have to become peaceful."

The social-worker devotee, Sanjaya, likewise asserted the importance of vegetarianism in telling me:

It is more eco-friendly to eat lower on the food chain. It is important to protect nature, even leaving spiritual reasons aside, because of the many negative human impacts on nature which harm us as they harm the natural world. We need to avoid poisoning rivers or worsening global warming and respond to our planetary home with more awareness. Little actions can help here, such as "Meatless Monday."

The longtime devotee Kaivalya Sundari Dasi echoed Mayapur's account that the cow is one of our Seven Mothers, and as far as she is concerned, eating cattle, whom she intentionally refers to as persons, causes many problems:

We must protect nature. Even bees and cows must be protected, because if we lose them, the ecosystem gets screwed up. Don't eat cows, meat, or eggs. Chickens and other animals are mass-produced and are treated very badly. Cutting down the rainforest to raise beef cows has enhanced [i.e., increased] greenhouse gases coming from the cows. We have to be conscious about everything we do.

Meat eating is the biggest cause of our calamities, whether they're natural disasters or whether they're wars, because meat eaters are racking up negative karma big time. It's a cycle that gets bigger and bigger and then hits hard. All that karma has an impact on things that happen to us. So if we [in ISKCON] are not part of that equation of the violence of meat eating, we're relatively protected. We don't agree with all of that violence, the killing of animals, or mistreating animals.

But in every region of the universe other than New Talavana's spiritual sky, there arise practical challenges to *ahimsa,* and Kaivalya recognizes this. She says that Krishna wants his human servants to be in good health; thus "it says in the scriptures that you can kill in self-defense. Let's take, for example, snakes. You can't just see a snake and kill it; it has to threaten you. But then killing it is ok. The same thing for mosquitoes: you have a right to protect yourself by killing them. God forgives you for that, as for accidental killings."

The devotee Mayapur mentioned that mowing the grass kills small beings and thus also violates *ahimsa,* potentially generating negative karma. But this is not a problem, he says, as one should offer the work to the service of Krishna with devotion, thus eliminating any human fault, and rely on Krishna to "take care of the karma." This belief of course reminds us of the famous formulation from the authoritative Hindu *Laws of Manu* 5:39 that "sacrifice is for the good of this whole universe and therefore killing in a sacrifice is not killing." Thus, while minimizing harm to natural beings, devotees may harm them in the service of religion.[19]

A longtime devotee named Bhima highlighted these limits of *ahimsa* by telling me that he once was behind the temple building potting some plants by the greenhouse when a venomous water moccasin suddenly appeared. This cottonmouth showed its fangs to Bhima and adopted an aggressive posture. Bhima grabbed a metal rod from nearby and killed the snake. To be fair to Bhima, poisonous snakes such as rattlesnakes, copperheads, and moccasins live near New Talavana, and other devotees told me that these snakes are killed when discovered, just as happened with Bhima. It appears that the *ahimsa* that is connected with serpent reverence in India failed to be transmitted to New Talavana as successfully as cow protection was, although even in India *ahimsa* often gets set aside for slithering ones when they are troublesome to humans.[20]

Whatever the limits of *ahimsa* regarding vipers may be, nonharm propels the cow protection that grounds New Talavana. In order to serve cattle and protect them from the slaughter that is the norm for American cattle, New Talavana houses a *goshala*, a "cow sanctuary." At least three thousand *goshala* institutions exist in India, most of which have developed only in the last two centuries. There are only six in the United States, and New Talavana is the largest of these. *Goshala*s provide old-folks' homes and clinical facilities for cattle, giving care to cows who are too old or infirm to be productive and therefore may be destroyed, which is an acute danger for both dairy and meat cattle in the United States. Planted within a larger beef-eating culture, ISKCON has an explicit policy that prohibits releasing cattle into situations in which they may be slaughtered.[21]

The New Talavana herd began in the 1970s when a devotee went to a livestock sale and bought a Holstein heifer, who then was named Kunti after the wife of King Pandu in the *Mahabharata,* and Kunti's calf. These two served as a reproductive seed for the herd. Jerseys were then added for the higher butterfat content in their milk, and devotees have bought milk cows when necessary to regulate the herd's natural dynamism. Several zebus, a breed native to India, arrived from ISKCON's farm in West Virginia. Some private devotees donated older cattle, and a vegetarian nondevotee donated a cow in order for it to avoid slaughter. On one occasion devotees found a calf from a beef breed inexplicably wandering in their forest, and they adopted it, saving it from the fate for which it was bred. But sometimes the well-meaning zeal of devotees at other farms to protect cattle can outstrip their resources or training and thus lead to overpopulation problems. For this reason, New Talavana took in eighty cows in 1986 and eight more in 1999 in order to reduce populations at other sites. New Talavana's norm hovers at about a hundred cattle, but as of the time of my fieldwork, in autumn 2014, there were only sixty-eight, because the big additions to the population of the 1980s and 1990s now are of an advanced age, resulting in twenty-six cattle deaths in just the last two years. Most of the herd is an elderly 15 to 20 years old, with Ishana, a 23-year-old ox, currently the oldest. Two calves were born during my two months of fieldwork.

These cattle are in three groups: bulls, milk cows, and everyone else. Devotees try to keep just enough bulls to maintain genetic diversity. At New Talavana one bovine mathematically occupies four acres, far exceeding the norm of one cow per acre, although the chief cowherd, Jayanti Sakhi Devi Dasi, told me that the grazing fields need more lime and fertilizer to improve botanical abundance. Even with this problem, in the semitropical climate and lush setting of New Talavana, it is easy for cattle to find edibles. Devotees grow winter hay in a neighbor's sixty-acre pasture as well as on about fifteen acres of hay pasture at New Talavana itself, and in some years there is a hay surplus.

Jayanti and her helper Bhakta Scott milk four cows a day at present, yielding the community a daily supply of nine gallons of fresh milk for drinking, making Indian-style *paneer* cheese, creating the sweet treat *burfi,* and for other uses. Jayanti and Scott milk cows by hand in a relaxed and friendly atmosphere, helping to make the dairy cruelty-free. Milk cows today are mostly purebred Guernsey, but there remain some Jersey genetics in the mix. Because of distribution logistics and other obstacles, New Talavana does not sell its milk commercially.

Keeping the cows healthy obviously remains important. The New Talavana staff personally minister to most bovine health-care needs, such as injections and worming regimens, with supplies procured from a veterinarian if necessary. More serious health issues are referred to a professional veterinarian. Overall, the herd appears to be remarkably healthy, especially given that most of the cattle are old.

Each cow receives a Sanskrit name with religious meaning, and name lineages have developed over time, with Surabhi V having the

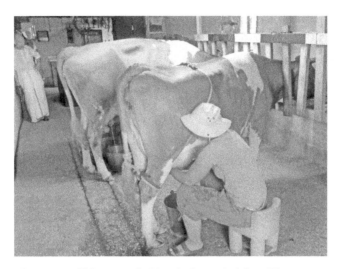

Figure 5. Milking cows in New Talavana's dairy. (Photo: Author.)

longest current lineage. Cows are never slaughtered and die only natural deaths. Before death, a cow typically will lie down and give up, so to speak. During this period devotees bring the dying cow food, water, and decorative garlands, and they chant beside the cow. Once dead, ideally the entire cow will be put to some productive purpose, as often happens in India; but this remains difficult in the United States because there exist few neighborhood markets for cowhide and other parts. New Talavana devotees wish that they could bury cows with a backhoe, but this is too expensive. So, instead, devotees bring dead cows to the back edge of the property in order to give them sky burials, in which vultures quickly dispose of the corpse, much in the same way as Zoroastrians, Tibetans, and some Native Americans, like traditional Choctaws, treat human remains. By the way, the no-kill policy of New Talavana devotees, as with many other Hindus as well as Jains, prevents euthanizing elderly cattle, and some commentators who claim that euthanization can be the most compassionate action for aged and suffering cattle criticize this practice.

Caring for the herd requires significant financial resources. New Talavana leaders recognize that running a *goshala* in the United States represents an economically irrational exercise, as capital resources are expended on cattle that will never provide a significant return on investment. This financial pressure means that one cannot protect cattle ad hoc, as there must be clear, interlocking plans for grazing, water, shelter, health care, births, milking, and fund-raising. New Talavana finances its cow protection through donations, especially through its Adopt-a-Cow program. Every penny of donations to this program goes toward cow maintenance and happiness, as program donors are asked to defray the following monthly cow expenses: grain for milk cows, $50; veterinary care, $50; equipment repair, $100; pasture maintenance, $208; hay production, $333; and diesel fuel, $400.

As a global organization ISKCON takes cow care seriously. ISKCON law 507 provides clear "minimum cow-protection standards," and its Ministry of Cow Protection and Agriculture publishes the *Cow Protection Book* as a how-to manual for affiliates. The Ministry of Cow Protection and Agriculture also teams with the International Society for Cow Protection (ISCOWP) to provide somewhat independent oversight for farms, as devotees visit farms that are not their own to produce annual reports. These reports list every single cow, specifying age, origin, use, and health status. Births, deaths, and other additions or subtractions also are listed, as are revenues and expenditures of the Cow Department. Reports detail serious individual health-care issues. In the report that I reviewed, for 2013, New Talavana's cow-protection program received approval without problems, reflecting the *goshala*'s long-term track record of energetic and intelligent operation. There is an advertisement that claims happy cows come from California, but the happiest cows of all may be the beloved and safe ones at New Talavana.

Although devotees do not worship cows as gods, they gratefully thank cattle, especially during *Gopastami*. This autumn holy day, celebrated in India as well as at New Talavana, marks the day that Krishna the boy cowherd went with the cows to the fields for the first time. At

New Talavana this day occasions one of the largest public celebrations of the year, the Festival of the Cow, also known as the *Go Puja Mela* (Cow Veneration Festival). Annually this event brings about seven hundred and fifty people to New Talavana, quite a large gathering for an alternative religion in the Bible Belt, with the colorful and beautiful Indian clothing of a number of these people adding to the merry atmosphere. Many of these people are devotees; some of them travel from far away for the event, and for the ISKCON people the festival serves as something like a reunion. But the Festival of the Cow also attracts many outsiders, such as those curious about Hinduism, folks interested in animal rights and cow support, and inquisitive college students. All these attendees have ample opportunities to aid the main goals of the event, which are to show thanks for and spiritual respect to cattle as well as to raise money for the *goshala*'s cow-protection activities.

Devotees gaily decorate the temple, outdoor pavilion, and central grounds of New Talavana for the festival. Large poster portraits of some of the community's cattle, complete with names, appear around the grounds. A vigil is kept featuring sacred chants and dances, a so-called *kirtan,* twenty-four hours long, via staggered watches by devotees, providing an ongoing stream of lively musical praises of Krishna, and sometimes big-name ISKCON bands donate their time to help with this. The priest keeps the daily schedule of temple rituals as usual, with everyone invited to join; and between services informational tours of the temple are given to newcomers. Booths dot the central grounds to raise money for cow protection by selling home-canned organic foods, books, CD's and movies, fresh-squeezed sugar-cane juice, curd (Indian cheese) burgers, South Indian snacks, Indian village food authentically cooked over burning cow dung, American and Indian sweets, spiritual accessories like crystals and herbs, and tarot-card readings.

However, one booth sells nothing, and instead disseminates free information regarding cattle, the need for their protection, and the joys of vegetarianism. It highlights the main theme of the day: the benevolence of Mother Cow. To increase knowledge and awareness of cattle,

Figure 6. Mother Cow at the Festival of the Cow. (Photo: Author.)

hayrides explore bovine pastures and allow people to pet and commune with cows in their home pastures. But the true cow veneration occurs with a mellow cow who is penned with her calf near the booths on the central grounds. This cow wears a festive flower garland of honor, and devotees ritually mark her face with the vermilion powder that decorates human faces and deities for sacred events. For wide-eyed

Figure 7. Poster of protected bull at the Festival of the Cow. (Photo: Author.)

Figure 8. Musicians at the Festival of the Cow play devotional songs. (Photo: Author.)

Figure 9. New Talavana provides a cattle sanctuary. (Photo: Author.)

children, the presence of this cow provides a pleasant petting zoo. For adults who are in touch with their Krishna consciousness, the cow supplies an opportunity to extend respect and reverence, as devotees make a point to gain good karma by petting the cow while chanting softly and sweetly *Go Mata ki jai!* "Glory to Mother Cow!" For its part, the tame cow, accustomed to human interaction, seems somewhat to enjoy being the center of attention, aside from making it clear that she would rather be petted on the neck than on the face.

Figure 10. Food cooked using cow dung at the Festival of the Cow. (Photo: Author.)

Whereas the celebrated cow plays a major role at New Talavana while remaining just an animal, not a deity, other natural forms actually are deities on earth and thereby receive due worship. One is Bhumi Devi, the Earth goddess, whom some New Talavana residents reverence. It was Bhumi Devi who, in the *Bhagavata Purana,* appeared in cow form to provoke Krishna to enter this world, and an Indian connection between an Earth goddess and cows may be traced back to ancient formulations in the Atharva Veda. This Mother Earth also appears in the annual ritual reverence of Goverdhan Mountain in Vrindavan. But more central at New Talavana is the plant goddess Tulsi, who serves as a stand-in for the forest of Vrindavan.[22]

Tulsi (*Tulasī*), the holy basil plant, receives veneration all over India, where she is a frequent fixture in the courtyards of homes to bring longevity and happiness. She has her own religious festival, Tulsi Vivaha, and her own famous temple in India, the Tulsi Manas Mandir, in

Figure 11. The Festival of the Cow offers interactions with cattle. (Photo: Author.)

Figure 12. Children learn how to milk a cow at the Festival of the Cow. (Photo: Author.)

Varanasi. She is an example of an Indian religious universe that invests a variety of plants with religious significance. For instance, the pipal or *bo* tree (*Ficus religiosa*) provides hermitages for the Hindu divine trinity of Brahman-Vishnu-Shiva, and for this reason its wood may not be burned. The Buddha also realized enlightenment under one of these trees, leading Buddhists to fashion rosaries from its seeds. Another tree, the *rudraksha* (*Elaeocarpus ganitrus*), supplies seeds to make rosaries for the followers of the Hindu deity Shiva. Banyan trees, numerous in India, are thought to be trees of immortality and famously gave Krishna shade. Further, the *neem* tree, which supplies a variety of medicines as well as an organic nonlethal pesticide, provides a home for Shitala, the goddess who battles smallpox. The sanctity of plants like these created one motivation for the famous environmental-protection efforts in India of the Bishnois and the Chipko movement.[23]

At New Talavana, Tulsi (*Ocimum sanctum lamiaceae*) reigns supreme among botanicals and is manifest as another sacred natural mother. Her very title, Shrimati, "Honored Mother," connotes divine motherhood, and one of her prayers directly addresses her maternally: "I am bathing goddess Tulsi Devi, who is very dear to Govinda and who brings life to all the devotees. She is the mother of the universe and the bestower of devotion to Lord Krishna." Like a caring mother she protects, leads away from sin, sponsors growth, and enables religious activities; and devotees recognize this maternal side in experiencing her as a divine person rather than a stationary thing.

A hero of the scriptural *Padma Purana,* Tulsi is a divine wife of the deity Vishnu. When they married, Vishnu told her:[24]

> Your hairs will be transformed into holy trees; and since the trees will be born of you, they will be known as Tulsi trees. All the residents of the three worlds will perform worship with the leaves and flowers of this tree. Thus, you, Tulsi, will reign as the best among trees and flowers. Whoever will be moistened or anointed with the water that has been sanctified by Tulsi leaves will reap the benefits of having bathed in all the sacred rivers and performed all kinds of sacrifices. Lord Hari [Krishna] will not be as pleased

with the gift of a thousand jars of honey as with one Tulsi leaf. Offering one such leaf as a gift will bring the same reward obtained by offering millions of cows. Anyone who leaves his body holding a Tulsi leaf in his hands will be saved from all sins.

Considered a mosquito repellent as well as a helpful base for many Indian medicines, Tulsi's material form cannot be liberated to the spiritual sky. But that is no problem for her, because as a goddess she never spiritually leaves the Heaven of Cows, where she enjoys a close companionship with Krishna's consort, Radha, and is recognized by New Talavana community members as one of Krishna's greatest devotees. The scriptural *Skanda Purana* states: "Tulsi is auspicious in all respects. Simply by seeing, simply by touching, simply by remembering, simply by praying to, simply by bowing before, simply by hearing about or simply by sowing this tree, there is always auspiciousness." This important role of Tulsi as a goddess in plant form was not lost on Chaitanya:[25]

> Chaitanya Mahaprabhu's disciples would keep a Tulsi tree beside Him, and He would sit taking *darshana* [basking in spiritual presence] of Shrimati Tulsi Maharani [Great Queen] and chant His prescribed number of *japa* rounds. Chaitanya Mahaprabhu would say, "Just as a fish cannot live when taken out of its environment, water, so I cannot remain alive in separation of Tulsi Maharani."

The lifeblood of New Talavana consists in making offerings to Krishna, but no offering is acceptable without the accompaniment of Tulsi, and thus she plays a part in each religious service. Even if one has no access to Tulsi except as a dried old sprig, all other offerings should be touched with that sprig in order to make them acceptable—such is Tulsi's vitality. More commonly at New Talavana, fresh Tulsi leaves adorn offering plates, fresh Tulsi *mañjaris* (buds) create blessed water— provided that Tulsi is not boiled—and Tulsi leaves are added to all *prashadam* blessed food that is to be eaten by devotees. Through consumption of Tulsi one becomes closer to her spirit as an ultimate devotee. Further, Tulsi wood is thought to provide protection from harm, especially to the head region of the human body, so New Talavana devotees wear Tulsi wood rosaries around their necks at all times.

Because of her sacredness and out of gratitude for her gifts, Tulsi enjoys her own *puja* (worship service) as part of every morning's practice at New Talavana, beginning at 4:30 A.M. This service involves many beautifully sung prayers and numerous rounds of chanting the *Maha-mantra*. The deities on the splendid altar in the temple first are presented with an *arati*-offering flame, with attendants passing the flame before the deities and then to the life-sized image of Shrila Prabhupada that sits next to the main altar. The flame then is passed to all in attendance, with each person waving hands over the flame and then over the head to partake of the blessing. Then attendants offer water using a holy conch shell, and after being passed before the deities and Prabhupada, the water is sprinkled on peoples' heads. After this comes a fragrant flower offering in the same pattern, followed by vigorous and enthusiastic chanting of the *Maha-mantra*. During the chanting the *pujari*, or temple priest, brings Tulsi in a pot to a spot in front of the main altar in the public temple space, placing her on a high stand. She appears lush, healthy, and about eighteen inches (46 cm) tall. Devotees decorate her pot with a beautiful maroon velvet cover with a gold silk lining and sequins, setting her off as special. The priest then sets up a *puja* altar on a lower stand next to Tulsi, with this temporary altar setting facing in the direction of Shrila Prabhupada. After this, devotees sing the *Tulsi-puja-kirtana:*

> O Tulsi, beloved of Krishna, I bow before you again and again. My desire is to obtain the service of Shri Shri Radha and Krishna. Whoever takes shelter of you has his wishes fulfilled. Bestowing your mercy on him, you make him a resident of Vrindavana. My desire is that you will also give me a residence in the pleasure groves of Sri Vrindavana-dhama [the Heaven of Cows]. Thus within my vision I will always behold the beautiful pastimes of Radha and Krishna. I beg you to make me a follower of the cowherd damsels of Vraja. Please give me the privilege of devotional service and make me your own maidservant. This very fallen and lowly servant of Krishna prays, "May I always swim in the love of Shri Shri Radha and Govinda [Krishna]."

Then devotees circumambulate Tulsi four times. During this time a container of water and a small spoon sit on the lower stand, in order that worshippers can show devotion by watering her with spoonfuls of water small enough that she cannot get waterlogged. Throughout these circumambulations devotees pray to Tulsi. When the circumambulations end, so does Tulsi's ritual.

Because Tulsi manifests such special qualities, New Talavana residents follow the rules for proper Tulsi care. *The Life of Tulsi Devi and Her Care and Worship,* an ISKCON manual for Tulsi practice, tells us that Tulsi should not be pruned unless she has health problems that pruning would help. She should be kept clean but never with nonorganic commercial sprays. While picking leaves or buds with the right hand only, one must recite Tulsi's *mantra* (sacred phrase), which translates into English as, "O Tulsi, you are born from nectar. You are always very dear to Lord Keshava [Krishna]. Now, in order to worship Lord Keshava, I am collecting your leaves and buds. Please bestow your benediction on me to serve the Lord." Devotees may not pick Tulsi leaves on *dvadashi* (the twelfth day after a new or full moon), the day following an *ekadashi* (a Vaishnava holy day that happens every fortnight) ritual fast. When she leaves her body, devotees use her wood to make rosaries or other sacred carvings.[26]

Devotees express considerable spiritual respect for Tulsi. One of the important teachers in the tradition, His Holiness Bhakti Visrambha Madhava Svami, even maintains an Internet site designed specifically to facilitate Tulsi worship. Closer to New Talavana, devotee Dandavats Dasa related to me that "Tulsi offers healing to the body, healing to our lives, and offers the greatest spiritual benefits. The care of cultivation of Tulsi is essential to our religious practices and observances." Mayapur Dham Dasa told me, "Tulsi is in a class by herself, and Krishna loves her so much ... she can bestow pure devotional service upon us. She can give us the ultimate benediction. So she nurtures us like a good mother." Like Mayapur, in conversation after conversation devotees effortlessly referred to Tulsi with the personal pronoun "she" rather than the impersonal "it" that most Americans use for plants. Devotees therefore extend in practice the teachings of *Laws of Manu* 1.49 that plants have "internal consciousness and experience happiness and unhappiness." At New Talavana, Tulsi retains respect as a valued subject, a person in her own right, not an object to be used thoughtlessly.[27]

At the same time, some Euro-American devotees confess that veneration for a plant did not come easy for them at first. After all, they were raised in a culture that does not include the worship of flora—excepting some historical relics whose sacred roots have been forgotten, such as holiday mistletoe decorations, whose importance derives from pre-Christian Celtic and Norse religiosity. Some devotees told me that they venerated Tulsi because Prabhupada instructed them to do so and that in the beginning botanical worship felt unfamiliar and hence uncomfortable. Mahindranath told me, "When I first came to the movement, I thought, 'What am I doing? I'm worshipping a plant!' This went through my head for a few months. Then after some time, I came to very much enjoy doing it, because Tulsi is the favorite spice of Lord Krishna." Another devotee, Sanjaya, explained to me that he came to Tulsi slowly, through a string of small spiritual insights, motivated by the thought that if it was important to Krishna, it was important to him also.

Certainly some readers will find treating a plant like Tulsi as a person or even a goddess to be strange, just as Mahindranath and Sanjaya did at first. The idea that plants are objects to be sown, killed, cut, shaped, eaten, chopped, moved, or arbitrarily declared weeds as we please has been a practical commonplace among humans from many different cultures. Many of us think that because plants lack brains, a central nervous system, specialized sensory organs like eyes, and locomotion, they must therefore lack thought, feeling, memory, communication, and awareness. Moreover, since we must eat plants to live, we tend to take them for granted, and thus plants routinely receive treatment similar to that of lifeless objects.

But closer inspection reveals that New Talavana's interaction with Tulsi as a person somewhat reflects contemporary botanical science.

Plants and humans share a number of biological traits, including adaptive modes modulated by electrochemical reactions. Humans think, feel, remember, communicate, and possess awareness because of electrical discharges modulated by calcium, sodium, and potassium. Plants, likewise, are electrical systems modulated through calcium, sodium, and potassium, and this allows plants to embody many of the same states as humans. Of course, these states are manifested differently in plants and humans, not least because of the differences brought about by a central nervous system or lack thereof. Nonetheless, contrary to common understandings, plants can, in a sense, see, think, and move because of electrochemical processes, as anyone knows who has seen a plant turn its leaves toward the sun, an action that when performed by a human would be taken to indicate sensory input, cognition, and motion. Although they may not suffer as do humans, plants can feel when they are being touched—the Venus flytrap providing just the most extreme example of an ordinary plant capacity. Plants move within their positions through chemistry and cell division, but they do this slowly and mostly underground, hence out of the notice of most humans. Memory appears obvious in plants that fruit in spring only after a cold snap in winter, and some new, controversial research proposes that changes in plant traits may be transmitted across generations, which also would be a form of memory. Additionally, plants communicate, as numerous studies have shown. For instance, when attacked by predators or disease, a wide variety of plants release "notice of damage" chemicals, which can warn other plants to deploy their own chemical defenses. We humans smell some of these distress signals in the odors of fresh-cut grass or cut flowers. As Daniel Chamovitz, director of the Manna Center for Plant Sciences at Tel Aviv University, tells us:[28]

> Plants are acutely aware of the world around them. They are aware of their visual environment; they differentiate between red, blue, far-red, and UV lights and respond accordingly. They are aware of aromas surrounding them and respond to minute quantities of volatile compounds wafting in the air. Plants know when they are being touched and can distinguish different

touches. They are aware of gravity: they can change their shapes to ensure that shoots grow up and roots grow down. And plants are aware of their past: they remember past infections and the conditions they've weathered and then modify their current physiology based on these memories.

In this vein, the biologist Brian J. Ford says this of plants:[29]

> Plants are bursting with movement. They are rich in sensation, and respond to the stimulation of the surrounding world every moment of their active lives. They can send messages to one another about overcrowding or a threatened attack by a new pest. Within each plant there is ceaseless activity as purposive as that in an animal. Many of them share hormones that are remarkably similar to our own. Their senses are sophisticated: some can detect the lightest touch (better than the sensitivity of the human fingertips), and they all have a sense of vision.... A plant in woodland may seem static to the casual observer, but inside it is a hive of activity.

Returning to the idea of personhood for plants, let us first turn to the anthropologist Irving Hallowell's influential notion that a person is a being with whom we have linguistic social interactions. Under this definition, Tulsi at New Talavana definitely exists as a person, as devotees have linguistic relations with her every day, even if she does not speak back in human language. But let us try a different standard as well. If I define a person as a being who in some way thinks, feels, remembers, communicates, and has awareness, current scientific understandings support our declaring plants as persons, as they meet these criteria. Thus, in treating Tulsi as a person, New Talavana devotees reflect contemporary science. In this case, both Hindus and botanists inform us that plants deserve much greater respect than they usually get for possessing their own sense of agency.[30]

Of course, regarding plants as persons poses a potential problem: if plants are persons, what do we eat? Is it moral to eat a fellow person, even if he is leafier than I? For instance, typically we pick a tomato without thinking of the outcome for the plant. But greater recognition of the plant's personhood alerts us to the fact that tomato plants produce their fruits to reproduce themselves, not to feed humans. When we pick a tomato, even if it doesn't make the plant feel pain, we still interrupt the natural striving of the plant to reproduce and, in a way, steal the tomato plant's potential children. Who among us wants a stranger to take away the results of our reproductive efforts and eat them? And the plant actively feels, in its own way, this theft. For this reason, in order to avoid harming a plant while picking edibles, strict members of the Jain religion will eat fruits and vegetables only once they have naturally fallen off the plant. Further, these strict Jains will not eat root vegetables at all, as doing so commonly kills them.

But this strict Jain lifestyle is difficult, and accordingly New Tala-vana shows us a different way out of the dilemma. Although a person and a goddess, Tulsi in some form appears on the menu for every meal at New Talavana, as an essential element of *prashadam*. Devotees consume their goddess because doctrine and myth pay homage to her greatness and sacredness, and rituals solemnly consecrate the harvest, preparation, and consumption of her as an edible. At New Talavana, if we approach her as a holy person, she allows us to eat her as part of her own service to Krishna. Put differently, devotees consume Tulsi precisely because of a deep recognition of her sacred personhood rather than in spite of it. New Talavana teaches us that we can both protect and eat elements of the natural world, provided that we do so with attitudes of gratitude, respect, intimacy, and reverence.

We have seen devotees experience cows and Tulsi as sacred natural mothers, but given the rich embrace of nature by many sects of the Hindu religion, devotees also experience rivers as holy mothers. Although the sacred rivers of India remain geographically far away from New Talavana, some devotees wish to experience river veneration in India or have done so, especially within the holy Yamuna River, which flows by Vrindavan. Daily prayers at New Talavana sing the praises of river Mother Yamuna, whom devotee Kaivalya describes as a living entity with a personality.

One specialist in the Hindu veneration of nature, David Haberman, tells us that, globally, rivers have been worshipped widely, with archeological evidence indicating reverence for the river Seine in pre-Christian Europe providing just one example. Haberman says that rivers typically are experienced religiously as sacred mothers, especially in India. For millennia Indians have adored rivers as boon-giving mother goddesses, and the scriptural *Padma Purana* puts this simply: "All rivers are holy" and "All rivers are the mothers of the whole world." Like a sacred mother, the river provides people with food and, through river rituals, helps to protect them from sin. This mother-river connection is perhaps most clearly manifest with Payoshni Mata, Mother Payoshni ("Warm Milk"), a holy river in Central India who is said to flow with actual milk. But to understand this sacred river–mother concept properly, we must step back from Western cultural conditioning, which may regard a sacred river as a physical river with some spiritual essence added. This concept does not capture Hindu rivers, who first and foremost are invisible, pure-spirit goddesses. These goddesses generously wear the clothing of earthly water forms for our benefit, being so maternally nurturing that they can appear in our drinking cups. Thus we owe them our gratitude.[31]

Sunderlal Bahaguna, an important Indian environmentalist who has combatted the unfortunate, rampant pollution that affects many of India's sacred waterways, says: "I love rivers because they are God; they are our Mother. In our philosophy we see God in all nature: mountains, rivers, springs, and other natural forms." But to Bahaguna, rivers do not serve just as objects of reverence, since they also supply models of self-lessness for emulative spiritual practice. He says: "Living in the company of nature, one learns many things. This river here flows for others. It is a model of loving service. Have you ever seen a river drinking its own water? Thus, nature sets an example for us human beings, and says that, if you want real peace and happiness, be in close contact with me."[32]

Although her divine sister river the Ganges gets more press, Yamuna, who Haberman says is "conceptualized religiously as a divine goddess flowing with liquid love," arises as a vital holy mother in her own right. Thought by some to be a female form of Krishna, she begins high in the Himalayas at the mountain Kalindi and then pours over 850 miles (1,376

Figure 13. Hindu holy men pay respects to a sacred river. (Photo: Author.)

km) past Delhi, Vrindavan, and the Taj Mahal before meeting her sister the Ganges at Allahabad, the confluence constituting one of the holiest spots in India. Whereas Ganga, the goddess of the Ganges, is perceived as a lunar deity who purifies from death, as daughter of the sun Yamuna appears as a rippling solar goddess who caringly purifies the living and so brings love, prosperity, and healing. As a goddess of the heart, from her banks she inspires both worldly and spiritual love. In this way devotees understand her not just as a good physical mother of the natural world but also as a spiritual mother of the seeker, a mother who teaches devotional love. Hence the North Indian saying, "Bathe in Ganga; drink Yamuna."[33]

Although river goddesses often have their own waterside temples, these buildings remain secondary in river worship, as the river itself is incarnate both as goddess and as temple proper. Bathing provides the best way to honor the holy mother, letting her intimately wash you clean on multiple levels. So each morning at sunrise the banks of the

Figure 14. Hindus venerate the Ganges with an *arati* ceremony. (Photo: Author.)

river become busy with life, as numerous Hindus enter the water, chanting *Yamuna Mata ki jai!* "Glory to Mother Yamuna!" Discreetly they cleanse themselves in her waters as they greet the break of dawn by chanting the *Gayatri* mantra (a widely used sacred phrase drawn from the Vedas), thus honoring the Sun deity as well. In addition, on the river bank around 5:00 A.M. and again around 7:30 P.M. believers, all the while singing lovely hymns of praise for their fluid Mother, perform *arati* (fire offerings) like those that we saw with Tulsi but this time directed toward the river. On her birthday she even has been offered new clothing to wear. Pilgrims stitch together 108 saris (108 being an auspicious number in Indian religions) and then, using a line of boats across the river, stretch the goddess's new outfit from bank to bank.[34]

Through these experiences of the Yamuna River, cattle, and Tulsi plants as sacred natural mothers, New Talavana supplies provocative models for understanding our relationships with nature, models that diverge significantly from those of the Abrahamic world. Although we may find a notion of human stewardship not identical with but not too dissimilar from Abrahamic concepts, New Talavana preaches the spiritual desirability of experiencing particular natural beings somewhat as we do human persons. Cattle, Tulsi, and Yamuna all possess thoughts, feelings, agendas, and rights, and demand our respect just as do persons in our human family. We find an emphasis on experiencing at least some natural beings with something like the same gratitude, respect, intimacy, and reverence as our experiences of our familial loved ones. In this way New Talavana makes real the idea of Mother Nature, who otherwise often emerges as a formless, lifeless, and pointless symbol. Moreover, New Talavana enjoins an ethic of *ahimsa,* nonharm, toward all natural beings, with some compromises, in ways unlike manifestations of Abrahamic faiths. Therefore cows, Tulsi, and holy rivers challenge us to expand our notions of spirituality and moral value beyond humans or even animals into the worlds of both plants and water.

At the same time, careful readers will have noted that cattle, Tulsi, and the Yamuna River may be maternal persons but are not fully human persons. At the Festival of the Cow, devotees may reverently decorate both their biological mothers and sacred cattle with vermilion powder, but no human mothers are kept in pens and fed hay. Human mothers of devotees live in solid houses and are free from the hunger of their children, whereas Tulsi winters in a greenhouse and is ritually eaten. Devotees honor their mothers by giving blessed bottles of Yamuna to their human mothers, not by giving humans to their maternal rivers. Thus at New Talavana we find vibrant examples of natural entities who are experienced as sacred mothers much like, but not exactly like, human, biological mothers.

Yamuna enjoys the nickname Daughter of the Sun, since the Rig Veda informs us that her father is Vivasvat, the Sun god. It was this Sun god, more commonly called Surya these days, who first received the *Bhagavad Gita* from Krishna, thus appearing first in the lineage of authority for the holy book. This Sun god also daily receives honor at sunrise river ablutions, thus hinting at the important role played by various solar deities in Indian history. But Gilgamesh's Sun god, Shamash, whom we saw beginning this chapter, teaches us that Indians are not alone in their veneration of the sun, and the Maya of Central America supply another brilliant example. Let's go to the highlands of Mexico and Guatemala to explore this reality next.

4

Sharing Mayan Natural Souls

The *Panchatantra* contains arguably the richest and most influential collection of stories in the world. Originating in India more than two thousand years ago and then translated into Persian, Arabic, and many European languages, the *Panchatantra* is the original source of many familiar folktales, including the story of the Christian St. Guinefort and many Uncle Remus stories. Of the *Panchatantra*'s myriad tales, "The Snake Who Paid Cash" is one of the more interesting. It seems that there once was a priest in India who was not a very good farmer. While out in his field one sweltering afternoon, he took a break to rest under a shade tree, when not far away he spied a giant, menacing cobra peeking out over an anthill. He thought that the cobra must be the guardian deity of the field and chalked up his failure as a farmer to his lack of reverence for the snake. He then poured milk into a saucer, laid it on the anthill, and apologized to the snake for not previously offering the proper amount of spiritual respect. When he returned to the spot the next morning, he found a gold coin on the plate. The priest then brought another saucer of milk and the next day found another gold coin. Needless to say, daily milk offerings and gold collections then became the priest's habit. But one day he had to go out of town and instructed his son to offer the milk in his absence. When the priest's son

142

found the resulting gold coin, he reasoned that the anthill must be full of gold, and he sought to destroy the snake so that he could abscond with the presumed hoard. But the cobra got the best of the boy, killing him, and his relatives cremated the son's corpse. Upon his return home, the priest discovered what had transpired and forlornly recited the following verse:[1]

> Be generous to all that lives;
> Receive the needy guest:
> If not, your own life fades away
> Like swans from lotus nest.

This sad yet intriguing story offers an instance of agricultural nature mysticism, a topic to which I will return, as well as the common practice of serpent worship. Snakes have been venerated perhaps as frequently and fervently as any other animal, given their intrinsic potency to affect human lives and their associations with dark waters and the world beneath the earth's surface. From the ancient Central Asian scripture Rig Veda to the Mochica people of Peru, the pre-Christian Norse, the contemporary Fipa people of Tanzania, and more, serpent reverence appears again and again. Perhaps we are hardwired to include snakes in religion; as the biologist Edward O. Wilson informs us: "The mind is primed to react emotionally to the sight of snakes, not just to fear them but to be aroused and absorbed in their details, to weave stories about them.... It pays in elementary survival to be interested in snakes and to respond emotionally to their generalized image." The religious studies scholar Laurie Cozad tells us that, across times, snake deities have been manifest as sovereigns, have exercised sacred power over earthly elements, and have responded both positively and negatively to human desires.[2]

In this light, C. F. Oldham tells us of villages in the lower reaches of the Indian Himalayas in which cobras, considered to be incarnations of the cobra deity Serpent King (Nagaraja), are protected from harm by custom. To curry their favor, Hindu villagers construct large sacrificial fires from logs of the sacred deodar cedar, which protects against evil spirits. On these pyres residents burn sacrificial gifts for Serpent King. When Serpent King's spirit arrives to celebrate the sacrifice in his honor, he enters and possesses the local priest, who mediates between the cobra god and the rest of the village. Using the priest as his mouthpiece, Serpent King speaks to members of the community to resolve disputes, answer questions, reveal the future, offer healing advice, and so on. For their part, the people use the occasion to petition Serpent King to bring opportune weather, especially rain, as Serpent King controls meteorological activity. In this way local prosperity depends on obedience to the cobra spirit, whose pronouncements are considered binding.[3]

We find similarly vivid serpent veneration among the Maya of Central America as well. The Maya have revered snakes for millennia, as the artwork at several old temple complexes reveals. In today's Maya world, serpents serve as emissaries of the spirits of the underworld and of local Mountain Lord sacred peaks. In these roles snakes help to bring the rains that are such blessings in a hot land that is joyfully dependent on the corn (maize) crop. As in "The Snake Who Paid Cash," therefore, some Mayan citizens offer food, incense, liquor, and candles to local serpent divinities, seeking their favor as part of the regimen for maintaining the health of the environment. These Mayan rituals for snakes display an essential element of the Mayan nature ethic, a relationship of reciprocity.

The Mayan universe may be fairly described as animist, one where individual natural beings are treated as persons. As one scholar of the Maya, Eric Thompson, says:[4]

> All creation is both alive and active. Trees, rocks, and plants are animate beings who aid or oppose [the Maya human]. The earth and the crops are living beings whom he must propitiate. When he cuts down the forest to make his *milpa* (agricultural field), he apologizes to the earth for "disfiguring" its face; when he kills a deer, he excuses the act on the grounds of his need.

This ecocentric model of the universe encourages human relationships with natural beings understood as peer persons; the Mayan writer Batz Lem claims that "there does not exist a classification nor a distinction in those who inhabit the cosmos: the rain talks. A dog, a plant, the wind, a rock, a comet is equal to a person because everything completes its specific function and must be respected with due deference and reverence." This leaves many Maya "seeing the animals and the landscapes around them not as 'objects,' but rather as 'subjects'—living entities with a spiritual identity and life-force of their own." We perceive this holy natural ambience in a story about complaining weeds:[5]

> Long ago, the people heard voices in their fields but did not know where they came from. The voices were those of the grasses of the field, who were protesting the pain that they suffered in being weeded and cut from the fields. Our Father [Jesus] talked to the grass and also to the people. He told the people not to worry, that he had already arranged with the grasses to protest no longer, for the people would not kill them altogether, although they did have to defend his body [corn is the earthly body of Jesus] from the weeds. Therefore, grass no longer protests.

Respecting many natural beings as sacred, the Maya may enjoy nature's fruits provided that they give to nature in return. The gods and natural beings must regenerate, and humans must help them to do so, just as they help humans. From ancient times Mayan religions have insisted that humans need gods, ancestors, and natural beings, and that natural beings, ancestors, and gods need humans, and so acting reciprocally has long been a religious obligation. This idea, that one must give back to nature, is written deeply into Maya ritual, thought, and feeling.

An example of this ethic of reciprocity may be found in house-blessing rituals. Before construction for a new home is started, the family solemnly speaks to the earth and petitions for permission to dig and build. Without such permission from the earth, the building will fail. As the family makes offerings, they address the earth: "We are just passing through this life, but we need shelter. We need a place to sleep, to be protected from the rains and from the dangers of night. Please understand us, that we are asking permission to change your face, the face of the earth."[6]

The ethic of reciprocity demands giving back for gifts received from sacred nature, but it does not mean that nature cannot be used. The Maya employ a variety of natural beings in order to live, thrive, and find happiness. Instead, the reciprocity ethic encourages taking from nature in a solemn, respectful way. Notice, for example, this contemporary Mayan hunting code:[7]

1. Do not kill animals without good reason.
2. Do not take more food than you need.
3. Do not take too many animals at once, and do not kill all members of a group of animals.
4. Do not kill more than a small number of animals in a year.
5. Minimize the killing of animals in a reproductive condition. If one accidentally kills a mother with young, he must adopt and raise the young.
6. Do not leave an animal wounded.

Through the ethic of reciprocity with nature, which may commonly be found in other indigenous religious forms, many Maya live within a deep network of interrelationships with sacred nature yet remain distinctly human. In a variety of ways, including the sharing of souls with animals, shamanic healing, and nature mysticism in the cornfield, the Maya world teaches that humans are distinct from but closely interwoven with the nonhuman natural world. Human fulfillment occurs not by overcoming nature but by entering nature more deeply, with an inherent understanding of oneself as a fundamentally relational being. This creates a different mindset for approaching nature than many Westerners are used to. As we will see, the Mayan networks of relations with nature collapse common distinctions between mind and body, the human and the natural, and the natural and the supernatural.

Here I focus on the present-day Mayan people from the highlands of southern Mexico and Guatemala. Among the Maya these are among the least enculturated to European ways, least likely to know Spanish, and most likely to speak their native Mayan tongue day to day. The anthropologist Jean Molesky-Poz informs us that these Maya currently are experiencing a pan-Maya resurgence, where time-honored Native American folkways and heritages increasingly flourish, with religious, social, and political overtones. I will focus primarily on these revived *costumbres,* or traditional lifeways, as currently lived by the vibrant Maya.

Although most of these people self-identify as Christians and would be upset if someone were to suggest that they are not, from the sixteenth-century Catholicism of the Spaniards to the current influx of evangelical Protestant missions from the United States, many Maya have chosen to be Christian in their own unique ways—to cite just one example, by continuing to follow the old Mayan 260-day ritual calendar. Sometimes Maya blend traditional religion with Christianity, whereas at other times the two religions are parallel alternatives. It would not be unusual for someone sincerely to enjoy singing hymns in church on Sunday and then, without missing a beat, on Monday seek shamanic healing, which invokes a litany of old, indigenous spirits. Saint James, or Santiago, may be the Catholic patron saint of a village, but he also is a nature deity of increase and abundance and thus is crucial in agricultural rites. In European images Saint Jerome is often depicted with a big cat that he tamed, as we saw in the chapter on Christianity; thus now Jerome is known as Father Jaguar and is a protector of souls that are shared with animals. Many Mayan people navigate these waters, admixed with both local tradition and Christian energies, by being Christian in public but traditional and indigenous in private, and especially in their inner worlds. The scholar of the Maya Eric Thompson stated that a typical Maya "has very little interest in the founder of Christianity; the crucifixion means almost nothing to him. . . . It is the gods of the soil and the protectors of the village who are enshrined in the heart of the Maya peasant."[8]

The mutual presence of traditional religion and Christianity affects Mayan relationships with nature. As an example, in the Mayan sacred book *Popol Vuh* (*Book of the Council*), the closest thing there is to ancient Mayan scripture, the two heroes XBalanque and Hunahpu defeat the lords of the underworld and, in victorious glory, ascend to become the sun and the moon. Historically this moon then was embraced as the maternal lunar deity Ix Chel, a leading Mayan goddess of old with a major ceremonial center at Cozumel, who is now as she was then a patron deity of childbirth. With the arrival of Christianity, some Maya identified the moon with Mary, mother of Jesus, known as Our Mother, Holy Mother, or Grandmother. This identification of Mary with the moon is not superficial or accidental, as some Westerners may imagine, but is deep and complete, with Mary remaining inseparable from the holy Moon. Thus Hail Mary prayers are directed toward the Rabbit in the Moon. (Like some Asian cultures, the Maya see a rabbit rather than a man in the moon.) If a Mayan woman worships Moon-Mary today, her operant mental image may be derived from images of Jesus's mother, from traditional Mayan lunar reverence, or quite likely, from both at once.[9]

As for the sun, it is understood by some Maya as the son of the moon, and of course Jesus is the son of Mary; accordingly, many Maya strongly identify Jesus with the sun. Sun-Christ loves his flock by bringing the life-giving warmth, both literal and spiritual, that makes Mayan life-ways possible. From this equation of Jesus with the sun, just as we saw sun veneration in India, so we find it in Central America as well. The contemporary Mayan practice of sun worship keeps alive a venerable and important manifestation of nature in human religions, as over millennia the sun has received reverence perhaps as much as any other natural being. Ancient sun veneration appears with the Egyptian solar god Ra, the Rig Veda, Zoroaster's teachings, Chinese shamanism, Persian and Roman piety toward Mithra, Japanese Shinto, and in many other settings. In the New World, many Native American groups have practiced sun worship, the Natchez and Aztecs famously connecting solar reverence with rituals of human sacrifice. In South America, sun worship was central among the Incas and their Andean predecessors, and in Central America historically it was embraced by the Olmecs, Toltecs, and others.

Traditionally the Maya worshipped the sun, known variously as *Kin, Ah Kin, Ahau,* or *Kih,* in a variety of rituals. Great kings during the Golden Age of 250–900 C.E. were called *Mah Kina* or Great Sun Lords, who ruled through the sacred power of the sun. Typically present-day Mayan people maintain this sun worship both in and out of church by fully blending Jesus with notions of a solar deity who is feared for possibly burning crops but also respected as a force of creation, healing, and spiritual insight. Sun-Christ created the universe, including the gods, as a Maya describes:[10]

> He made the trees. He planted the corn fields. He planted everything there is, animals and everything. He made birds, cows, sheep, horses, birds, chickens, whatever. He made everything. "I guess I'll make a lump of mud. I'll make a person, I'll make one out of mud," he said. He made one. He blew on it three times. The mud turned into a person.

Sun-Christ provides essential orientation in time and space, participates in some way in almost every Mayan ritual, and resolves disputes between corn and weeds, as we have seen. Sun-Christ lovingly cares for his flock by bringing practical and spiritual supports for happiness. Every night Our Father, Sun-Christ, traverses the underworld, just as the sun did in traditional Mayan cosmology, and as it did in ancient Egyptian mythology. Moreover, Venus, the Morning Star, becomes deified for her role of clearing the path each day for Sun-Christ, saying, "'It's me, I sweep Our Lord's path.' The path of the holy sun."[11]

Besides Moon-Mary and Sun-Christ, the cross also unifies traditional and Christian points of view. The Mayan cross, unlike the European one, has four arms of equal lengths and so symbolizes totality, even infinity, in the four cardinal directions. The intersecting lines joining these directions symbolize the interconnectedness of everything in the universe. Taken together, the cross denotes powerful sacredness, whether as an icon of Jesus or as a cross-shaped floral offering of pine tops and geraniums for a Mountain Lord deity. Because of the multifaceted sacredness of the cross symbol, crosses dot the highland Maya landscape not just at churches but also at *encanto* (sacred) natural spots such as holy lakes, stones, mountaintops, and caves, where they serve as conduits for communicating with a variety of divine figures. Some Mayan crosses have been thought to be so full of spiritual charisma that they may talk and prophesy.[12]

Through history and into the present, the Maya have allied cross symbolism with their understanding of *Wacah Chan,* the World Tree. As one finds in some other Mesoamerican cultures as well as in historical China, Egypt, Mesopotamia, Europe, and parts of Africa, many Maya envision the universe as a holy tree whose trunk, branches, and leaves are manifested as physical reality. The material universe in fact is the World Tree; part of its trunk is, for some Maya, visible in the night sky as the Milky Way. According to one Mayan story, in the beginning a sacred, cosmic ceiba tree stood in the center of primal chaos. It began to flower and fruit:[13]

> Not only were there gross physical objects like rocks, maize, and deer hanging from the branches of this tree; there were also such elements as lightning and even individual segments of time. Eventually this abundance became too much for the tree to support, and the fruit fell. Smashing open, the fruit spread their seeds, and soon there were numerous seedlings growing at the foot of the old tree. The great tree provided shelter to the young "plants," nurturing them, until finally the old tree was itself crowded out by the new. Since then, this tree has existed as a stump at the center of the world. This stump is what remains of the original "Father/Mother" [creators], the source and purpose of life. Moreover, this tree stump constitutes that force which allows the world to flower anew.

The roots of the World Tree reach into the underworld, the place that the *Popol Vuh* calls *Xibalba,* the destination of the dead presided over by nine lords. Despite the presence of antithetical European concepts of heaven and hell, the idea of an underworld afterlife common to all remains a Mayan standard. The uppermost reaches of the World Tree define the realm of the heavenly gods, like the Sun and the Moon, who exist in thirteen regions. The divinity of these heights is symbolized by a supernatural bird perched at the top of the tree. The vertically middle trunk area of the tree is our terrestrial habitat, symbolized by the cross's horizontal bar, and the tree trunk enables interactions between the upper and lower realms. By embodying upper, middle, and lower levels of existence in totality, the tree connects and unites all beings and powers in the universe. Employment of the idea of the World Tree, with still-practiced rituals of regeneration and fertility, emphasizes Mayan religious notions regarding the sacredness of the entire universe, including all natural beings, as well as the profound webs of relationship constituting that sacred universe, all portrayed in floral cross imagery.

Previously I mentioned Mountain Lords, who serve as one type of sacred mountain in the ecocentric Maya universe. One story says that a group of great Christian saints came from the East and settled among the Maya. Those saints who found their own villages became village patron saints; the other saints, without their own villages, became Father/Mothers, or Mountain Lords. Mountain Lords, like the Tibetan local mountain gods we will encounter in the next chapter, are holy peaks who care for and protect the people who live in their environs. Hence they are worshipped, since they strongly influence local rain, other weather phenomena, and flora through their activities, while also acting as de-facto Masters of Animals. Having inherited old Mayan rain beliefs regarding lightning, clouds, and snakes, sharp-backed mountain gods are male, whereas smoother mountains are female, and these divine mountains marry. When the alpine Father-Mother marital couple experiences concord, so does the surrounding valley, whereas marital discord between mountain deities brings problems. Therefore mountaintop prayers and sacrifices of chickens, incense, candles, and liquor are directed precisely toward making the pair happy with humans and with each other. Mountain Lords also may be reached through the mediation of Earth deities living in caves, lakes, cenotes, and streams, and for this reason altars and sacrifices exist in these places. The gods of these locations, the serpent spirits who frequent them, and nearby good-luck toads help in rituals requesting rain.[14]

Protecting these Mountain Lords is a sacred duty, as we detect in a story from the anthropologist Gary Gossen. When a new automobile road was being constructed, some non-Mayan engineers aimed to destroy a certain large rock, Owl Rock, which served as a Mountain Lord. But a Mayan engineer with a "very strong animal soul" dissented and changed the plan, saving the rock. For this the Mountain Lord rewarded the engineer with wealth.[15]

The *Popol Vuh* informs us that the gods created humans specifically because the gods want to receive offerings and be worshipped, and when offerings are withheld from Mountain Lords, they may retaliate. The anthropologist Dennis Tedlock relates a Quiche Maya story wherein "Just as people have dogs [as pets], so mountains have coyotes. When someone has not offered to the Father/Mothers on their altars, then a coyote comes to the house, enters the yard to take away the chickens, or the pigs, or sheep, whatever people have at their houses. He grabs them and eats them."[16]

Of interest here is Mayan respect for these Mountain Lords as parents, exhibiting kin ecocentrism like that we saw with rivers in India. Maya commonly approach these Mountain Lords and their local emissaries on intimate terms, with respectful forms of address like Honored Father or Nurturing Mother, since they are experienced as familiar and potent social actors, not just as hunks of stone. In this way, if a person is defined as a being with whom one has linguistic social relations, a Mountain Lord and her emissaries may be called "persons," cautioning us to use the word "person" carefully.

A second type of Mayan sacred peak is the soul mountain, a concept that brings us to the heart of Mayan spiritual relationships with the natural world, beginning with the notion of the natural soul. Based on his fieldwork in the highlands of Chiapas, the anthropologist Pedro Pitarch tells us that many contemporary Tzeltal Maya believe that humans possess three souls. First among these souls is the Bird of the Heart (*mutil otan*)—so named following a long Mesoamerican tradition—who is the vital essence, the life force, of a human. The Bird of the Heart supplies the energy that makes bodily existence possible, like the battery that enables a mobile phone. Apart from its appearance as a hen in females and a rooster in males, everyone has exactly the same Bird of the Heart, and for this reason it does not delimit individuals. Loss of this Bird through witchcraft or another cause brings illness and possibly death. At death the Bird of the Heart leaves the body and is eaten by an animal or a *lab* (animal spirit) like those that we will encounter below.

The second soul is the *chulel*, which is a small shadow, a spiritual facsimile, of the person. It is the seat of emotion, memory, and language, and thus serves to differentiate individuals as the basis of personality. At night when the body rests, the *chulel*, not bound by time and space, leaves the body and travels through the universe, and we experience the adventures of the roaming *chulel* as dreams. At death it is the *chulel* soul that goes to the afterlife in the underworld.

This interior *chulel* exists simultaneously in another, doppelgänger aspect. A double of the inner *chulel* dwells within one of four *chiibal* mountains, one mountain for each of the four lineages of the Tzeltal Maya. These soul mountains, unlike holy Mountain Lord peaks, are not worshipped in themselves. Inside they possess spiritual amenities not found in empirical Mayan villages and provide five-star care for the souls of humans and animals alike. Soul mountains contain residences, foods, schools, and clinics, as well as social and political organizations for souls. Ritual candles burned in the physical world smell like flowers in the soul mountain. Because of a segregation of adult souls from youthful ones, the souls of children dwelling in the mountain are vulnerable because of a lack of parental oversight, and parents invest time and money in rituals to ensure that the Great Mother of the soul mountain and her assistants take good care of their children's souls. Soul mountains also contain spiritual courts, complete with soul jails, where lineage councils may dispense punishments for miscreant souls who misbehave in the soul mountain rather than in the empirical world. These soul punishments may result, by extension, in illness or death for physical humans. In Mayan soul mountains, animals and other natural beings inhabit a heaven on earth, and these heavenly beings influence the material realm.[17]

The anthropologist Evon Vogt tells us that among the Maya, almost anything of value may possess a *chulel* soul: corn, beans, squash, salt, homes, household fires, crosses, saints, musical instruments used in religious ceremonies, and traditional deities. Thus Mayan soul beliefs present us with an animist reality in which a wide variety of things are regarded as persons and thought to be animate, whether they are considered animate in other worldviews or not.[18]

The third type of soul, the *lab,* also called *way* or *chanul* in various Mayan dialects, deeply integrates Mayans with the natural world. Just as the *chulel* has two aspects, within the heart and within the soul mountain, the *lab* also exists simultaneously within a human and also in the everyday natural world. All people possess a minimum of one and a maximum of thirteen *lab* souls, these being shared with a wide variety of beings: a vast array of animal species, meteors, lightning, winds, illness-giving beings in human or animal form, and bizarre water snakes with metal tools for heads. These connections of *lab* natural soul-companions are purely between individuals, rather than with a species. One may share a *lab* companion-soul with one specific pigeon, for instance, rather than with any number of pigeons. It is of interest that some of these soul relationships are with meteorological phenomena; Mayan religion enshrines religious experiences with weather, unlike some other religious forms in this book.

Souls are shared with common *lab*-soul animals, including house cats and big cats; pigeons, hawks, eagles, woodpeckers and humming-birds; opossums, foxes, coatis, coyotes, and weasels; as well as caterpillars, army ants, butterflies, and some spiders. Individuals among these alter-ego animals connect through an invisible *lab*-soul tie to specific humans. Most wild animals are just wild animals, but a few are animal soul-companions of humans, and ordinarily it is impossible to tell from appearance or behavior which animal is which.

The Chamula Maya rank animal soul-companions according to a social hierarchy that obtains in both the human and the nonhuman worlds, so that not all animal soul-companions are created equal. The upper classes of Mayan society, such as kings of old or present-day shamans (traditional spiritual healers), share souls with jaguars. (This connection between shamans and jaguars will be important later in this chapter.) Members of the middle class share souls with ocelots, coyotes, foxes, and weasels. Lower classes share souls with rabbits, opossums, or skunks.[19]

These *lab* natural soul-companions have the same sex as their human counterparts, and their destinies are tied, too. What happens to one member of the partnership happens to the other as well. As a jaguar who is my soul companion prospers, so do I; when my rabbit soul companion gets sick, so do I; and when I die, so does my coyote soul companion. Exhibiting this connection, one Mayan tale describes a woman who got fed up with a weasel who raided her hen house, eventually shooting the weasel dead. The woman then got sick and died three days later, because the weasel actually was her animal soul-companion. In another story, a healer treating a sick boy successfully prescribed snakebite medication despite an absence of snakebites on the boy's body, because the boy's animal soul-companion had been bitten by a snake. Another boy, who was unable to swallow, was cured when his healer went into the bush to free his animal soul-companion, who had gotten caught in vines and was strangling. One can appreciate that in this religious form, the fates of humans and animals are spiritually interlinked, with real-world ramifications. There is an inbuilt incentive for some measure of nonharm, as one would not wish to hurt the natural soul-companion of oneself or a loved one. This situation makes real the words of Ecclesiastes 3:19: "For the fate of the sons of men and the fate of beasts is the same; as one dies, so dies the other. They all have the same breath, and humanity has no advantage over the beasts; for all is vanity."[20]

It is necessary to emphasize here that the natural soul-companion tie is purely individual, not communal, and thus this complex of belief and practice differs from totemism as classically understood. As described above in the introduction to this book, totemism is almost always a communal affair. Individuals have totems, but only because they are members of groups that adhere to certain totems. Moreover, totemism involves a connection with all members of a type or species. So, with totemism, my entire clan may have a spiritual connection to all rabbits. But Mayan animal soul-companions pertain strictly to individuals. Within one Mayan family we should not be surprised to find connections to multiple species, and all these connections will be with specific animals, not the entire species. With Mayan soul sharing, I may have my own unique spiritual connection with one specific rabbit, and my brother may have a different tie with one specific fox. Also in contrast to totemism, many Maya remain hesitant to reveal anything about their animal soul-companion or may disseminate false information, even if they do not know who their animal soul-companion is. They do this to protect themselves from physical or black-magic harm.

Set in broader context, this complex of locally variable beliefs in animal soul-companions, known generically as *nagualism* or *tonalism,* is still found geographically stretching from northern Mexico to the Andes. The anthropologist Weston La Barre tells us that such beliefs emerged in the Americas at least by the Mesolithic era, perhaps around 10,000 B.C.E., and may have been reformulated or standardized under the Olmecs (ca. 1500–400 B.C.E.). Among lowland Mexican groups the term *nagualism* may pertain only to witches, but usually for the highland Maya everyone has at least one animal soul-companion. It is of interest that one may find similar belief schemas regarding the sharing of souls with natural beings among Tibetans.[21]

Because the bond between natural soul-companions is invisible, many Maya, such as the weasel-killing woman mentioned above, do not know their natural soul-companions. Such information may be communicated through a powerful dream, especially one that repeats three times. A *lab* relationship also may be deduced, as a template animal soul-companion can be passed on through an inheritance that skips generations. Or a shaman, a religious healer, may be able to detect one's natural soul-companion through visions. Lorenzo Lot tells an interesting story about a rare man who actually knew his *lab* animal and communicated with it:[22]

> The man lived alone, with no family, in an isolated house on the riverbank. His *lab,* an animal in which he took fierce pride, was a jaguar. It lived in the jungle, but every year it came to pay him a visit. To get to Cancuc it traversed underground passageways until it surfaced, always at night, at a cross near his house. On its arrival, the old man would give it something to eat (raw turkey), he would stroke it, and they would play for awhile as if it were a dog. Then the old man would give it the odd bit of advice, the most important thing not to go anywhere near humans, because jaguar pelts are highly valued and they might kill him for it. Finally, they would bid each other farewell until the next year.

Natural soul-companions are *yuel,* sacred power, and because they are shared with humans, they empower humans and grant them certain characteristics. Individuals with jaguar or puma soul-companions tend to be stout and strong; those with hawk *labs* will have excellent eyesight; those with water soul-companions swim well; those with wind *labs* will be stormy, and those with hummingbird soul-companions will peer insightfully into spiritual realms. Moods and psychological states within humans may be attributed to the activities of soul-companions. Thus having more natural soul-companions (a human may have up to thirteen *labs*) makes one more spiritually powerful, but it also makes one more vulnerable, as there are more conjoined soul-companions who may get sick, die, or just ruin one's day by sharing a sour disposition.[23]

Sharing souls with natural beings in this way collapses the distinction between humanity and the rest of the natural world. The natural soul-sharing complex sponsors a notion of the self that is not independent of others but instead is inherently relational. The human self is expansive, as it encompasses the natural world, while it is also humbled by the recognition that human beings occupy just one niche in the vastness of sacred nature. With natural soul-sharing, we are not separate from nature in a final way, as our spirits and our fates intertwine, weaving us humans ever more deeply into an ecocentric fabric. From the point of view of natural soul-sharing, the human is the natural, and vice versa. Rather than trying to overcome nature, becoming more human means entering nature more deeply.

But Mayan natural soul-sharing does not simply collapse humanity into the natural world in an unrecognizable stew. Although interwoven with nature, humans retain a sense of separateness, because humans remain superior to natural beings and—not unlike what we saw with Abrahamic religions—act as stewards of nature. We see this, for instance, in the creation stories in the *Popol Vuh*. Once upon a time there existed just sky, water, and gods, including opossum, coyote, peccary (native American pig), coati (a type of raccoon), and bird-serpent deities. Then the twin gods, Heart of Sky as well as Sovereign and Quetzal Serpent, created the earth, complete with mountains and rivers. Animals were created, with birds and deer anointed as Masters of Animals. But when the gods demanded that the animals speak and offer praise to their creators, the animals proved incapable. The disappointed gods told them: "You shall be replaced, because you were not successful.... Your calling will merely be to have your flesh eaten." In this way in the *Popol Vuh* animals were made to serve: "The animals that were on the face of the earth were eaten and killed."[24]

Still wanting to be worshipped, the gods then created humans from mud, but the mud people just fell apart when wet. Then the gods made humans from wood but found them too dim-witted, these wooden people then transforming over time into spider monkeys. A fox, coyote, parakeet, and raven then discovered corn. After this, the gods formed yellow and white corn into human flesh and water into human blood, creating the first four human beings. Because these humans could praise the gods in speech, the creators were finally content. In the *Popol Vuh* creation ended when the best forms, humans, were finished.

A Tzotzil Maya tale further displays a sense of human superiority, as animality is a punishment in the origin of monkeys like capuchins. Once upon a time an evil people existed, who clubbed their children to death at puberty. After killing their children, they ate them. In punishment for this behavior, Sun-Christ sent a great flood, which killed many of them. Sun-Christ then appeared to the survivors and asked,[25]

> "What are you doing here?"
>
> "Nothing," the people replied. "We're just lighting a fire."
>
> They had spoken but three or four words when at once they were given monkey tails and monkey fur. Once they had monkey tails and monkey fur, they were banished to the woods forever; these monkeys were never given corn to eat again.
>
> "I shall never again let you have corn," said Our Lord Sun-Christ. "From now on you can find your own food there in the woods."
>
> "All right, then," said the newly minted monkeys.
>
> When Our Lord Sun-Christ went back up to the sky, the monkeys began searching in the woods for their food. These monkeys had been people long ago. They were changed into monkeys because they had done evil.

In part of another story, Mayan humans are portrayed as superior to both *ladinos* (non-Mayan Mexicans) and dogs. It seems that there once was a stinking human woman who engaged in marital relations with a dog. The lady became pregnant and gave birth to the first *ladinos*, who then multiplied. Thus offending typical Mayan sexual conservatism,[26]

> That is why ladinos have no shame.
> They flirt and speak with each other on the road.
> They hug and put their arms around each other in public.
> They even kiss each other in public.
> This is all because they had a dog for a father long ago.

In these approaches to the natural world one may even get a sense of human dominion over nature such as we saw in the book of Genesis. Eric Thompson relates an oral story in which[27]

> The jaguar existed before humans were made. The creator ... started to fashion humans. The jaguar was watching, but the creator did not want him to observe the process. He gave the jaguar a jar and a calabash full of holes and sent him to fetch water from the river, hoping to finish the creation while the jaguar tried to fill the jar with water scooped up with the leaking calabash. The jaguar was unsuccessful in filling the jar till the frog said to him, "Smear mud over the holes." By the time the jaguar thus filled the jar, the creator had made thirteen humans and twelve guns. The jaguar learned after being shot twice in the paw that humans were to be masters.

A basic Mayan attitude toward the natural world emerges in these stories. Humanity is better than the rest of creation, since the creators were not satisfied until humans had been made, and animals specifically were directed to serve humans. This perspective fuels a sense of human superiority, a boundary marker between the human and the natural. In this way, indigenous Mayan sensibilities of superiority to and dominion over nature are not dissimilar from those that we saw in Augustine's Christianity, although they have roots in pre-Christian Mayan cultural forms. The Mayan worldview diverges, however, when it comes to regarding natural beings as sacred. Natural soul-companions have the same sacred souls that we do; mountains are gods; lakes and caves are blessed churches; and so on. Further, insofar as the indigenous Mayan worldview was not nurtured by the Great Chain of Being, superior humans are interwoven with natural beings rather than simply remaining categorically better. Hence the ethic of reciprocity, in which one does not solely take from nature: one takes but returns a gift. This ethic of reciprocity creates outcomes for real natural beings and humans in the Maya universe that do not arise in strictly Abrahamic realms.

To illustrate this last point, let us return to the Bird of the Heart life-force soul and the *chulel* personality soul. These souls may be lost in a variety of ways: through capture while wandering in a dream, sexual intercourse, fright, excitement, anger, spiritual sale to a slave-making Mountain Lord, or an accident. Loss of the Bird of the Heart, which provides life energy, almost always means quick death, because of the difficulty in retrieving such souls as well as the inability of the human body to live long without this soul. Things are a little different when the *chulel,* the personality soul, gets lost. An absent *chulel* may simply be disoriented, but it also may be captured by a witch or demon for use in black magic or by a *lab* for food. A Mountain Lord may also enslave a *chulel* to work chores. The loss of one's *chulel* soul can result in a number of illnesses, such as depression, paranoia, psychosis, or epilepsy. Loss of one's *chulel* soul for an extended period also may result in death.[28]

If you are sick because you have lost your soul, you need someone to find your soul and return it to you. This activity is the specialty of the Mayan shaman, called *ajcuna, hiloletik, h-men,* and other terms. Shamans, sometimes mistakenly called diviners or witch doctors, may be found in virtually all places at virtually all times in human history, as shamanism could be the world's oldest extant religious form. As described by scholars of religion such as Mircea Eliade, Åke Hultkrantz, and Sergei Shirokogoroff, a shaman is a religious specialist who in a trance of varying intensity can soul travel out of the body to visit nonhuman realms of the cosmos. Besides this terrestrial world, shamans' souls can voyage to the upper world of the gods as well as the underworld of the dead. The shaman gains this power through the mastery of spirits, as more powerful shamans will have potent soul-companions who aid them in the tasks of locating souls and dealing with demons.

Relationships with these helper spirits develop during the process of shamanic initiation, during which shaman candidates often fall ill and must cultivate friendships with spirits as part of self-healing. Once the shaman can spiritually heal herself, she knows the path for spiritually healing others; thus shamans everywhere typically are spiritual healers. In the Mayan world, shamans heal through the use of prayer, massage, plant pharmacology, plant magic, dream interpretation, and Western medicines. They may communicate with healing spirits through the use of dreams, a divinatory staff, a bundle of sacred seeds and stones, or a divining crystal or stone known as a *sastun* or *am*. Communication with spirits also may be aided by the consumption of *balché*, a honey mead brewed with the bark of the *balché* tree.[29]

Part of shamanic practice involves the recovery of lost souls by enlisting the help of spirits and their invisible gossip networks. When the soul captor is mild, such as a relatively weak demon, the shaman may simply verbally demand, with appropriate threats, the return of the soul. The shaman may make an offering to a more vigorous soul captor as a form of ransom. Or, in serious cases, the shaman may have to do spiritual battle against a powerfully malevolent witch or demon. The successful shaman will return with the lost soul and, coming out of the trance, restore the soul to its proper owner, who then should feel healed.

By healing people of serious illness and defending the community from negative forces, shamans perform valuable services for the public. Shamans also may be fortune-tellers and respected sources for advice, and so a good shaman is always in demand: shamans may work seemingly unending hours. Among today's highland Maya, shamans may be more prosperous than other people, but usually they earn their extra pay with a sometimes extra-demanding lifestyle.

In working their magic of befriending and cajoling spirits, there is a close symbolic connection between shamans and jaguars. For example, a shaman may wear jaguar clothing while engaged in ritual. Shamanic tools and paraphernalia, including talismanic spirit bundles, may include jaguar teeth, hair, jawbones, or other body parts. Shamans admire jaguars in these ways because of their power. The largest, most successful nonhuman predators in the Americas, jaguars can live in a variety of habitats but prefer jungles near water sources. They are big cats, fast and agile, with large, sharp teeth set in muscular jaws and pointed claws at the ends of strong limbs. As such, they are excellent land predators, commonly feasting on armadillos, peccaries, pacas, and deer. Because they enjoy swimming, they also hunt in the water.

Figure 15. Jaguars are apex predators in the Western hemisphere. (©iStock. com/ Number: 22721606, 2013, Artist: Dirk Freder.)

Additionally, they climb trees, allowing them to eat the birds of the air. And they can do it all day or night because of their mirrored eyes, which allow excellent vision in darkness. All in all, the magnificent features and effective actions of the jaguar make for a vivid symbol of power.[30]

A shaman of necessity has a jaguar as an animal soul-companion, so the shaman shares dreams, health, and experiences with a physical jaguar. With shamanic training, the shaman can and should also come to share thoughts and feelings with the jaguar so deeply that the shaman becomes the jaguar. That is, enabled by the jaguar soul-companion relationship, a hallmark of the Mayan shaman is the ability to become a jaguar. The shaman needs to hunt for lost souls, and the jaguar is the best hunter. The shaman at times needs to fight evil, and the jaguar is the best fighter. Moreover, some Maya say that witches can shape-shift into jaguars, leaving the shaman who fights them without the same capacity at a decided disadvantage. So the shaman becomes more powerful at her vocation by exploiting the innate jaguar-human soul connection to assume jaguar form. By identifying with the jaguar as hunter, the shaman becomes a great hunter of souls, too. This skill of theriomorphic (animal-form) transformation into a jaguar is so essential that some Maya regard a shaman who lacks this ability as an impostor.

The notion that humans transform into animals, and especially shamans into jaguars, is ancient in Mesoamerica. More than three thousand years ago the Olmecs, so foundational in Central America, symbolically connected earthly and divine power through the medium of the jaguar and bequeathed to us artifacts of were-jaguars, which are part human, part jaguar, and perhaps also part divine. The *Popol Vuh* symbolically equates *balam* (jaguar) with both magical power and strength while describing a variety of theriomorphic transformations, including into jaguar form. The ancient Maya used jaguar names for nobility and personal titles, and rulers covered their thrones with jaguar pelts. Thus, in common Mayan sensibility, the jaguar evokes the powerful as sacred and the sacred as powerful. It is of further interest that the ability of religious professionals to theriomorphically transform into power animals may be found in many other cultures, such as the antelope transformations of San shamans in southern Africa, the wolflike skinwalkers of the desert southwestern United States, vulture-formed possession mediums in Niger, were-bear Ojibwa holy people in the Great Lakes region, or Arctic shamans who shape-shift into holy reindeer so that they may fly to be blessed by the creator Sun god Hövki—these reindeer perhaps contributing to legends surrounding Santa Claus.[31]

We get a sense of the antiquity of such beliefs in the Mayan world if we consider a report from 1629 by the Spanish priest Fray Hernando Ruíz de Alarcón y Mendoza, wherein two friars said,[32]

> A large bat flew into their cell one night. The two chased it by throwing things at it until it finally escaped through an open window. The next day, an old woman sought them out, found one of the monks, and asked him why they had tried to kill her. He thought she was insane, but she described the previous night's conflict in detail. Then she claimed that she was the bat and that she was still exhausted from evading them.

These transformations prompt a quick look again at the question of whether animals practice religion. If to be manifest as a deity is a religious practice, then the entire Mayan natural world practices religion. If possession of a soul demarks religion, then natural soul-companions practice religion. If praying is religion, then crickets are religious, as a folk belief tells us that "when crickets sing, they are really praying. Our Father left it that way because people do not know the prayers; the crickets help them pray. That is why there are crickets all over the earth." Needless to say, jaguars who emerge from shamans who shape-shift in ritual also practice religion as well, although arguably they do so because of their humanity. Jaguars who are not shape-shifted do not practice human religion.[33]

We may think of Mayan shamanic transformations into jaguars as occurring in two ways. The first happens when the shape-shifting transformation is spiritual and is at least largely immaterial. For example, while the shaman is soul traveling, you may see the shaman's body, perhaps slumped in a trance in a hammock or prone on the floor, reflecting an altered state of consciousness. For some Maya this fact militates against a sheer material interpretation of the transformation and leads to the idea that the shaman becomes a purely spiritual jaguar. The spiritual jaguar remains potent, as in the Mayan perspective spirit precedes and thus can control matter. And if the shaman must fight against a witch's or demon's soul, a solely spiritual body suffices.

The notion of a purely spiritual jaguar transformation also makes sense in light of the shaman-jaguar soul-companion relationship. In a spiritual sense, from birth shamans are already jaguars, and some jaguars are already human. The shaman has the jaguar's power through the *lab* soul; the shaman need only activate this power. Therefore, in shamanic training the disciple attempts to integrate his innate jaguar nature as much as possible, trying to get in touch spiritually with the jaguar within. In a profound and numinous mystical consciousness, a shaman-to-be must commune with jaguar elements of his own experience.

Shamanic training aims to produce this mystical communion. Through the ordeals, initiations, and learning experiences of the training process, one must entertain rich experiences of nature mysticism while uncovering one's preexistent spiritual enmeshment in the natural world. As the Mayan shaman Martín Prechtel describes it, the shaman does not draw on the power of nature; the shaman *is* nature. He says:[34]

> When you finally understood that nature was the imagination of the Gods, you realized that your nature hunted your own soul inside this enormous imagination. Your own soul was the imagination of the ancestors living inside the imagination of the Gods. The discovered nature of your soul caused the shaman's soul to survive ... a shaman had to become nature, not just an observer of nature.

The shaman works toward this goal using techniques such as the ritual known as calling, designed to produce both animal power and proper shamanic consciousness. In this ritual one rests alone in a wild mountain forest without food, water, or other necessities, as one would in a northern Native American vision quest. Being the only human in an otherwise nonhuman field of experience, one invites mindful awareness of the forest as it is. Then one meditates, in a sense, on beings within one's surroundings, with the idea of attracting them. Prechtel claims:[35]

> Calling with your heart, your nature, means you cannot use speech or your native language. Noises were technically okay, but they had to come from your own natural soul, not be a creative contrivance of your mind.
>
> Each shaman had to remember what worked best for him. The main point of calling was that it was not *chasing*. You could not order life to come to you, nor did you actively *go after* it. The secret was to get behind the eyes of what you wanted to call, become that being's vision, likes, and dislikes; understand by being what your subject wanted to go toward. Then you became the object of that animal's desire. One had to become fascinating to nature so nature would come! Becoming irresistible to what one called meant making yourself *visible* and delicious.

Prechtel goes on to say that it is not difficult to call dangerous or poisonous animals if one addresses them using *Rilaj Vinaq* (Venerable Deity), a term of great respect connoting the Mayan ideal of a complete being.

Through the practice of calling you must "tune your abilities to be in nature instead of around or drawing on nature-to be nature." Although the practice bears resemblances to meditation, in nature's embrace one does not contemplate or think discursively. As Prechtel put it:[36]

> You couldn't think about your life, or the life of others. There would be plenty of time for that, because to have time and place to just think about this and that is heaven to us. This exercise, however, was to make sure you didn't think. It was not like some Asian meditation where you empty yourself exactly, but rather was where you filled yourself with all the senses, with every cricket chirp and birdsong, every creak, crack, pop, and twitter. You were not to focus on what happened as an observer, but rather to hear, see, and allow it to all sink into the bottom of your body and bones like silt and seeds dropping into your river of liquid bone from the overhanging

trees, while you gazed from the bottom of the water, very still, hardly moving, like an alligator.

Honing consciousness in this way, one enters a momentous experience that can be described as nature mysticism, the direct experience of sacredness in and through the natural world:[37]

> If I did the exercise right, my soul would begin to merge with my entire diverse surroundings, and the edges of who I was would get increasingly blurred until my mind would jump and snap me back like a dog on a leash, scared of how far I might wander, and maybe never come back. Then I'd calm my mind, send it off and slowly begin to listen and see, until I started to merge again with nature and be snapped back again by my mind. Each time, however, I'd get a little farther into nature and a little better at staying there.
>
> A current began to pulse between the mind of self-preservation and the mind of the natural instinct to become part of the life around me. After a year of practice, that pulse became so fast and habitual that it took on the character of a unique "third thing." That third thing that appeared was what I would need to have in order to survive my initiation as a shaman. While immersed in nature, not analyzing, not understanding exactly but becoming nature, one really did begin seeing how vast the human soul can be.

By resting in this third consciousness and calling an animal, one can pluck a whisker or hair from the animal, even a jaguar, and not get killed, thus obtaining a charged talisman of the animal's power. As a shaman in training, Prechtel especially treasured such a prize from a jaguar, so that he could enter more fully into the world of jaguar power. One day in the forest he surprisingly got his chance, as he felt warm liquid on his leg and smelled something foul. Turning to look, he saw[38]

> There next to me, knocking me with his powerful, spotted leg, was a big old male jaguar spraying my leg as if I were a tree. Gracefully, I found that middle place in my being between human and animal, a pure grinning awareness, neither fear nor courage, because for the most part human courage is just educated fear, and animals can sense that, too. Quickly I reached down, grabbed a long white whisker on the right cheek of this fine spotted Child of a Woman Valley, and deftly popped it out of his face with great

belly force, no breath, and a minimum of movement. He coughed and grumbled, tossing his deadly playful head to one side, showing a little tusk, then leisurely trotted off into the misty thicket.

Completing his spiritual identification with the jaguar, one night Prechtel dreamed that[39]

> A spotted old lady jaguar held me tenderly but inescapably in her grip while she licked my face with her big rasping tongue. In the intervals between great washings of my weeping face, she whispered secrets into my ear in a low rumble like a far-off rainstorm. She filled me with knowledge and the substance of my unopened destiny. I woke up shaking and happy in the middle of one of those washings, knowing the jaguar was my spirit wife, the talker whose secrets from the original earth have kept me alive to this day.

In these remarks Prechtel discusses the shaman's transformation into a jaguar as a spiritual one, without a catalytic physical component. But other Maya maintain that the transformation of the shaman is physical, and proponents of this idea describe alternative ways that this transformation is achieved. The first explanation relies on pure magic: the shaman is so imposing that his spirit can become manifest as a physical jaguar body. The second explanation involves possession, as a shaman's spirit displaces that of a material jaguar, allowing the shaman to lodge his soul within and take control of a physical jaguar body. In this view, the shaman's human body may be slumped in a trance in a hut while his other, controlled jaguar body simultaneously prowls. In either perspective, the physically shape-shifted shaman-jaguar is considered especially ferocious, as it is more skilled, cunning, and vicious than an ordinary jaguar, which is not shape-shifted.

A shaman-jaguar is necessary for fighting witchcraft, because while soul traveling, the shaman can uncover hidden witches and force them to recant their spells. Particularly malignant witches may require violence to eliminate, and the shaman-jaguar meets this challenge by fusing the predatory, strong nature of the jaguar with the spiritual prowess of the shaman. A Tzotzil Maya shaman told his godson about how he utilized his shared animal soul (his *lab* soul) in dreams to possess a violent physical jaguar in order to battle what he considered to be evil:[40]

> A jaguar [the shaman] walked towards a road. When he arrived at the road, he climbed a tree. When he saw a man coming, he climbed down and bit him quickly; then he suddenly grabbed him. He cut out his heart and ate it along with the tongue; but he didn't eat all of them. He just ate a little bit. He carried them to his cave. When he arrived at the cave, he gave little bites to his friends because they were hungry. They were afraid to go out to look for their own food, so every night he went out to look for food. He did nothing but eat people. Every night he went to the place where the big tree was.
>
> Finally the people realized that there was a jaguar by the road. They went at night to kill him. When they arrived at the place where the jaguar was, they turned on their lights and found him in the tree. They fired the gun but the he caught the bullet in his paw. The gun roared again and this time he did not stop the bullet. It hit him in the ribs. A third time the gun fired and he caught the bullet in his paw again. Finally he realized that he was not going to be able to escape the bullets. He scrambled down the tree, fleeing. He went to hide in the hills. He didn't die. When my godfather saw the jaguar flee to the hills, he woke up. He was really trembling! He was very scared but he was still lying there in bed. His animal soul had been scared. His body was still asleep in his bed.
>
> But when my godfather woke up, he had a terrible headache. He had a fever, he couldn't get out of bed. He almost died.... Since his animal soul had defended himself with his hands, they looked as if they had been burned. Just imagine, all the skin peeled off of his hands! My godfather said, "They went to kill the jaguar, but he was my soul animal. That is why I almost died."

In this story the shaman-jaguar does not kill randomly or gratuitously. Instead, the godfather explained, "That is how I defend my friends." Intriguingly, we find a similar belief in dream possessions of violent tigers in tribal India.[41]

Whether the jaguar is a spiritual or a material transformation, or both, in jaguar form the shaman can quickly and effectively lead his posse of spiritual friends to hunt down lost souls. Once the soul is found, the shaman-jaguar is threatening enough to intimidate, bargain with, or defeat any demon or witch while also making an ideal escort for the soul to the body of the human patient. Ideally the illness then disappears, and the patient returns to health.

These shaman-jaguars represent the spiritual virtuosos of the Mayan world, but one does not need to be a shaman to be deeply involved in nature mysticism, since numerous Mayan farmers offer us an interesting example of an often-overlooked subcategory of nature mysticism: agricultural or field mysticism, or what we may wish to call in the Mayan world milpa mysticism. A milpa is a traditional Mayan slash-and-burn field planted with corn, beans, and squash, commonly providing a Mayan family with most of its food for the year as well as barter material. But a mystical Mayan farmer does not just thoughtlessly plow and plant his milpa, as he must recognize, embrace, and create teamwork with the spirits of the earth, the spirits of the plants, the Mountain Lord who controls rain, ancestors, the spirits of serpents and vermin, and so on. In these ways the Mayan farmer typically develops intimate spiritual relationships with numerous natural forces, and this is as true today as it was two hundred fifty years ago, when a Franciscan friar said of the Maya: "The enchantment and rapture with which they look upon their milpas is such that on their account they forget children, wife, and any other pleasure, as though the milpas were their final purpose in life."[42]

In this agricultural nature mysticism there obtains a deep partnership and spiritual love between the farmer and the corn, understood as the earthly body of Sun-Christ. The farmer, made of corn as the *Popol Vuh* tells us, benefits the corn by planting it, protecting it from weeds and predators, and quenching its thirst with rain-bringing rituals. In return, "our mother maize" generously feeds the farmer's family for another year. This reciprocal relationship is marked by prayers and rituals. For example, should birds eat part of the corn crop, the soul of the eaten corn must be ritually returned to the field for the corn to be healthy and happy. Thus one prays to the corn spirit: "Señora Xob, bring back the soul of the maize that has been carried away; do not allow it to forsake us because animals have eaten it; call your companions together so that the soul of the maize be undivided, so that we have strength to eat of it." Through the prayers and rituals, the corn is thought of as a peer friend, and so despite the numerous sacrificial opportunities elsewhere in Mayan religion, no offerings are made to the corn spirit itself.[43]

Often when we think of nature mysticism we think of folks like John Muir alone in the wilderness, but with their agricultural mysticism the Maya pursue a domesticated form of nature mysticism that can be practiced in any home garden, as we saw in the tale "The Snake Who Paid Cash." Although this agricultural nature mysticism lacks the spectacle of a shaman transforming into a jaguar, it is perhaps more fundamental and widespread in the Mayan world. Much as the shaman seeks to *be* the jaguar, so the farmer seeks to *be* the spirits of the sun, rain, earth, corn, beans, and squash. What is sought is a rich, moving nature mystical experience of sacredness, along with a good harvest. While profoundly communing with nature, the human remains distinct from but nonetheless increasingly interwoven with elements of the natural world. Agricultural nature mysticism beautifully exhibits fundamental Mayan notions of the myriad holy relationships between humans and other natural beings.

Therefore in Mayan natural soul-companions, shamanic theriomorphic transformations, and agricultural nature mysticism, we find models of human perfection in which personal empowerment arises precisely because of deepened experiential connections with the natural world. In these examples humans and nonhumans remain intimately and spiritually linked, with the result that no human stands apart from or over nature. These Mayan beliefs portray close, interdependent partnerships between all human beings and all nonhuman natural beings, since nature is the foundation for humanity, not an obstacle for humanity to overcome.

Mayan shamans and farmers live out this worldview. The shaman gains her power to begin with by training in naturalness, finding the psychological and emotional sweet spot between human and nonhuman consciousness to become an animal like a jaguar. In becoming a jaguar, the shaman gains the resources to complete her duties to herself, her family, her village, and the gods, as does the farmer with the agricultural spirits. In fact, in ordinary Mayan perspective it is only because the shaman and farmer are so connected with nature that they have any power at all. Here humans are only fully human when they embrace the nonhuman relationships and realities of their lives. Life is meaningful only when one becomes more spiritually enmeshed within nature rather seeking to conquer it. Human fulfillment is achieved in concert with nonhuman nature rather than in juxtaposition to it.

Of course, there are limits to this happy interweaving with nature. The Maya use natural beings to fulfill human needs, unavoidably placing some stress on the natural environment. And with human wants and needs being what they are, even amid an ethic of reciprocity, human use of the natural world can become problematic, as we know from historical Mayan experience. The Maya began linguistically around 2,000 B.C.E., and between around 300 B.C.E. and 800 C.E. they built one of the great empires in world history, with mathematical and scientific advances to match those of India, China, Europe, and Middle East; cities with giant populations for the time; and strong kings who built the magnificent and famous temple-complex cities of the greater Yucatan and the highlands. But then, in one of the more remarkable stories in history, Mayan cultures crumbled over a relatively short period of time, first in the south and later in the north. Numerous reasons have been offered for this transition, for which many divergent factors must have contributed. One of the more accepted explanations involves soil exhaustion. In this theory, the Mayan municipalities got too large, and the earth could not carry the load. While mild use of the Mayan slash-and-burn agricultural technique can contribute to sustainability, too much use can inhibit forest regrowth, leaving infertile patches rather than renewable plots; this was a problem in 800 C.E. as it is for the Maya today. In another example of ancient Mayan human-caused environmental problems, the gorgeous quetzal bird was nearly extinct by the ninth century, just as some species struggle to survive in Mayan country today. Elsewhere in the ancient world, humans appear to have aided the extinctions of wooly mammoths, saber-toothed tigers, and Egyptian wild Cape dogs, although climate changes helped these extinctions as well.[44]

Because of these historical environmental struggles, the Maya supply notice that we should avoid some frequent misunderstandings regarding indigenous religions, human history, and the environment. Many people, perhaps inspired by the philosopher Jean-Jacques Rousseau, have claimed that long ago humans lived in primal harmony with the natural environment in a kind of Eden. In this perspective, primal religions and their reflections in current indigenous traditions like those of the Maya inspire humans to live in a paradise of happiness, concord, and unity with nature and therefore are of necessity much more nature-friendly than Abrahamic religions. There are at least two problems with these views.

First, they appear to be factually incorrect. Numerous archaeological studies have shown that humans, indigenous or otherwise, have negatively impacted their environment for as long as we can trace human history, eliminating any notion of a primal utopia. Easter Island provides a poignant example of this reality. As the anthropologist Charles L. Redman explains, Polynesian settlers, armed with "nature-friendly" indigenous religious sensibilities, arrived at this isolated Pacific island around 400 C.E., calling it Rapanui. With rich volcanic soils, a warm, semitropical climate, and an absence of humans, Rapanui teemed with multiple species of flowers, brush, trees, and animals. In fact, the island possessed arguably the Pacific's highest concentration of seabirds, along with six flightless land-bird species. In this land of flowing milk and honey, the settlers prospered and eventually built a civilization capable of creating the eerie, giant, stone heads for which the island is famous.

But by the time European explorers arrived in the sixteenth century, Rapanui was completely deforested because of both human action and serious drought, its rich soils eroded or incapable of regeneration; and the diversity of life declined to near zero. The tiny human population that remained lived in the greatest poverty, devoid of economic resources and incapable of escape from their self-made predicament, since there were no trees left to build boats. Like Mayan history, Easter Island teaches us that, because of human needs and desires, even peoples armed with supposedly nature-friendly religions do not now and have not ever lived in utopian harmony with nature. I may add that this includes the human-centered practice of animal sacrifice, which commonly appears in Native American religions, including that of the Maya. Many more instances of this lack of utopian harmony exist.[45]

As is also problematic, these mistaken ideas of a primal harmony with nature inhibit our ability to learn about human environmental impacts. If the only way to be nature-friendly is to live a simple, indigenous lifestyle, which is impossible for many people in the contemporary world, then indigenous religions fail to offer us practical advice and direction, and their lessons remain curious museum pieces. But if indigenous peoples do not live in effortless harmony with nature and instead endure their own struggles to be nature-friendly, then we may learn from our shared history with our indigenous cousins.

Therefore despite the ecocentrism, even kin ecocentrism, built into Mayan religion, and its ethic of reciprocity with sacred nature, human needs and wants nonetheless intrude, compromising an otherwise ecocentric notion of sacred environment with human concerns. Because of these differing influences, Mayan traditional religion leaves us with strong ecocentric elements admixed with a dose of anthropocentrism, as cream blends with coffee. This turn to human-centeredness should not surprise us, for—as we have seen and will see more fully in the next chapters—pure ecocentrism globally is hard to find.

But this situation notwithstanding, Mayan shamans, steeped in a rich and ancient culture, will continue to be jaguars, and farmers will continue to be corn. In so doing they both define and blur what makes humanity distinct from the rest of the natural world. These Mayan mystics remind us of the sage Zhuang Zhou, from the Chinese Daoist classic *Zhuangzi*, as he is confused about his species:[46]

> Once Zhuang Zhou dreamed he was a butterfly, a butterfly flitting and fluttering around, happy with himself and doing as he pleased. He didn't know he was Zhuang Zhou. Suddenly he woke up, and there he was, solid and unmistakable Zhuang Zhou. But he didn't know if he were Zhuang Zhou who had dreamed he was a butterfly or a butterfly dreaming he was Zhuang Zhou.

The Maya and Zhuang Zhou offer cases where the line between humans and natural beings is unclear because of the possibility of transforming from one form of life to another. However, this line may be muddied other ways, such as through permanent hybridization. Now we jet to the other side of the planet to explore that reality.

5

Friendly Yetis

Judges 16:23 in the Hebrew Bible tells how the Philistines, enemies of the ancient Jews, enthusiastically thanked their central god, Dagon, when they had captured the powerful Jewish warrior Samson. Then in 1 Samuel 5 the Philistines spirited away the Jewish Ark of the Covenant and hid it in the temple of this same Dagon. In worshipping Dagon like this, the Philistines continued a tradition that stretched back to the middle of the third millennium B.C.E. in the central Euphrates region, Syria, and Palestine. Known to some as the father of the gods, Dagon included among his progeny the prominent Near Eastern god Baal.

Despite this eminence, the identity of the god Dagon remains uncertain. *The Anchor Bible Dictionary* explains that Dagon may have been a storm god, a god of grain, a god of fish, or a half-fish, half-human deity. Whatever the historical truth about Dagon may be, this last interpretation took root, and by the Middle Ages the Jewish rabbinic tradition regarded Dagon, now without divinity, as a human-fish hybrid creature. Speaking of Dagon, the medieval French biblical commentator Rabbi Shlomo Yitzchaki (1040–1105 C.E.) wrote of mermaidlike human-fish hybrids known in Old French as *sereine*, and the *Moshav Zekeinim*, a medieval Jewish scriptural commentary, includes discussion of a "creature in the sea which is similar in part to a person, from the navel upwards, and it is similar to a woman in all aspects, in that it has breasts and long hair like that of a woman, and from the navel downwards it is a fish. And it sings beautifully, with a pleasant voice." Thus it appears that the ancient god Dagon, understood as a human-fish, lost his divinity and transformed over the centuries into the legendary mermaid of Western culture.[1]

A god becoming a mermaid highlights the numerous important symbolic uses of natural beings in religions, since imaginary natural beings fulfill many functions. Among these are innumerable instances of imaginary beings, including gryphons, the ancient Near Eastern bird-lion blends that adorn Jewish arks containing the Torah and that are said to have decorated Solomon's throne, and Chinese Daoist temple protector dragons, who bring rain, good luck, and prosperity. Often imaginary animals take the forms that they do in order to provide specific moral instruction, as we see in the description of the phoenix in the medieval Christian bestiary *Physiologus*:[2]

> There is a species of bird in the land of India which is called the phoenix, which enters the wood of Lebanon after five hundred years and bathes his two wings in the fragrance.... Then the bird enters Heliopolis laden with fragrance and mounts the altar, where he ignites the fire and burns himself up. The next day then the priest examines the altar and finds a worm in its ashes. On the second day, however, he finds a tiny birdling. On the third day he finds a huge eagle which, taking flight, greets the priest and goes off to his former abode.
>
> If this species of bird has the power to kill himself in such a manner as to raise himself up, how foolish are those people who become angry at the words of the Savior, "I have the power to lay down my life, and I have the power to take it again."

Some of the most interesting of these imaginary beings are specifically were-animals, or human-animal hybrids like the mermaid. Chiron, in Greek myth the learned teacher of the likes of Achilles and Asclepius, was a human-horse centaur. The devil once assailed the Christian saint Anthony Abbot in the form of a human who was a donkey from the legs down. Hindu temples to Vishnu always are guarded by Vishnu's *vahana*, or animal spirit companion, the human-eagle Garuda; and Vishnu himself defeated evil by incarnating as the human-lion Narasimha. Further, there is the curious example of a Lithuanian man named Thiess, who confessed to judicial authorities his becoming a werewolf in order that he might fight against the devil and his evildoing human minions.[3]

Adding to this fascinating list of religious were-animals are the yetis of the Himalayas, who are sacred human-animal hybrids that make an interesting case study. In contrast to the generally strong separation between humans and animals that we saw typifying Abrahamic traditions, Himalayan folk-cultural images of yetis present a model in which powerful divinity is manifest simultaneously as both human and animal. Further, as we saw with phoenixes, yetis offer forms of moral instruction.

Before we go too far into the world of yetis, though, I should offer a few remarks about my approach. Some people concern themselves with a search for physical yetis, but in this book I do not. Here I speak simply about cultural images of yetis without fretting about affirming or denying their material existence. Some Himalayan residents believe that yetis exist, and I simply examine these beliefs. But since some Himalayan citizens do not believe in material yetis, an attitude of agnosticism seems appropriate. And we may learn a great deal about human interactions with the natural world from beliefs and practices regarding things like alleged yeti scalps yet not be too worried about the authenticity of those scalps.

Unless and until undisputed physical remains of a yeti emerge, we may consider yetis to exist in the human imagination alone, with little restraint from reality in the creation of images of them. As such, yetis make excellent screens for understanding projected human attitudes toward the natural world. Just as a therapist may show you an amorphous Rorschach inkblot and discern your psychological state from how you describe it, so yetis show us what we think about nature, especially a facet of interactions with nature everywhere: experiences of ambivalence. Scholars of human-animal interactions universally describe our experiences of animals as fundamentally ambivalent. We eat natural beings, but they also eat us, and so we are drawn to them yet also fear them. We love some animals as family members but kill others simply for bothering us. Many of us think cows are cute and innocent but also deserving of the knife when we want steak. The scholar of human-animal interactions James Serpell puts this ambivalence this way:[4]

> At one extreme are the animals we call pets. They make little or no practical or economic contribution to human society, yet we nurture and care for them like our own kith and kin, and display outrage and disgust when they are subjected to ill-treatment. At the other, we have animals like the pig on which a major section of our economy depends, supremely useful animals in every respect.... By rights, we ought to be eternally grateful to pigs for the extraordinary sacrifices they make on our behalf. Instead, the quality of life we impose on them suggests nothing but contempt and hatred.

Yetis also exhibit this ambivalence, because in the Himalayas they have existed as cultural realities for centuries in ways quite different from what Western culture would have us believe. In Western popular culture yetis, also known as abominable snowmen, are huge, bloodthirsty, secular monsters. But in the Himalayas, yetis have a human side and an animal side. Their human side allows them to be friendly, compassionate, and sometimes religiously pious. Their animal side can be ferocious, as in Western images, but it is so because yetis may be incarnate gods on earth who must keep community order. To many Himalayan peoples, yetis profoundly symbolize what it means to be human, what it means to be an animal, and what it means to be a visible incarnation of the sacred—all at the same time.

The first mention of yetis in the English-speaking world came from Brian H. Hodgson, a British representative at the court of Kathmandu from 1820 to 1843. His Nepalese assistants told him of a wild man who "moved, they said, erectly: was covered with long dark hair, and had no tail." Major Lawrence A. Waddell added to the lore in 1889 when he observed alleged yeti footprints. Around 1904 a British soldier named William Hugh Knight claimed to physically encounter a yeti near Gangtok, Sikkim. In describing this yeti to *The Times* in 1921 Knight said,[5]

> He was a little under six feet high, almost stark naked in that bitter cold—it was the month of November. He was a kind of pale yellow all over, about the colour of a Chinaman, a shock of matted hair on his head, little hair on his face, highly splayed feet, and large, formidable hands. His muscular development in his arms, thighs, legs, back and chest were terrific. He had in his hands what seemed to me to be some form of primitive bow. He did not see me, but stood there, and I watched for some five or six minutes. So far as I could make out, he was watching some man or beast far down the hillside. At the end of some five minutes he started off on a run down the hill, and I was impressed with the tremendous speed at which he travelled.

Western encounters with yetis continued when members of the Howard-Bury Everest expedition of 1921 found strange humanlike footprints in the snow at around twenty-one thousand feet. Their report prompted Henry Newman, a British writer for Kolkata's *The Statesman* newspaper, to shape yeti tales into a story about a mysterious danger lurking in the Himalayas. Misunderstanding the meaning of a Tibetan-language appellation of this creature, *miteh kangmi*, "human-bear of the snow," Newman unfortunately named this being the abominable snowman. Perhaps because of the regrettable appearance of the word "abominable" in Newman's description, the vast majority of Western notions of yetis since his time have depicted them only as secular, predatory beasts.[6]

Yetis appear in a different guise in their Asian homeland. Yetilike beings appear in the folklore of many societies along the length of the Himalayas, from an eastern location in Sichuan, in China, all the way west to the Pamirs, in Uzbekistan, and so there are many names for and understandings of this creature. The word "yeti" itself comes from the Sherpa dialect of the Tibetan language, the Sherpas having migrated from Tibet to eastern Nepal in the fifteenth and the early sixteenth century. "Yeti" derives from the Sherpa *yehteh*, "cliff-dwelling bear," and the Sherpa recognize two varieties of yetis. The larger is the *dzuteh*, "livestock bear," which walks only on four legs and preys on goats, cattle, and yaks. Sherpas explicitly recognize this as the Himalayan red bear. The smaller of the two is the *miteh* or *mehteh*, "human-bear." Many Sherpas have shown scientists that they can easily recognize bears but still insist that the *miteh*, which is said to walk upright on two legs, is separate from all bears. It is this *miteh* that provides fodder for yeti legends, artwork, physical relics, and so on.[7]

In central Tibet one finds that the creature is called *miguh*, "wild human," more often than "yeti," and in Bhutan this becomes *mirguh*. Other Tibetan names include *kangmi*, "snow man"; *mishompo*, "strong man"; and *michenpo*, "big man." Many Tibetans claim that its footprints resemble those of the Himalayan brown bear, known in Tibet as *teh-mong* or *miteh*, and often in Tibet the yeti is called *miteh kangmi*, "human-bear of the snow." All these names imply closeness to humans in their use of the word *mi*, which in Tibetan means a human being.[8]

The Rong (also called Lepcha), a Tibet-influenced indigenous group who live in the Sikkimese Himalayas, call the yeti *chumung*, "snow goblin"; *hlomung*, "mountain goblin"; or *Pongrum*, "benevolent god Pong." More or less human in form and covered in hair, the *chumung* lives on the high slopes of the sacred peak Kanchenjunga.[9]

Since at least the eighteenth century some Himalayan residents have thought that yetis are real, and tales of encounters continue to this day. Tibetan cultural images portray yetis as apelike rather than bearlike, with long arms, a powerful torso, a conical head, and a full covering of reddish-brown hair (thus differing from Western images of yetis, which typically are white). This long, dark hair is a trademark; on one occasion a Tibetan lady at Drepung Monastery, in Lhasa, Tibet, good-naturedly joked with me by calling me a yeti because of my long, brown head hair, bushy beard, and dark-upholstered arms.

The yeti's face is simian, as it lacks hair and is said to have the flat nose of a primate rather than the protruding nose of a bear. The biologist Charles Stonor tells of showing photos of apes and bears to Tibetans and each time the Tibetans identified orangutans, not bears, with yetis. The insistence of Tibetans that yetis are apelike and not bearlike is remarkable, given that there are no apes known to live high in the Himalayas, but there are red, brown, and blue bears, and perhaps in the distant past a relative of the polar bear. Stonor further highlights that yeti reports can occur in winter, when bears are hibernating.[10]

Nonetheless the mountain climber Reinhold Messner says that yetis are mistakenly perceived bears. The anthropologist Jeff Meldrum states that this may be true for some yeti sightings but others may stem from sightings of relic populations of an ancient Asian ape classified as *Gigantopithecus*. Myra Shackley postulates that yetis could be relic populations of Neanderthals. Personally, I wonder if some yeti sightings are not mistaken perceptions of Himalayan holy people like Hindu *sadhus* or Tibetan yogis who, after years of wandering in homeless mountain solitude far from human populations, have become shaggy and somewhat desocialized and thus may appear both wild and human at the same time. But my theory does not account well for the times when yetis are said to possess superhuman strength.[11]

Yetis are said to move on two or four legs as they please. Some say that their feet point backwards. They live not in the snows but in the forests just below the snow line, and during the winter they may move to lower altitudes, bringing them nearer to human settlements. They may, however, visit the high-altitude snows to cross to another valley or to feed on alpine mosses. Yetis also are said to eat frogs and pikas, which are small mouse-hares abundant in the Himalayas. They may steal food such as potatoes from humans as well.[12]

Said to be nocturnal, yetis are rarely seen, and in Bhutan they may be thought to possess a *dipshing*, a twig that makes them invisible. They are more often heard, being widely credited with a high-pitched screech or whistling sound. Some sources tell us that yetis have their own language and female-led social groups. Female yetis are famous for their low-hanging breasts, which are "so large they have to throw them over their shoulders before they bend down," an attribute that often helps to distinguish yetis in Tibetan art.[13]

Stories of yeti encounters help to clarify these descriptions. One day a Sherpa named Pasang Nima was with friends at a religious festival when a group returned to their camp to report sighting a yeti. Intrigued, Pasang Nima followed directions to the spot of the encounter to ascertain the truth behind the story. The area was flat and sparsely covered in small rhododendron bushes. Upon arrival Pasang Nima spotted a figure, about the size and build of a strong man, some two hundred yards away. Long hair covered its head, torso, and limbs, although its face and chest were not very hairy. The color of the hair was both dark and light but overall was reddish. The being walked on two legs and often reached down as if scavenging for roots. Pasang Nima and his friends watched it for some time, during which the creature was entirely upright, never moving on all four limbs. Eventually the yeti caught sight of its audience and scurried off into the brush on two legs while emitting a loud, high-pitched cry.[14]

Another Sherpa named Phorchen tells of seeing a yeti near the town of Namche Bazaar. In midwinter he set out for some yak pastures, where he was hoping to find some wax left over from beehives that he had seen the previous summer. While he was climbing over some rocks he spied a brown animal coming down the slopes. At first he took no further notice, as he assumed that it was a musk deer. However, as it came closer he noticed that it was no deer, since it moved only on two legs. The yeti had not seen Phorchen, who remained dead still so that he could watch the creature. The yeti walked on two legs on the flat portions, just like a human, but sometimes dropped to four legs to navigate the difficult patches of ground. It was the size of a small man, with long, reddish-brown and black hair, which was lighter and thinner on the chest and face. Its head was conical and pointed, and the brown face was like a monkey's.

After watching the yeti for a while, fear overcame Phorchen. He began to bang his knife on a tree, hoping that noise would scare the creature away, and eventually the creature bounded off in a manner unlike that of a deer or a *tahr* (Himalayan mountain goat). The next morning Phorchen returned to the spot with a friend and discovered what looked like a bare human footprint in the snow.[15]

Two Norwegians named Thorberg and Frostis share a tale from eastern Nepal in 1948. They were part of a group that discovered two sets of what appeared to be bare human footprints in the snow leading up a valley. Their curiosity piqued, they followed the prints until they came across the print makers: a pair of yetis. Members of their party tried to lasso the yetis, who were angered by this approach and attacked. One of the group members was knocked down and mauled, and while other group members attended to their fallen friend, the pair of yetis slipped away. Everyone in the group agreed that they had encountered two large apes.[16]

Both Sherpas and central Tibetans use the word *miteh,* "human-bear," to denote the yeti in language, yet they typically think of yetis as human-apes. But whether were-apes or were-bears, yetis are composite beings rather than simple life forms, as they combine human and animal traits as a hybrid species that straddles the boundary between human and animal. The *Mani Kabum,* a twelfth-century religious and historical chronicle of Tibet, describes how yetis got this hybrid character. According to the *Mani Kabum,* there once was a great lake that receded, leaving behind Tibet with all its animals, forests, and mountains. On one of these mountains, Hepo Ri, the Tibetan people were born. This mountain was inhabited by a female mountain ogress who was an incarnation of Drolma (also known as Tara), the Tibetan deity of mercy. This ogress met and mated with a monkey who was an incarnation of the deity of compassion, Chenrezig. Their six children were human-monkey hybrids who were the ancestors of the six original Tibetan clans. The human-monkeys were short and covered in hair, had flat, red faces like primates, stood erect, and perhaps had tails. Over generations their progeny evolved, becoming more human and less simian, until they became the Tibetan people. But, according to Tibetan oral folklore, a subgroup had their evolution curtailed early and instead of becoming human they remained hirsute wild people, or yetis.[17]

Thus in Tibetan lore yetis and humans stand apart from the rest of the natural world, as their special relationship includes common ancestry and, to a point, common development. Yetis share much with humans and differ from other animals. Yet with their animal side they are not fully human, either. They exist in a vague, liminal region between humans and animals and, of especial interest, they do so in accordance with stable species characteristics.

The constancy of their hybrid character separates yetis from some other animal-human mixtures. The Mayan shaman may shape-shift into a jaguar for ritual purposes but then returns to human form, the theriomorphic transformation in this case being merely temporary. Tibetan religions also provide cases of such temporary hybrid characters. For example, the Tibetan mystic Milarepa once spent the winter in meditation retreat in the remote Cave of Conquering Demons on Chomolangma, also known as Mt. Everest. The harsh winter included a brutal storm when it snowed for eighteen days and nights, cutting the cave off from all communication and commerce. The weather was so bad, in fact, that Milarepa's disciples in town decided that no human could have survived it on Mt. Everest and held a sacramental feast in honor of Milarepa's presumed death. When the winter was over Milarepa's disciples set about the grim task of going to the cave and recovering his corpse. Surmounting a mountain pass near Milarepa's cave, the disciples stopped to rest, when a snow leopard, an ethereal Himalayan big cat, climbed upon a nearby boulder and stared at the disciples for a few minutes before disappearing. The disciples continued their walk, noticing that human footprints stood on the path alongside the leopard's, and eventually the disciples reached the cave. Milarepa, surrounded by freshly prepared food, immediately chastised his otherwise joyful disciples for arriving so late and thus allowing the food to get cold. He insisted that they begin feasting right away and worry about other things (like his surprising survival) later. His disciple Dunpa Shajaguna responded, "Indeed, it is dinner-time for us, but surely you must have known that we were coming." Milarepa replied:[18]

> "When I was sitting on the rock, I saw you all resting on the other side of the pass." "We saw a leopard sitting there," said Dunpa Shajaguna, "but we did not see you. Where were you then?" "I was the leopard," Milarepa answered. "To a yogi who has completely mastered the union of wisdom and energy, the essence of the Four Elements is perfectly controlled. He can transform into whatever bodily form he chooses. I have shown you my occult power of performing supernatural acts because you are all gifted and advanced disciples."

Yetis don't shape-shift like this. Unlike Milarepa, werewolves who appear only at full moons, and Mayan shamans who become temporary jaguars during rituals, yetis stand apart as perpetual were-apes or were-bears. This constancy inhibits any sharp division or clear distinction between animal and human worlds in a way that temporary hybrid transformations do not. Images of permanently hybrid yetis demonstrate to some Himalayan residents that humanity is seamlessly integrated into the larger natural world, not just distinct yet interwoven as we saw with the Maya. Yetis do not cross the line between human and animal only to return, as instead they define the line between human and animal as necessarily blurry.

In some folk stories the ancestral kinship between humans and yetis as described in the *Mani Kabum* is so close that it allows interbreeding between humans and yetis. For example, a Sherpa informant told Dr. Charles Stonor this story, which is a variant of a commonly told tale:[19]

> A woman of our people had her little girl kidnapped by the yetis, who took her off with them, far away into the mountains. For three years she sought her child by every means she could think of; but, try as she would, not a scrap of news did she get. Then one day she found her, quite by chance. The girl had forgotten how to talk and no longer knew her mother, who was greatly troubled how to reach her. So, as a forlorn hope, she went up into the rocks with the clothes and little playthings the child had used long ago. These she left in a prominent place, near to where the child was living with the yetis.

The girl found them and they brought back memories of her former life. Slowly she became human once more and her speech returned to her. She was living with a male yeti by whom she had a child; this took after its father and was scarcely human at all. Although she was now longing to return to her own people, she could think of no way to escape. So her mother gave her some strips of fresh yak skin, not yet dry; and with these she stealthily bound his hands and feet as soon as he had gone to sleep: tying them loosely, so that he should feel nothing. By morning the thongs had dried and tightened, and the girl could escape home to her parents, abandoning her yeti-child to its own kith and kin, who lost no time in killing it.

Besides displaying a close kinship between yetis and humans, this story reveals another important yeti-folklore theme: in Himalayan cultures parents may wield the yeti as a bogeyman for disciplining the young. Children who misbehave may be told that if they do not reform, they will be abducted by a yeti.

Some pieces of Tibetan sacred art affirm the understanding of yetis as were-apes. Tibetan Buddhism possesses a variety of *mandalas*, elaborate artworks that aid in advanced meditation practices, as well as *thangkas*, meditational paintings that depict deities and spiritual teachers. Showing their debt to the influence of Tibetan folk traditions, most of these artworks that depict yetis do so by portraying them as apelike in some way and existing in a realm between the human and the animal. From the Buddhist side this is heterodox, as the Buddhism that Tibet inherited from India does not include a realm of rebirth between humans and animals. Nonetheless, folk beliefs alter the shapes of high religions everywhere, and the same is true with Tibetan yetis, who adhere to their folk tradition as were-animals even in the most prestigious of Buddhist monasteries.

The mountaineer Reinhold Messner offers an interesting story on this count. While hiking in Bhutan he came upon Gangtey Monastery. In the monastery he found a wall covered with the preserved heads of several animals. Such taxidermized animal heads are common in Tibetan monasteries, as they are thought to lend nature's power to the spot. But this wall was different, as a mounted yeti head adorned the

Figure 16. Animal head in a Tibetan monastery. (Photo: Author.)

top of the display. The monks confirmed for Messner that the yeti head (which Messner says was fabricated) was on top because yetis occupy an intermediate space lower than humans but higher than animals.[20]

Recognizing that yetis are human-animal hybrids allows us to understand the surprising ability of yetis to practice religion in the Tibetan folk tradition. As we have seen, often in spiritual traditions animals cannot practice religion, and this is true in the Buddhism of Tibet. Also, Buddhist rules explicitly state that monks and nuns must be human beings, and the tradition generally holds that nonhumans lack the self-reflective capacity required to tread the path to enlightenment. In most Buddhist thought, only humans practice religion. But some elements of Tibetan folk religion that entertain the yeti's partial humanity got integrated into Tibetan Buddhism and reveal that yetis may at times be pious Buddhists.

Stories from the life of the great seventeenth-century religious leader Lama Sangwa Dorje illustrate such a Buddhist yeti. In his youth Lama Sangwa Dorje left Sherpa country to study Buddhism in southern Tibet. He became skilled in both intellectual and practical aspects of Buddhism and so was recognized as the fifth incarnation of the spiritual teacher of Rongphu Monastery. Then he returned to the Sherpa Khumbu region with the desire to build monasteries. Before commencing, he sought a blessing from his tutelary deity Gombu, so he retreated alone to a cave near Pangboche to intensely meditate.

Hermit meditators like Sangwa Dorje are highly revered in the Tibetan world since it is thought that they bring good luck and do the hard spiritual work for everyone else. Typically, therefore, local lay people provision meditators with gifts of food, clothing, medicine, and the like, in support of their retreats. Such generosity to hermits is considered an important spiritual practice of devotion that creates good karma. In the case of Sangwa Dorje, his devoted patron was a yeti, who regularly brought food, water, and fuel to the monk. Over time this yeti even became Sangwa Dorje's Buddhist disciple. When the yeti died, Lama Sangwa Dorje retained the yeti's scalp and hand and enshrined them in Pangboche Gompa, a monastery that Sangwa Dorje founded in 1667.[21]

Yeti relics sometimes have spiritual charisma, as is true for the relics of Sangwa Dorje's yeti also. For centuries these yeti relics, charged with spiritual power, were paraded around the village at least once a year by Sangwa Dorje's successors, the Drogon lamas. This parade was thought to bring auspicious energy and especially fertility for a good harvest, and the yeti relics blessed humans, animals, houses, and fields alike. Unfortunately the yeti hand was stolen from the monastery in 1999.[22]

As for the authenticity of yeti relics, we have seen Messner encounter a yeti head which he thought was fabricated. The famous yeti scalp from Khumjung Gompa in Nepal was shown by Western scientists to be formed from serow antelope skins that had been sewn together. Before it was stolen, the yeti hand of Pangboche Gompa was described as antelope and human bones that had been wired together. But of course, for some Himalayan people, if an article functions ritually as a yeti scalp, it is a yeti scalp, regardless of DNA constitution. An object fabricated centuries ago to encourage religious belief may have its origins forgotten and now appear to people as old, traditional, and therefore real. We see a similar situation with the myriad supposed bits of the cross of Jesus, which provide devotional support to many Christians yet, in the most charitable perspective, are far too numerous for every single one to be authentic. Thus yeti artifacts may perform serious and profound religious work even if they perhaps are not at all authentic.[23]

Lama Sangwa Dorje's story from Sherpa country is not the only one in which yetis practice religion. In another tale, from Bhutan, a group of yetis expressed religious devotion by serving as the attendants for a Buddhist shrine. These yetis would sneak into a temple for the deity Palden Lhamo in the dead of night lest any human could take notice. Night after night the yetis would clean and refill the bowls and plates that contained water and food offerings, replenish the butter in the temple butter lamps, dust, sweep, and then disappear into the presunrise darkness. Like Sangwa Dorje's yeti, these creatures practiced acts of religious devotion very similar to those of Tibetan humans. Many theorists have told us that the difference between humans and animals is the practice of religion, but these yetis strain this understanding.[24]

These stories highlight why some Tibetans told both Charles Stonor and René de Nebesky-Wojkowitz, a scholar of religion who resided in the Himalayas, that yetis are placid beings who need not be feared unless they are injured. In the stories of both Lama Sangwa Dorje and the Bhutanese temple keepers, we find yetis who are much kinder and gentler than any in Western depictions. These yetis are peaceful,

Figure 17. A friendly yeti as portrayed at the Norbulinka Institute. (Photo: Author.)

devoted Buddhists who practice religion and contribute to Tibetan society. This way of thinking about yetis is brilliantly displayed at the Norbulinka Institute, the Dalai Lama's own monastery, temple, and museum in Dharamsala, India. In one of the murals there that display the people and fauna of Tibet, one can find a yeti who has a medium build, long, brown hair, and an amiable apelike face adorned with a large smile. It is a friendly yeti.

In other tales yetis behave not as Buddhist practitioners but as religious allies of humans. One such story tells of a yeti who exhibits the Buddhist virtue of gratitude, although perhaps in a way less human and more animal than our yeti temple attendants showed. This story is quite common, known in several variants across Himalayan communities. In this story, a Tibetan Buddhist meditator or yogi wandered through the mountains. Then,[25]

One day he was crippled by an attack of gout and was unable to walk. He established himself in a pleasant place at the edge of the forest, where he found some goats, who eventually followed him everywhere like pets. There he remained.

On the other side of the hill were some abandoned shacks. Every day he would see a huge dark man coming and going between the shacks and the river. Apart from this, there was no other sign of life.

One week he no longer noticed his strange neighbor on his daily walk. Having become intrigued by that mysterious man and feeling a bit better, the yogi decided to investigate the man's dilapidated dwelling.

Inside, the yogi was startled to come face to face with a *migö*, or wild man, as Tibetans call the yeti. The hirsute behemoth was lying outstretched on the floor, eyes closed and fangs apart, seemingly unaware of the intrusion. He was feverish and obviously ill.

One of the yeti's feet was grossly swollen and full of pus. The yogi immediately noticed, protruding from the infected area of that vast foot, a sharp splinter of wood that could easily be removed. He thought, "I know he can jump up and devour me at any moment, but now that I have come this far I might as well try to help the poor creature."

While he gently extracted the long splinter, the yeti—aware that the lama was helping him—lay as still as a patient etherized upon an operating table. The kindly yogi cautiously cleaned away the pus. He washed the wound, using his own saliva as a salve; then he bandaged the bizarre foot with a rag torn from his own clothing.

On tiptoe he left the yeti, returning to his goats, which were tied to a tree in the forest. Days afterward, he saw the yeti limping down to the river, presumably for water, and then slowly returning to his house. Eventually the creature's gait improved to the point where he could walk without difficulty. Miraculously enough, the yogi's crippling gout also began to subside so that his painful stride began to return to normal, until he, too, was completely cured. After that, he no longer saw the yeti.

One day the ferocious yeti suddenly leapt down like a giant gorilla from the trees, grimaced at the yogi, then sprang back into the trees and was gone. A few days later the same thing happened—but this time the yeti was carrying a dead tiger on his shoulder. Placing the magnificent carcass in front of the lama as if in a token of his gratitude, he again bounded off into the dense jungle.

The yogi did not wish to eat the meat, but he skinned the beautiful beast with meticulous care. Eventually, upon his return to the Shechen Monastery, he offered the splendid tiger skin to the monastery for use during tantric rites.

This story's yeti showed his gratitude to the yogi by giving him a gift in an act of Buddhist devotion. Thus this yeti helps humans practice religion. We see another such helper yeti, although in symbolic form, in a ritual from the Khumbu region of Sherpa country. At Khumjung Gompa monastery an annual religious festival called Dumche memorializes the death of Lama Sangwa Dorje. An important figure in the festival is the *gyamakag*, whom I will call scapegoat yeti. The scapegoat yeti is a human who symbolizes the yeti, as he dresses in a sheepskin coat with the fur turned outside, paints his face black, and wears the scalp of a supposed yeti that is kept at the monastery. Posted at the gates of the monastery, his job is to chase away evil, since malevolent spirits are thought to fear yetis greatly. Thus the scapegoat yeti performs a protective function.

But the scapegoat yeti does more than guard the community; he also enacts a crucial ritual role. On the second day of the festival, lamas, or Tibetan spiritual teachers, make a special effigy called the *lokpar torma*. Such effigies are common in Tibetan rituals. While there are wide variations, *torma* effigies commonly are conical, about eight inches tall, sculpted from butter and flour, and colorfully decorated. Unlike all other effigies at the festival, though, only the *lokpar* effigy is made from buckwheat rather than barley, is colored red and black, and bears decorations of hellish flames and miniature human skulls. Its special characteristics identify the *lokpar* effigy as a trap for evil spirits as part of a ritual of exorcism.

During the sixth day of the festival lamas sit near this effigy and chant the invocation of the Red Wrathful Guru, infusing the effigy with the misdeeds of the community while also attracting like a magnet, and then trapping, any evil spirits that may be waiting to attack the village in the future. By the end of the chant, the effigy contains within itself the fullness of the village's negative energies and forces.

Following this chanting, in the courtyard of the monastery monks wearing colorful silks and spectacular masks perform a series of vivid, sacred *cham* dances amid villagers crowded all around. Then the scapegoat yeti, brandishing a sword in one hand and the exorcism effigy in the other, leads the community out of the monastery gate to a pit dug outside the village, all the while chanting loudly, *Ho! Ho!* He wears a mask over his mouth to prevent his breathing in evil energy from the malevolence-laden effigy. The scapegoat yeti places the effigy in the pit, after which townsfolk throw stones at it and the scapegoat yeti stabs it. As the yeti kills the demons in the effigy with his sword, lamas chant invocations to beneficent deities in order to enjoin their help in banishing the evil energy. Thus this ritual yeti is a scapegoat, as lamas and townspeople are spared the negative karma from killing the demons that are trapped in the effigy but the scapegoat yeti is not. This makes the scapegoat yeti role an unpopular, if necessary, one. Then the community burns the effigy, thus completing the removal of negative forces, and the people return to the monastery for more religious dances and holiday frivolity. Thus the symbolic human-as-yeti creates a sense of well-being within the community by taking its negativity upon himself. This martyr yeti helps humans by bearing their sins.[26]

The yetis we have surveyed so far have been humanlike religious practitioners or helpers for humans practicing religion and have not really shown the animal side of their constitution. But there are quite a few stories that stress the animal side of the yeti's hybrid character. One of the most common of these tales, which admits of many variants, involves the need to remove yetis who are acting like animal pests:[27]

> Nowadays the yeti is a scarce animal in our Sherpa country. Time was, many generations back, it was much commoner and a great nuisance, raiding fields, digging up roots, and plucking the grain. The villagers were reduced to serious straits, and tried every way they could think of to get rid of them. Snares and traps of every sort failed; the yetis sat high up in the crags above the fields, watching everything and laughing to themselves at the puny efforts of the Sherpas. Then one day someone hit on the idea of putting out jars of the best *chang* [Himalayan barley beer]. The yetis came down at night and greedily drank it up. So the next night a strong dose of a poisonous root was put in the beer, and the raiders all died. All of their race was extinguished except one female, who was heavily pregnant at the time and could not manage to climb down to the fields. So it was that the yetis were not quite exterminated and still survive to this day.

Although this story treats yetis like ordinary vermin, some animal yetis embody intense holiness, since sometimes yetis are not just were-animals; they are divine were-animals. As one Sherpa said, the yeti is both a beast and a spirit. Previously I mentioned one of these essentially sacred yetis, the *chumung* of the Rong people. The hairy, humanlike *chumung* is the god of hunting and the owner of all forest animals. In this attribute the *chumung* resembles the Master of Animals that we have seen in other contexts. Both before and after the hunt, the *chumung* must be propitiated with offerings to secure present and future hunting success. When displeased, the *chumung* retaliates with poltergeist behavior such as throwing stones at people or their houses. But since it is a humanlike Master of Animals, the Rong *chumung* ambiguously participates in both sides of the human-animal divide in form and function.[28]

Aside from the *chumung,* it is fascinating that the most innately sacred of hybrid yetis is simultaneously the most animal in form and the most ferocious. Take, for example, a ritual that Myra Shackley describes from the Himalayan region of Lo Manthang. Every year the Tibetan Buddhist Sakya monastery of Ngon-ga Janghub Ling Monthang

Choedhe hosts a five-day festival called Deje in which negative forces, whether understood as external malevolent spirits or as internal obstacles to enlightenment, are driven away. The ritual itself involves a plethora of sacred dances in which the central figure is the deity Dorje Phurba. At the end of the ritual drama, danced over many hours by trained monks in fantastic costumes, Dorje Phurba overcomes a major demon in part because of the help of four monks dressed as Dorje Phurba's sacred animal protectors: a tiger, a wolf, a snow leopard, and a *miteh* yeti. Here the yeti is not a central deity but rather is a powerful protector deity who embodies intense sacred energy and performs a fierce religious function. This more animal yeti retains more essential sacredness than the other, more human, yetis that we have seen and also is more ferocious than some other yetis.[29]

This yeti conjunction, exhibiting greater animality combined with innate sacredness and greater ferocity, is nowhere more visible than in the context of the veneration of sacred mountains in traditional Tibetan folk religion. Many Himalayan people consider a great mountain in their vicinity to be their regional *yullha,* "local deity." In Tibetan folk belief the magnificent mountains of the Himalayas are gods who appear as magnificent mountains. These gods could appear as yaks, lakes, or whatever else they please, but they have chosen to become incarnate as awe-inspiring snow-capped peaks. As the patron gods of communities, these mountain gods provide positive boons as well as defensive care. But, in turn, local mountain deities exert control over their vassal people through taboos, informal laws, and a sense of omniscience.

Such Tibetan beliefs spotlight the long-term, crucial roles played by mountains in human religions. We have already seen evidence for such mountain veneration in Mayan respect for sacred peaks as either cities for souls or prosperity-bringing Mountain Lords. Perhaps one reason for mountains' sacred appeal arises from sheer altitude. If the divinities we wish to contact are in the sky, then the higher we are above the sea, the closer to the gods we are. For example, in the first millennium B.C.E. Minoans, in Crete, constructed temples on the tops of mountains such as

Petsophas and Juktas. These temples appear to have been oriented toward subjugating agricultural pests such as beetles, weasels, hedgehogs, and tortoises by appealing to a spirit, perhaps the Master of Animals, who could be contacted on the mountain top. Other examples of this attitude of reaching for the sky include the Temple Mount in Jerusalem, the location of the ancient great Jewish temple and today's Dome of the Rock, as well as the homologies between mountains and religious architecture, such as church steeples, frequently encountered across traditions.[30]

Sometimes mountains are sacred because they provide homes for gods, their relative isolation from human settlements giving divinities a residential buffer zone, as with the familiar example of Mt. Olympus. In this regard Scott Schnell describes instructive attitudes toward *yama no kami*, the mountain gods of Japanese Shinto. Some lowland Japanese rice farmers invite the *kami*, the nature spirit, of the sacred Mt. Kasa to leave its alpine abode each spring and descend to spend the summer in their rice fields, since they rely on the deity to provide them with irrigation water. After harvest, the god is ritually released back to the top of the mountain. Because the *kami* may send way too much water or none at all, the lowlanders approach the god with an attitude of fear, and there remains a sense that it is best for farmers and deity alike that the default home of the deity is on top of the holy mountain, away from human populations.[31]

The Himalayan peak Kailash deserves mention here. One of the holiest spots in Asia, the snow-covered Kailash, in western Tibet, is the home of the great Hindu deity Shiva. Annually many Hindus invest significant time and expense into long pilgrimages to this place and the accompanying sacred lake Manasarovar. But in contradistinction to this Hindu tradition, in the Tibetan folk belief that we have been exploring, Kailash is not the dwelling of a deity; it is an ancient and very powerful *yullha* local deity. Kailash is both a home to a deity and a deity in itself, depending on perspective, and Tibetans adopt the latter understanding. Thus Kailash, or *Kang Rinpoche* in Tibetan, also attracts many Tibetan pilgrims as well.

A visitor to Tibet may easily understand the divinity ascribed to mountains. Many peaks, rising four miles or more above sea level, demand respect for their majesty, immensity, and control over weather and sunlight: Are these not the qualities of gods? In emphasizing that the mountains themselves are deities, Tibetan beliefs resemble others found in folk traditions of the Andes and East Africa as well.

Embodying power, these mountain gods maintain order in their surroundings. In Tibet, local mountain gods function as divine judicial systems, sentencing malefactors to punishments such as illness, bad luck, or death. When it becomes necessary for a local mountain deity, playing the role of sheriff, to send out a deputy as a physical enforcer, the deity chooses to emanate as an apelike yeti. This mountain-deity yeti is the god incarnate and is extremely holy. It punishes rule breaches by bringing illness, property damage or theft, crop destruction, depredation of livestock, and even death, like the killer tigers of Javanese lore who are sent by Muhammad to punish adultery, bears sent by Kutenai shamans to chastise miscreants, or Thiess, the Satan-hunting werewolf mentioned previously. This is why among the many Buddhist artworks of the revered Drepung Monastery, in Lhasa, Tibet, one finds a black, gold, and red mural painting of a numinous she-yeti carrying a decapitated human corpse.[32]

Because mountain-deity yetis function as punitive keepers of community order, Himalayan people frequently regard hearing or seeing a yeti as a bad omen, and some mountain dwellers may seek the aid of a Buddhist leader to dispel negative forces and accumulate merit if they have encountered a yeti. Further, because some yetis are deities, it is said that yetis should not be photographed, and a yeti may kill a photographer who violates this taboo. Western popular-cultural notions of yetis typically portray them as secular beasts devoid of religious significance, whereas these yetis, like some Native American characterizations of Sasquatch, represent powerful manifest deities.[33]

The Tibetologist Toni Huber presents us with a specific example of this function of the mountain-deity yeti's keeping order in the community. Dakpa Sheri is a high Himalayan mountain god who, perhaps for

Figure 18. A fierce yeti as portrayed at Drepung Monastery
in Lhasa, Tibet. (Photo: Author.)

millennia, has served as a major pilgrimage destination for Tibetans.
Following Tibetan tradition, pilgrims worship the deity of the mountain through preliminary rites of purification and then through the
practice of *korra,* clockwise circumambulation. To enable this practice
at Dakpa Sheri, there exist paths around the mountain at various altitudes, with protocol stipulating that women avoid the upper paths and
instead use a defined women-only path. One day a woman defied this
discrimination by dressing as a man and successfully traversing a *korra*
route meant for males only. Afterwards she openly gloated about her
accomplishment. In response the mountain deity, offended by the lack
of respect shown to what it considered to be a holy gender distinction,

got to work. After nightfall a divine yeti, exhibiting an animal strength far beyond any human, abducted the lady, split open a tree, placed her in the gap, and then resealed the tree, entombing the poor woman inside.[34]

A similar story comes to us regarding a man named Ap Rinchen, who lived in the region of Sakteng. He had suffered a difficult winter beset by trouble, especially the recurring bad dreams that caused him light sleep by night and great fear by day. Finally he could take it no more and decided to consult his spiritual teacher, Lama Wokpo, for advice. Unfortunately for Ap Rinchen, the winter had been very cold, and the largest storm in years had just left high drifts of snow everywhere. Nonetheless he decided to brave the hostile elements and set out for the home of Lama Wokpo, who lived with his family up the valley. The lama's family welcomed Ap Rinchen in and offered him hot food and tea. But he felt restless with his worries and so he waited impatiently to see Lama Wokpo. Finally he spoke to the lama, who soothed Ap Rinchen with his words. After they had finished the discussion, Lama Wokpo implored Ap Rinchen to stay and spend the night in his home because of the weather. Calmer but still agitated, Ap Rinchen politely but firmly refused the invitation, eventually disappearing into the frosty, forbidding night.

Still obsessing over his concerns, on his way home Ap Rinchen was surprised to suddenly encounter a yeti not far from Lama Wokpo's house. Not thinking clearly, tragically Ap Rinchen pulled a knife in self-defense. But this was no ordinary yeti; it was a mountain-deity yeti, a sacred enforcer, and there is a taboo against threatening this divine character. Thus Ap Rinchen violated a sacred precept, and the yeti reacted accordingly. The yeti chased Ap Rinchen, grabbing at him and slowly ripping off his clothes. Eventually Ap Rinchen fell helpless, after which the yeti played with him as a cat might play with a mouse, repeatedly tossing him in the air and thereby lacerating him and breaking his bones. More large animal than human in power, the yeti left Ap Rinchen's naked, misshapen corpse covered in huge black-and-blue bruises. Ap Rinchen broke a taboo and paid for it with a thrashing meted out by a violent, animallike mountain-deity yeti.[35]

By themselves, punishments like these do not define the divine character of the mountain-deity yeti, who also issues spiritual challenges to humans. For example, as the story goes, there once was a young monk named Gelong Dorje who lived a meditative lifestyle in Himalayan wilderness solitude like others we have seen in this chapter. He stayed in a simple one-room wooden cabin situated, like many Tibetan Buddhist retreats, atop a promontory on the edge of a steep cliff. Living there so long that his shaved monk's head had become home to long, flowing locks of hair, Gelong Dorje spent every available minute absorbed in religious practice. One winter night a terribly powerful snowstorm erupted outside his cabin. During the storm Gelong Dorje heard the footsteps of a creature repeatedly circling his cabin and, amid the din of the gales, he also heard an eerie, animallike rather than windlike whistling sound: the high-pitched voice of a yeti. Early the next morning, he found giant humanlike footprints twice the size of his own in the snow all around his cabin. Gelong Dorje reasoned that sometimes mountain deities send tigers or bears to test the motivation and resolve of hermits and this time the local mountain deity had sent a yeti.

Apparently the local spirits felt that Gelong Dorje required a stiffer challenge. A few nights later his hut was suddenly shaken by a terrifying, turbulent earthquake:[36]

> He heard the rumbling and crashing sounds as if the entire hillsides were shaking loose. The trees seemed to crash. Then he recognized the whistle, a sharp shrill one, exactly the same whistle people had warned him about, the yeti's call. All at once he felt his hut being pushed towards the precipice and he was tossed about his hut. He could actually make out the heavy breathing and the occasional grunt of a creature as it pushed and heaved against his hut. Unperturbed and perhaps slightly amused, he called upon his root guru and said, "Look at what they are doing to me. I take refuge in you. Guide me." Then he sat in determined meditation, oblivious of the destruction of the world around him.

As dawn broke, Gelong Dorje took his break. He was rather surprised to see that everything was intact. The hillsides that had crashed and rumbled were tranquil and pristine as before and the trees stood tall and undisturbed. The only evidence of last night's destruction was his own hut, which had been pushed toward the crest and leaned precariously over the precipice. The unmistakable footprints of the yeti were all around the house.

Undaunted, Gelong Dorje continued his meditation in the tilted house. Not only had he overcome all forms of fear but he realized also that there are no limits to the kinds of tests that the spirits present to human beings. He wondered whether the yeti's appearing to him was the ultimate divine test.

Such mountain-deity henchmen are the most innately sacred of yetis, as they embody the powerful, numinous divine charisma of the local mountain god. As I mentioned, this leads to an interesting conjunction of themes, wherein the most essentially divine yetis also are both the most animal in form and the most violent. Although they possess the dangerous animal quality found in Western popular-culture representations of yetis, they also retain a divine side that is missing from purely secular Western monsters. They are not the mindless, bloodthirsty beasts of Hollywood movies. Instead, they are shaggy constables of the holy who defend sacred law.

This conjunction of sacredness, animality, and ferocity teaches us about Tibetan folk religions. The sacredness of mountain-deity yetis highlights how, since ancient times, Tibetans have regarded various animals such as yaks, trees such as junipers, birds, crystal mountain lakes, turgid alpine rivers, and of course mountains to be sacred beings that at times are at least as spiritually powerful as humans. Tibetan religions thus show religious respect for a wide variety of natural forms from the animal, plant, and mineral worlds. Like John Muir, Tibetans live in an environment in which many natural beings enjoy a spiritual value relatively equal to humans'. Given this valuation, ecocentric relationships with nature result in a place for yetis within Tibetan religions.

But mountain-deity yetis do not simply embody sacredness in a more-animal form; they also at times threaten humans. As we have seen, though, this dangerous behavior represents not random wickedness but the implementation of the commands of a divine being. Therefore their behavior is not unlike the stringent disciplinary action of the divine that we see in other religious contexts, such as the destruction of sinful Sodom and Gomorrah, the conquest of demonic Lanka in India's *Ramayana,* and God's words in Leviticus 26:22: "I will send wild animals against you, and they will rob you of your children, destroy your cattle and make you so few in number that your roads will be deserted." Sometimes the sacred will scourge people with tough love, as is true in the case of mountain-deity yetis. Reminding us of nature red in tooth and claw, these more-animal yetis perform holy judicial activities and issue well-intentioned religious challenges. They separate agency for divine discipline from the purely human sphere of activity, ethically indicating that enacting divine discipline is a mission for gods and animals but is not a path for humans to emulate. In this way, negative purported experiences with animalistic yetis create unique outcomes for Tibetan folk religions. Such influence also reverberates within the world of the many wrathful deities of Tibetan Buddhism, which are shaped by such indigenous understandings of sacred ferocity despite their having been imported originally from Indian Buddhist traditions.

However, as we know, some yetis are friendly practitioners of religion rather than punitive mountain gods, and if we return to their example we may learn about how Tibetan folk religions alter relationships with nature, as they do more than merely explode Western myths that simply depict dumb, predatory yetis. The more-human yetis practice acts of religious devotion to great religious leaders, serve as attendants in temples, provide charismatic talismans with their body parts, express gratitude to humans, martyr themselves for the sins of a human community, and drive away evil forces. They fill these religious roles, usually reserved for *Homo sapiens* alone in the Tibetan universe, because of their humanness. Here animal and human worlds remain not sharply divided or clearly distinct, as instead the human and the animal seam-lessly blend into each other. Yetis who practice religion remind some human Himalayan residents that they are integrated into an organic whole as part of rather than separated from the natural world. These yetis inform Tibetans to approach the natural world with an attitude of sacred, ecocentric respect. This reinforces the overall ecocentric flavor of Tibetan folk religions through dialectical interactions whereby religion influences experience with nature and vice versa.

Yetis thus present a unique model for religious experiences with nature in which the sacred is manifest in a constant hybrid human-animal form. Humans keep no monopoly on holiness, as an animal may embody sacredness, too, thus collapsing any strong divisions between the human world and the animal world. Because of its stable hybrid character, the yeti may simultaneously practice religion like a human, express holy animal ferocity, and embody intense divinity. Yetis teach us that sacredness may appear in both human and animal forms at the same time.

Further, because yetis so vividly show us what is in the human imagination, they highlight the sense of ambivalence that always seems to accompany human approaches to nature. The historian Gerald Carson taught that "The human view of the beast world has been ambivalent, a knife-edge balancing of fear with fascination, affection with exploitation, kindness with cruelty, the whole complicated by theological explanations of the universe and clouded by self-deceit." Being simultaneously revered and feared, loved and despised, holy and base, as well as admired and insulted, as projections of the human imagination yetis help to show us these ambivalent, multifaceted attitudes that we humans carry with us when we encounter the natural world.[37]

6

Enlightened Buddhist Stones

According to a Lakota Sioux creation story, Rock always existed and had no beginning. His spirit was the Great Holy, and he was the first of the superior gods. Since only Rock lived, there was no one to witness his awesome power, and he felt lonely. So, for partnership, Rock created Earth from his own substance in the form of a disk. Rock gave her the spirit of the Earth Goddess, who remains part of Rock yet is the second highest deity. The strain of this creative act caused Rock to bleed, and his blood formed the oceans and rivers. From this blue water another god, Sky, separated. Sky then took parts of himself, Rock, and Earth Goddess to form the fourth great deity, Sun. After this, Sky wished to create humans. So he took some of Rock to make bones, some of Earth Goddess to make flesh, and some of the waters to make blood. From these he shaped male and female figures and gave them animation, intelligence, affections, and the ability to reproduce, naming them the Bison People. Because of Rock's preeminence as a creator god, in reverence the Lakota decorate large boulders with paint and colored swan down, consider the stones in a sweat-lodge ritual to be manifest spirits, and keep special stone talismans thought to be charged with the power of one's visions.[1]

Unlike the Lakota, many people in the West remain unfamiliar with the practice of reverencing stone as the highest god, or as any god for that matter. Western cultures, with their inheritance of the Abrahamic disregard for the mineral world, which we saw earlier, generally find that things like stones and water are inanimate (from the Latin for "soulless") and hence devoid of relevance for religion. Stones, at the bottom of the Great Chain of Being, are thought to lack feeling, consciousness, and the capacity for spiritual enlightenment.

But the Lakota are not alone in their reverence for stony things. We have already seen John Muir worshipping with granite heaps and Tibetans and Mayans respecting stone mountains as gods, a practice shared by many alpine peoples. The Hindus of New Talavana reverence Goverdhan Mountain in Vrindavan and its stones as the physical presence of Krishna as well as small, black *shalagrama* stones from the Gandaki River Valley of Nepal and East India, as these are thought to embody Vishnu, the divine husband of Tulsi. In addition, a visit to Magnolia Grove, a Vietnamese Buddhist monastery in Mississippi in the United States, reveals that stones may be enlightened Buddhas and spiritual teachers to humans. But, instructively, Magnolia Grove's eco-centric vision does not come without compromises.

Magnolia Grove arises from East Asian Mahayana Buddhism and hence a distinct place in the Buddhist world, as Buddhism exhibits a variety of attitudes toward nature depending on approach. Some scholars describe Buddhism as anthropocentric, as the worst human birth is better than the best animal birth, killing a human is a higher monastic offense than killing an animal, reciting the *Patimokkha* monastic ritual in the presence of animals is an offense, monastics are forbidden to imitate animals or keep them as pets (this latter rule is sometimes broken), and animals may not ordain as monastics. In terms of diet, the Buddha appears to have permitted his followers to eat meat and fish, explicitly stating that it is one's self-restraint, not one's food, that makes one pure, although eating the flesh of an elephant, snake, dog, horse, lion, tiger, leopard, bear, or hyena is forbidden for various reasons. Finally, although Buddhism may encourage kindness to animals, it sometimes does so through an attitude of instrumentality, in which the practice seeks the religious benefit of a human more than the worldly benefit of an animal.[2]

Other commentators argue that Buddhism is essentially biocentric, and such elements clearly emerge when we consider the Buddhist practice of animal release. The Buddha found no offense in monks' releasing animals from hunting traps out of compassion, provided that the animals were set free rather than eaten. Over time rituals of animal release, whereby Buddhists seek beneficial karma through the freeing of animals intended for death, became part of the tradition, and such rituals may be found all over the Buddhist world. I once went with a few Tibetan Buddhists to buy live fish for the *tsethar* ("life release") animal release ritual from the markets on the mostly Han Chinese west side of Lhasa, Tibet's capital. These Tibetans felt remorse for some personal action and were hoping that they might lighten their karma by initiating a pescatory liberation. In the Chinese markets fish are kept alive in large pools so that customers may buy and then eat fresh fish. Instead of buying the fish for food, the Tibetans purchased freshwater fish, took them to the banks of the Kyichu River which runs through the city, and released the fish to freedom, all the while chanting the six-syllable mantra of compassion (*om mani padme hum*, or *om mani pemay hoong*, as many Tibetans pronounce it) and praying for the happiness of the fish.

This animal-friendly dimension of Buddhism extends into the scriptural Jataka tales, although not without ambiguity. There are more than five hundred of these tales, most of which are found in the *Sutta Pitaka* section of the Pali canon. These stories have influence throughout the Buddhist world, including in the construction of the great monuments at Ajanta and Borobudur, and are often employed as devices for teaching humans. The Jatakas relate biographies of the Buddha in his previous lives before he lived as Siddhartha Gotama, the Buddha in India in the middle of the first millennium B.C.E. In many of these previous incarnations, the Buddha-to-be was an animal and taught others, both by word and by example, while he was in animal form. Thus the world of the Jatakas inspires us to take animals as our spiritual exemplars. But this respect is not without ambivalence; sometimes the Jatakas portray animals quite negatively, too.

Concern for animals appears quite vividly in one of the most famous of the Jataka stories. In this tale, the Buddha-to-be in a previous life was born as a human into a Hindu Brahmin family. Assiduously cultivating wisdom and compassion, the Buddha-to-be was such a model of gentleness that his presence "had a calming effect on the wild beasts, who stopped preying on each other and began themselves to live like hermits." One day while enjoying the forest, the Buddha-to-be found a cave that contained a tigress and her newborn cubs. The tigress was fatigued from the birth process and emaciated with hunger, and she began to look on her own cubs as so much food. This pained the compassionate Buddha-to-be, who then voluntarily plunged to his death from an escarpment, intentionally depositing his lifeless corpse at the cave's mouth as a food offering for the tigress. This story highlights the moral value of natural beings and the need to extend our concern to animals.[3]

In another story, the Buddha-to-be took birth as a quail in a jungle. He refused to eat the bugs fed to him by his quail parents, preferring a vegetarian fare, and thus had not developed the ability to fly. Once a great fire broke out, threatening the Buddha's family's nest. The rest of his family flew away in terror at the fire but the Buddha-to-be, being flightless, remained. The Buddha-to-be then spoke truly to the fire, saying that he had nothing to offer the fire as an honored guest, as mandated by codes of hospitality. With this, the fire immediately subsided and disappeared, so moved as it was by the Buddha-to-be's regard for truth. Thus in this story a Buddha-quail teaches what would become the national motto of India, *Satyameva Jayate*, "Truth Alone Triumphs."

The Jataka story of the Buddha as Dhrtarashtra, king of the geese, is especially animal-friendly. As geese the Buddha-to-be and his general, Sumukha, presided over Lake Manasa with such gentleness and insight that they became famous, and Brahmadatta, king of Benares, longed to meet them. To attract them, Brahmadatta had a beautiful lake constructed and then announced that the lake would be a safe refuge for all birds, in time attracting the Buddha-to-be and his general to visit. Once the two celebrated geese arrived, the king of Benares then set traps, and the Buddha-to-be became caught, but Sumukha remained free. Sumukha loyally refused to leave the Buddha-to-be in his time of distress, amazing the king's trapper. Therefore the trapper did his duty by bringing the geese to see the king, but he did so leaving the birds unfettered. The king was impressed, befriended the Buddha-to-be and his goose general, and gave the merciful trapper a big bonus. The two geese taught humans with their wisdom, insight, and love, as "only the spiritually mature can behave so unassumingly and with such sound sense." The two birds modeled the virtue of honesty, as in this tale honesty is common in animals but lacking in humans, just as we found in the Islamic *Book of the Superiority of Dogs over Many of Those Who Wear Clothes:*[4]

> When humans appear to have tender compassion in their hearts, it is usually deceptive. They affect charming ways and say nice things, but underneath it all you find a thoroughly nasty character. Just consider, my lord: and beasts express what they feel by their cries. Only human beings are clever enough to express the opposite.

Thus a goose Buddha-to-be became a spiritual teacher for King Brahmadatta.

As throughout the Buddhist religion, such animal-friendly sentiments in the Jataka tales are admixed with negative symbolic uses of animals. Perhaps we see this most clearly in the Tale of the Woodpecker. In this story, the Buddha-to-be incarnates as a woodpecker. One day he notices a lion in severe pain and, courting danger, the Buddha-to-be helps the lion by removing the bone that is stuck in his throat. But the lion remains ungrateful, as later the Buddha-to-be asks the lion to share his food, but the lion rudely refuses. Then a forest sprite reproaches the Buddha-as-woodpecker for putting up with the lion's rudeness. The Buddha-as-woodpecker responds by teaching the sprite about unselfish generosity, explaining that good deeds should be done for others without concern for later reward or punishment, comparing those who wish to punish the ungrateful with elephants who seem haughty, since they first spray themselves with water before rolling in the dust rather than just rolling in the dust as other animals appear to do. The sprite then commends the Buddha for his saintliness, specifically remarking that species affiliation is not relevant for possessing good spiritual qualities. Hence this story teaches that animals can be wise and compassionate unless they behave like ungrateful lions or pompous elephants.[5]

Buddhist concern for animals also appears when we consider that Buddhism, like Christianity, bans animal sacrifice, and Buddhism further discourages injuring or killing animals, such as with an injunction against butchery. Moreover, as with Hinduism, Buddhism posits a universe of reincarnation with five or six realms: hell, ghost, animal, human, (demigod), and god. Humans reincarnate as animals, and animals reincarnate as humans, eliminating sharp distinctions between humans and animals and creating a sense of comradeship within a cosmic network of living beings. But as Tibetan yetis showed us, humans also retain a sense of superiority to animals by occupying a higher level of rebirth and generally remaining more capable of the pursuit of nirvana. Thus Buddhism does have biocentric dimensions, although not without ambiguity.

This marriage of anthropocentrism and biocentrism further emerges in the contemporary tree-ordination movement in Thailand. The anthropologist Susan Darlington tells us that the rate of deforestation in Thailand is higher than in any other Asian country except Nepal and (maybe) Borneo. The causes of deforestation are complex, ranging from poverty in rural areas to economic development and consumerism in Bangkok. In response, some Thai Buddhist monks have reinterpreted scripture and developed new rituals in order to create a conservation movement, seeking to reduce suffering and quell the Buddhist three poisons of greed, aversion, and ignorance, which they view as the roots of the environmental crisis. Most of these *phra nak anuraksa* (conservation monks) come from rural areas that may be the hardest hit by environmental degradation. Appearing on television and in newspapers, these monks have considerably raised awareness of environmental issues and motivated many people to act.

An example of this movement is a monk named Phrakhru Pitak Nanthakhun, of Nan Province, who created an innovative tree-ordination ceremony by reformulating the ritual of *thaut phaa paa*, the annual giving of robes to monks. In Phrakhru Pitak's ceremony, laypeople offer seedlings to be planted both in temples and in clear-cut former forests. These seedlings, having been ritually accepted by the monks, are thus sanctified, and villagers will be reluctant to cut them once planted. Moreover, they tend to be fruit trees, which are economically productive without having to be cut down.

Then, with great pomp, a monk's robe is offered to a grown tree rather than a human. The robe is tied around its trunk as if the tree were a monk, enriching the message that trees should be specially protected. The ordained tree receives blessed water and the installment of a small shrine with a Buddha image. When the monks who lead the ceremony are liberal, they may even appeal verbally to the traditional nature spirits of Thai belief, which fall outside Buddhism proper. Throughout the ceremony, Buddhist symbols are used to stress the religious connection to conservation, the villagers' interdependence with the forest, and the moral importance of ecological action. But of course, as much as this ritual evinces arboreal love, it retains a human-centered foundation, as only humans may become monks, and Phrakhru Pitak maintains no pretense that the trees are literally rather than just symbolically ordained. Moreover, some conservation monks explicitly state that one of the motives for the movement is to keep Buddhism relevant within contemporary Thai human society rather than to raise the spiritual status of trees.[6]

Along with anthropocentric and biocentric perspectives such as these, Buddhism, especially in the East Asian Mahayana world to which Magnolia Grove belongs, also maintains ecocentric approaches. East Asian Mahayana Buddhism achieves its more ecocentric flavor by placing greater emphasis on the scriptural Diamond Sutra, to which we will return momentarily, and the Lotus Sutra. The fifth chapter of the Lotus Sutra describes Dharma (spiritual) rain, which falls on plants and enables them to sprout and grow according to their own capacities. This passage has been interpreted to mean that plants have Buddha nature, the capacity for Buddhahood; and East Asian Buddhists who employ the Lotus Sutra are more likely than other Buddhists to ascribe intrinsic value to many forms of existence.[7]

The writings of Dogen, whose Japanese Soto Zen is a historical and textual cousin to the Buddhism at Magnolia Grove, exhibit this dynamic. In his Mountain and Waters Discourse, Dogen indicates that mountains and rivers are sacred texts themselves, being animate, conscious, and enlightened. Dogen writes:

> Mountains and waters ... are liberated in their actual occurrence.... It is not the case simply that there is water in the world; within the world of water there is a world. And this is true not only within water: within clouds as well there is world of sentient beings; within wind there is world of sentient beings; within fire there is world of sentient beings; within earth there is world of sentient beings. Within the dharma realm there is a world of sentient beings; within a single blade of grass there is world of sentient beings; within a single staff there is a world of sentient beings. And wherever there is a world of sentient beings, there, inevitably, is the world of buddhas and ancestors.

For Dogen mountains "lack none of their proper virtues" because "the virtues of the mountain are high and broad, the spiritual power to ride the clouds is always mastered from the mountains, and the marvelous ability to follow the wind is inevitably liberated from the mountains." Further, "the mountains become the buddhas and ancestors, and it is for this reason that the buddhas and ancestors have thus appeared." For its part, water is virtuous, sacred, and enlightened as well, since

Water is neither strong nor weak, neither wet nor dry, neither moving nor
still, neither cold nor hot, neither being nor nonbeing, neither delusion nor
enlightenment. Frozen, it is harder than diamond; who could break it?
Melted, it is softer than milk; who could break it? This being the case, we
cannot doubt the many virtues realized by water.

Thus, citing the Buddha, Dogen tells us that all natural beings are enlightened: "The Buddha has said, 'All things are ultimately liberated.'"[8]

This inclusive East Asian Buddhist environment of an enlightened
natural world, broadly conceived, is strongly manifest at Magnolia
Grove. Magnolia Grove began in 2000 when some Vietnamese immi-
grant families in the southeastern United States purchased a 140-acre
rural property with a farmhouse to use as a community center and
ultimately a monastery. The largely undeveloped property included
beautiful meadows interspersed within pine and oak forests. Seeking
a spiritual leader, the community approached the eminent Vietnamese
Thien Buddhist monk Thich Nhat Hanh, who consecrated the land
for monastic use in 2005. An American couple, Caucasian followers of
Nhat Hanh, offered the considerable resources of their construction
company, and over the next few years the community added a new
kitchen, small meditation hall, large meditation hall, bookstore, and
several residential buildings to create the physical necessities for a
monastery.

Then, on September 27, 2009, the Vietnamese government forcibly
closed the Bat Nha Temple in central Vietnam, leaving four hundred
monks and nuns, all affiliated with Thich Nhat Hanh, without homes.
International fund-raising campaigns brought as many of these monastics as possible to other locations in Europe and the United States, and
some of them found a new home at Magnolia Grove. By 2011 the monastery consisted of roughly twenty nuns and ten monks, all Vietnamese
by birth, along with about one hundred nonresidential lay supporters
from the Vietnamese-American community. In part because Nhat
Hanh is so well known in the Buddhist world, several hundred non-
Vietnamese American practitioners joined the community as well.

Figure 19. Meditation Hall at Magnolia Grove. (Photo: Author.)

Commitment within this group runs along a spectrum from rare visits to everyday care of the monastics. Almost every weekend there are public teachings at the monastery, delivered alternately in English and in Vietnamese, with real-time translation always available.

Buddhist practice at Magnolia Grove emphasizes mindfulness meditation for everyone in the community, meditation through work, the chanting of sacred texts, and several retreats a year. Devotional practices found in some other Buddhist settings are minimized, except for prostrations to the Buddha image in the meditation hall and meritorious financial donations. The monastery celebrates Tet (the Vietnamese New Year), the Buddha's birthday, and less formally, the American holidays Thanksgiving, Christmas, New Year's, and the Fourth of July.

The religious leader of the community, Thich Nhat Hanh, was born in central Vietnam on October 11, 1926. After ordaining as a monk at age

Figure 20. Statue of the deity Quan Am in the Lotus Pond at Magnolia Grove. (Photo: Author.)

17 at the Tu Hieu Temple, he became an influential Buddhist scholar and leader in Vietnam during the 1950s and 1960s. In 1965 he founded a new monastic order, the Tiep Hien (Order of Interbeing) as part of the Thien school of Vietnamese Buddhism. Thien Buddhism is a cousin to the Zen of Japan, as both forms may be traced back to the same Chinese masters, but they flowered differently in their respective adopted countries.

Figure 21. Sunday chanting at Magnolia Grove. (Photo: Author.)

In response to the turmoil of the 1960s, Nhat Hanh helped to instigate a nonpartisan antiwar movement, and for his efforts he was nominated for the Nobel Peace Prize by Dr. Martin Luther King, Jr. Unfortunately, his attempt to create peaceful dialogue between the adversaries resulted in his developing enemies among people from both sides who favored the war, and he was forced to flee Vietnam in 1966. Being resilient, he moved to France, taught at the Sorbonne, and founded a monastery and retreat center called Plum Village. The Plum

Figure 22. Dragon to celebrate the Vietnamese New Year at Magnolia Grove. (Photo: Author.)

Village community then exploded in size, and now there are hundreds of affiliated practice centers on every continent but Antarctica. Nhat Hanh himself is a prolific author, with almost one hundred titles in numerous languages. Along with the Dalai Lama, Nhat Hanh remains one of the most visible and influential leaders in the Buddhist world today.[9]

Because of his time in France, Nhat Hanh has been strongly influenced by Western ecological thought, and so he argues that concern for the environment is inherent in the practice of Buddhism and that every Buddhist should be a protector of the natural world. This environmental sensibility—indeed, like all the practices within his network of centers—revolves around the Buddhist concept of *pratitya-samutpada,* "dependent origination," the interconnected nature of all things. This foundational Buddhist notion describes a universe in which everything that exists in creation rises or falls based on one or more interrelated external causes, so that the universe is manifested not in isolated individuals but in a web of interconnections. Everything exists as an effect of a prior cause and serves as a cause for a later effect, so that everything ends up being interrelated to everything else. This renders any sense of absolute independence in space or time illusory, as individuality appears to exist only because of the larger web of connections. A classic analogy of this concept from Buddhist texts describes three sticks standing upright by leaning on one another. Take one stick away, and the other two fall. None, in the end, is independent.

Nhat Hanh translates the Sanskrit concept of *pratitya-samutpada* into Vietnamese as *tiep hien,* which he then translates into English as "interbeing." As an example of interbeing, Nhat Hanh chooses a sheet of paper. In one sheet of paper we can see the tree that the paper came from, the rain clouds that fed the tree, the logger who felled the tree, the bread that the logger ate for breakfast, the parents of the logger, and so on; and thus in the end we see not just a single sheet of paper but a universal web of interconnections. Nhat Hanh writes: "In one sheet of paper, we see everything else, the cloud, the forest, the logger. I am; therefore you are. You are; therefore I am. That is the meaning of 'interbeing.'" *Tiep,* he further tells us, means "be in touch," in the sense of being in touch with ourselves in addition to "the Buddhas and the *bodhisattvas* [Buddhist saints], the enlightened people in whom full understanding and compassion are tangible and effective." It is important for his environmental views that *tiep* also means "be in touch with everything that is around us in the animal, vegetable, and mineral realms." *Hien* denotes "present time," but it also means "make real, make manifest." In Nhat Hanh's Buddhist philosophy, therefore, interbeing implies manifest sacred contact with a natural world ecocentrically consisting of interrelated humans, animals, plants, and minerals.[10]

For Nhat Hanh the Diamond Sutra, "the most ancient text on deep ecology," depicts interbeing from within the Mahayana Buddhist scriptures. This choice of text, along with the influential Lotus Sutra, helps to create an ecocentric dimension for East Asian forms of Buddhism, such as at Magnolia Grove, which is lacking in other forms of Buddhism. Nhat Hanh claims that the Diamond Sutra teaches us that because all things inter-are, or exist only within a web of interconnections, discriminating on the basis of species is foolish, since no species exists independently. Today the human eats the carrot that consumes mineral nutrients from the soil, but later the decomposing human body will provide the minerals for another carrot—How can we favor one element of this chain when each element depends on the others? Thus the preference of one species over another ignores basic facts of existence according to Thich Nhat Hanh. Even more, preferring animate things over inanimate things falls prey to the same error, since inanimate things depend on animate things and vice versa. The Diamond Sutra thus reads: "If, Subhuti, a *bodhisattva* holds on to the idea that a self, a person, a living being, or a life span exists, that person is not an authentic *bodhisattva*." Eschewing biocentrism in favor of ecocentrism, Nhat Hanh says: "Atoms and stones are consciousness itself. This is why discrimination of living beings against non-living beings should be discarded." Even water "is a good friend, a *bodhisattva*." To Nhat Hanh a true Buddhist is "one who sees no demarcation between organic and non-organic, self and non-self, living beings and non-living beings." At Magnolia Grove, Buddhists ecocentrically should seek to protect all elements of the natural world and be as concerned with streams and boulders as they are with humans or cats.[11]

Thich Nhat Hanh spends most of his time in France, and so he has appointed senior monastics as teachers to fill his day-to-day role at Magnolia Grove. Brother Phap Kong is one of these senior teachers. He told me that with the Diamond Sutra in mind, any sense of human superiority to natural beings is "an illusion." Since literally "we are what we eat, we must recognize that we are animals, plants, and minerals," as without these human life is impossible. He told me that usually we think of stones as inanimate, but actually they are "organisms which store and release energy." Humans are "equal partners in a larger system," so that considering humans to be separate from or superior to natural beings and acting for human benefit alone leads to "destructive outcomes." Instead, "the most powerful compassion is that which does not discriminate" across species or natural categories. Just like his master, Nhat Hanh, Phap Kong stresses an ecocentric point of view within Buddhist practice.

In the theory of Magnolia Grove, just as humans possess Buddha nature, the innate capacity for enlightenment, so do all things in the natural world with which humans inter-are, and so practitioners are instructed to consider all elements of the natural world as essentially enlightened. On this note Sister Dang Nghiem, the most senior teacher at Magnolia Grove, told me: "Natural beings are already in nirvana. Everything has Buddha nature, even stones." She said that we easily can see this inherent enlightenment in animals, who in her view lack human greed and craving, as most species will stop feeding when full. They may store up food for the winter, but they do not take more than they need, unlike humans, who hoard endlessly "to fill an inner void with stuff." Animals may not lead "reflective, intelligent, spiritual lives," but they still may be teachers to humans through their effortless spirituality. In this way, just as all animals in Islam are naturally surrendered to God, so at Magnolia Grove the entire natural world is already enlightened. Here, stones are Buddhas.

In a similar vein another senior teacher, Sister Chan Hy Nghiem, said to me: "You must prepare your heart to accept the condition of learning from nature." When I asked her if animals could realize the Buddhist goal of nirvana, Chan Hy Nghiem said yes, offering me the following story:

Once there was a saintly monk named Hai Duc who lived alone in a hut in the high mountains of Vietnam, where he meditated in a cave. Recognizing his saintly gentleness, every day a tiger and a monkey would bring food offerings to him. One day lay people came, took teachings from Hai Duc, and built a temple at his hermitage. After some time, however, Hai Duc passed away. The tiger, who always lounged around the temple's stupa [reliquary monument], became depressed, stopped eating, and eventually died, too. This tiger revealed that it knew how to love and care for others and thus showed its Buddha nature [capacity for enlightenment].

Humans need to learn how to love and could learn from this tiger, according to Chan Hy Nghiem.

Animals may offer spiritual lessons in other ways according to another teacher, the Venerable Phuoc Tinh. Wild animals, he taught, use medicines within themselves. When they face illness, they find safe places to lie down, rest, self-heal, and recover their energy. For example, cats eat grass to make themselves vomit impurities and then take time to recuperate. However, humans do not follow these lessons, according to Phuoc Tinh. Human beings rush around and stress themselves, thus causing themselves illness, so that parties, games, and other distractions can become health hazards. For Phuoc Tinh, people need to find more time for silence and peace in their lives so that they may, in a sense, lie down and self-heal. And in such self-healing, "learning to enjoy the natural world can be very nourishing," since "communing with natural beauty can be enriching on an inner level," Phuoc Tinh said.

But it is not only animals who serve as spiritual teachers at Magnolia Grove. In a public teaching session Dang Nghiem encouraged the community members to recognize their similarities with trees. Just as trees reach for sunlight and water, so humans seek nutrients. Just as trees have roots that ground them, so do humans have grounding, enriching roots in parents, ancestors, cultures, bodies, foods, and education. People even exchange gases with trees through respiration, and trees look like human lungs upside down, so that for Dang Nghiem it is appropriate to think of an interconnection: "the trees, my lungs." And "just as trees need healthy roots, so do humans, [and] so people must take care of their roots, making sure that they are as wholesome as possible and offering them gratitude for their positive contributions to life." In order to extend such gratitude, she used a further botanical reference in encouraging the community to "water flowers." This practice involves grateful recognition of the positive influences of others through open and vigorous praise of them. In this way, she said, the practice of "watering flowers" generates happiness, serenity, and cooperation.

Dang Nghiem told me that trees also teach us to accept our own mortality and imperfections. In the winter trees may seem dead, yet every spring they return to vitality and manifest the blooms of summer. Then in the autumn they let go of their leaves and again embrace quiet inactivity. In this process, no leaf is perfect, and neither is any tree. Humans live the same way, according to Dang Nghiem, who said: "People have life cycles of birth and death during which no one is perfect." For Dang Nghiem, when we get in touch with trees we respect and value these facts, an attitude allowing us to better accept our own impermanence and imperfections. Such acceptance enables us to face life in calmer, more peaceful ways, leading to greater happiness and less fear of death. Furthermore, humans can better care for earth's impermanence "without fear or despair" if people accept their own impermanence. But such lessons are difficult to learn in today's world, because "our lives are so full of things that are dead or unchanging," according to Dang Nghiem.

Sister Chan Hy Nghiem, who previously told us that we should learn love from a tiger, also taught that we should learn from trees. Trees make oxygen for humans to breathe, she said, and without trees we would die. Therefore, to her, humans inter-are with trees, and because of this interrelation, humans may learn about compassion from trees. Trees, she stated, compassionately offer us shade and teach us to appreciate the beauty of the natural world. When she sees trees standing solidly, she is called back to herself to solidly withstand the trials of life. Trees teach her to avoid jealousy and anger, as trees lack both these emotional states, and the firmness of trees in a strong wind reminds her to mentally remain in the present moment. Through trees she can learn the fact of impermanence, a fundamental Buddhist notion, since despite their firmness trees are always changing. Chan Hy Nghiem related that meditating on nature in these ways has strengthened her own spiritual practice over many years and that she teaches others to meditate in the same way.

During Chan Hy Nghiem's interview a stray dog who had made the monastery its temporary home playfully stole her hat from the chair next to her. It took a few minutes for Chan Hy Nghiem and me to retrieve the hat from the dog's possession. Seated again to resume the interview, Chan Hy Nghiem used the event as grist for the Buddhist pedagogical mill. With a mix of humor and seriousness she expressed how the dog reminded her to return to inner peace and thereby avoid an angry response.

Chan Hy Nghiem extended these insights in a public teaching she offered as a commentary on the scriptural Mahaparinirvana Sutra. In this teaching Chan Hy Nghiem taught community members to extend four forms of gratitude: to parents, to teachers, to supportive friends, and to "animals, plants, and minerals." This last gratitude, she asserted, is necessary because without animals, plants, and minerals, we humans cannot live. They are part of us. She strongly encouraged members of the community to experience these gratitudes as deeply and intensely as possible as part of the Buddhist spiritual path.

In order to learn these spiritual lessons from animals, trees, and stones, Buddhist walking meditation occurs each day at Magnolia Grove. Just as quiet sitting meditation encourages mindfulness, or a deep experience of the present moment, so in walking meditation one develops mindfulness of the present moment by ambling slowly, silently, and with focused awareness of each footstep. Rather than walking with a distracted mind full of worries about work, family, and so on, walking meditation requires a moment-by-moment immersion in the simple act of walking. Such an awareness, of course, includes a rich appreciation of the environment of the walk.

Most of the 140 acres of Magnolia Grove consists of undeveloped forests and meadows, and there are a number of trails that lead through these wilderness surroundings, lending many beautiful sylvan scenes to the walk. Teachers at Magnolia Grove actively encourage the incorporation of these bucolic experiences in walking meditation to more profoundly and selflessly realize interbeing. For instance, within instructions for walking meditation during a winter retreat, monastics asked for silent attention to nature as part of the practice. Buddhists heard that leaves were on the ground because trees were taking care of their bodies ahead of new growth in the spring and, from this, practitioners should learn to take care of their own bodies. Teachers also asked meditators to silently contemplate a tree. A tree is rooted, grounded, unwavering, and does not get distracted from the present moment. Practitioners were taught to persist similarly rooted, grounded, and unwavering in their meditation, whether they were sitting, walking, or amid the bustle of everyday life. Perhaps most important, practitioners were taught to use such experiences to realize their interconnectedness with natural forms and thus their interbeing with nature.

These lessons from walking meditation extend into another form of meditation called touching the earth, which involves prostrations before a Buddha image or other sacred object. In this practice one chants phrases from scripture and then stretches out on the floor face down, showing one's supplication to interconnected realities that are bigger than oneself. Dang Nghiem told me that when one touches the earth in this way, one contacts the earth's capacity for forgiveness, compassion, forbearance, and healing. One then practices to integrate these earthy qualities into oneself—because, Dang Nghiem said, we humans are made of earth.

Meditation works best not as an isolated practice but as part of an overall lifestyle, and so the nuns and monks of Magnolia Grove implement a number of lifestyle practices that are designed to help Buddhists to realize their interbeing with nature. To anyone staying at the monastery, consuming food mindfully is the most obvious of these practices.

Figure 23. Thich Nhat Hanh leads walking meditation at Magnolia Grove. (Photo: Author.)

The vow of Nhat Hanh's Fifth Mindfulness Training delineates contours for mindful eating:

> Aware of the suffering caused by unmindful consumption, I am committed to cultivating good health, both physical and mental, for myself, my family, and my society by practicing mindful eating, drinking, and consuming.... I will contemplate interbeing and consume in a way that preserves peace, joy, and well-being in my body and consciousness, and in the collective body and consciousness of my family, my society, and the earth.

Figure 24. Walking meditation at Magnolia Grove. (Photo: Author.)

Like all monasteries in the Plum Village network, Magnolia Grove is vegan. Food consists of plant products without meat or dairy, and protein is provided through the copious use of nuts and soy products like tofu. Such a diet allows the community, it feels, to eat in a more environmentally friendly way. In his remarks to UNESCO on October 7, 2006, as recounted in his "Letter from Thich Nhat Hanh," Nhat Hanh offered material reasons for such a diet. According to Nhat Hanh, more than half the water used in the United States is used to raise animals for food. It takes 2,500 gallons of water to create a pound of beef but only twenty-five gallons to produce a pound of wheat. Raising animals for food produces more water pollution than any other industry. Nhat Hanh further tells us that animals raised for food eat 80 percent of the maize crop and 95 percent of the oat crop though these grains could meet the caloric needs of 8.7 billion people, which is larger than the current human population. If lay members of the community want to eat beef at home, that is acceptable to Nhat Hanh, who nonetheless encourages them to reduce their consumption of beef by 50 percent in order to limit the load on planetary resources.[12]

Along with these environmental reasons, there exist spiritual reasons for following such a diet. Brother Phap Kong tells us that because "we are what we eat," in consuming factory-raised animals and eggs one also consumes the anger and fear of the animals that experience the horrific conditions of factory farms. The anger and fear of the animals become a part of the person, according to Phap Kong, and later realize expression as modes of environmental destruction. Buddhists must break this chain if they wish to protect humanity and the planet. Thus Phap Kong views eating plants, and especially environmentally friendly organically grown plants, as more compassionate, because plants as food suffer much less than animals raised for food. Of this mindful eating he said: "We try to overcome anger and fear and in so doing try to restore our planet to equilibrium."

Mindfulness of what one eats is important for a meaningful experience of interbeing, but how one eats is important, too. At Magnolia Grove most meals provide exercises in meditative, mindful eating. At the beginning of the meal eaters recite the Five Contemplations:

1. This food is a gift of the earth, the sky, numerous living beings, and much hard work.

2. May we eat with mindfulness and gratitude so as to be worthy to receive it.

3. May we recognize and transform our unwholesome mental formations, especially our greed, and learn to eat with moderation.

4. May we keep our compassion alive by eating in such a way that we reduce the suffering of living beings, preserve our planet, and reverse the process of global warming.

5. We accept this food so that we may nurture our brotherhood and sisterhood, strengthen our *sangha* (community), and nourish our ideal of serving all beings.

As one eats, one meditates on these Five Contemplations, and the meal is taken in silence in order to enhance the sense of meditation. One should think, "I am eating with the aim of preserving my life. The aim of my life is to study and practice to transform my afflictions and to liberate people and all other species from their suffering." Teachers instruct eaters to chew food slowly and completely, up to thirty chews, until solid food becomes liquid in the mouth, so that eaters may contemplate gratitude for both the food and the source of the food. This practice can foster a deep, affective, and vibrant realization of the nonduality of the eater and the nature-based eaten that ideally leads to a powerful sense of one's interconnectedness with the natural world.[13]

Magnolia Grove implements other practices with both spiritual and planet-friendly reasons in mind. Monks and nuns make their own shopping bags. In order to save trees the monastery supplies no paper napkins, and washed hands naturally dry in the warm Mississippi air. Monastics use but one mug of water each for washing faces and brushing teeth in order to conserve resources. The ideal shower takes less than seven minutes. Residents wash dishes by hand and then machine-sanitize them, saving water over using a dishwasher, and the nonsoapy water from the process is offered to flowers and trees. Clothes are washed only in full loads for efficiency and then air-dried. The monastery composts leftover food to serve as fertilizer for the center's organic gardens. What can be recycled is recycled. Most impressive, in the cruel, humid heat of a Southern summer monastics still will not use air-conditioning. Of this conservation of resources Sister Dang Nghiem said: "We need to reduce consumption as a concrete act of love"—because not only does this help our planet; it also "gives us a sense of confidence and empowerment in the face of what can seem like overwhelming environmental crises."

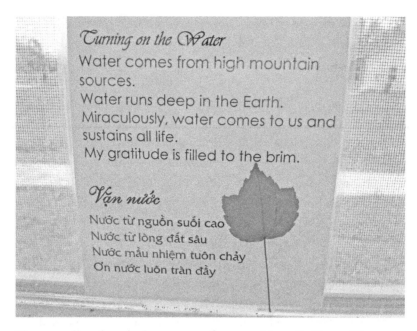

Turning on the Water
Water comes from high mountain
sources.
Water runs deep in the Earth.
Miraculously, water comes to us and
sustains all life.
My gratitude is filled to the brim.

Vận nước

Nước từ nguồn suối cao
Nước từ lòng đất sâu
Nước mầu nhiệm tuôn chảy
Ơn nước luôn tràn đầy

Figure 25. Sign above bathroom water faucets at Magnolia Grove. (Photo: Author.)

These concrete acts of love at Magnolia Grove include the practice of the India-derived *ahimsa* (nonharm), which we have seen before. It is of interest that teachers at Magnolia Grove do not invoke the idea of reincarnation often, and so they do not justify nonharm with the argument of other Buddhist schools, that one may have been a different organism in a previous life. Instead, because of the focus on interbeing, teachers promote nonharm because one is indeed all other beings in this, our present life. The First Mindfulness Training delineates the path of nonviolence:

> Aware of the suffering caused by the destruction of life, I am committed to cultivating the insight of interbeing and compassion and learning ways to protect the lives of people, animals, plants, and minerals. I am determined not to kill, not to let others kill, and not to support any act of killing in the world, in my thinking or in my way of life.

As a result, acts of nonviolence commonly occur at Magnolia Grove. As a case in point, once the community met in a meditation room for a talk, during which a daddy longlegs insect visibly came crawling across the ground into the midst of those seated on the floor. In other settings this creature may have elicited screams and then a killing swat. Instead, a monk coaxed it onto a piece of paper and then carried it outside, gently freeing it into the grass.

To form a generally nonviolent lifestyle, monastics use no poisons to kill kitchen bugs and no pesticides in the garden. Kitchen workers try to keep things clean so as not to invite unwanted visitors. Residents deploy chili pepper and vinegar as vermin repellents. Monks and nuns avoid noxious chemicals in everything, right down to the dish soap. They trap mice live for later release and follow the same practice with snakes, poisonous or not, whenever possible.

Chan Hy Nghiem tells an interesting story in this regard. One day while on walking meditation she came face to face with a rattlesnake. At first she felt nervous and frightened. But she meditatively returned to mindfulness of her breath, allowing her to feel calm and centered. She says that she then spoke to the snake lovingly and eventually the serpent decided to move away, thus ending their encounter without incident.

By the way, besides avoiding the harm of even poisonous snakes like this, Magnolia Grove residents also avoid killing mosquitoes, placing them on this count in stark contrast to the Hindus of chapter 3, who defend the killing of these creatures for religious reasons despite also cherishing *ahimsa*. Since both groups abstain from eating meat, this crucial difference, along with myriad other possible examples like it, highlights how vegetarian attitudes toward the natural world can vary significantly, apart from refusing to use animals for food. While compassionately concerned with preserving animals that otherwise might be eaten by humans and thus at least somewhat nature-friendly, many vegetarian concerns do not extend intrinsic value across ecosystems to a broader conception of the natural world, not even to nonfood creatures like snakes or mosquitoes (or even less unpleasant ones like geckos or fireflies), not to mention plants, water, or minerals. Indeed, whereas meat eating implicitly condones the killing of animals, many vegetarian lifestyles likewise implicitly condone the destruction of nonfood animals, plants, or mineral formations, and from ecosystem points of view such acceptance results in potential problems for natural beings—even taking into account the fact that humans need to consume not animals but rather plants for nourishment.

While nature-friendly variants of forms of vegetarianism do not invalidate the practice, nor do they support meat eating, they alert us to avoid the too-easy equation of vegetarianism with broad nature-friendliness that many people make, even animal-rights scholars. What we see here is that vegetarianism (and, as we will see later, veganism) does not automatically result in wholesome approaches to nature, despite the many claims to the contrary. Instead, differences in meatless worldviews invite us to more closely examine dietary perspectives for their implications for the natural world beyond animals used for food. These differences teach us that eating in a fully nature-friendly way involves deeper insights that extend value to wilderness as well as barnyard or factory farm, leafy as well as furry, and inorganic as well as organic, as we have seen in many places in this book. Or, as Gandhi put it: "Though the question of diet is very important for a religious person, yet it is not the be-all and end-all of religion or nonviolence; nor is it the most vital factor. The observance of religion and non-violence has more to do with the heart."[14]

These limits to meatless worldviews notwithstanding, practices of nonharm and respect for nature as sacred must be taught to the next generation if they will be sustainable, and Magnolia Grove strives for this goal. In retreats and classes specifically designed for visiting children, monks and nuns teach that humans consist of and connect to nature. Monastics frequently help children to understand how humans depend on other beings and how other beings depend on humans because, they emphasize, humanity cannot survive damage to animals, plants, and minerals.

The education of the young begins within the practice of walking meditation. Although the children frequently excuse themselves from formal teaching events that are boring for them, they seem to delight in a nice stroll through the countryside. The children appear to do little actual meditation on these walks, but the nuns and monks hope to serve as role models, enabling the children to slowly imbibe an appreciation for nature.

Nuns and monks educate children more directly through the practice of the Two Promises, the version of the adult Mindfulness Trainings adapted especially for young people. At youth and family retreats children learn and recite the Two Promises:

1. I vow to develop my understanding in order to live peacefully with people, animals, plants, and minerals.
2. I vow to develop my compassion in order to protect the lives of people, animals, plants, and minerals.

Monastics ask children to engage in the practice of the Two Promises during the retreat and continue that practice at home when the retreat has finished. Retreats reinforce this practice with discussion groups in which youngsters may share their experiences and learn from their peers. Dang Nghiem told me that children offer very positive reports of their practices, as they say that during their retreats "I learned to walk with nature (from walking meditation)" or "I learned to live without my phone and Facebook (and contact nature instead)."

Throughout such retreats children sing a song by Joe Rilley to enrich these lessons. Then at the end of the retreat, the entire community, children and adults alike, together joyfully sings this song:

I love nature; nature is cool.
The forest is my classroom; the earth is my school.
Trees are my teachers; animals are my friends.
And on this school all life depends.

These elements of Magnolia Grove teachings and practices lead us to appreciate that they encourage experiences with animals and other nonhuman natural forms in which boundaries between individual existences are blurred. Because humans experience interbeing with nonhuman natural forms, broadly conceived, no clear line demarks human from nonhuman. Rather than sharp subject-object distinctions, human realities dissolve into those of animals, plants, water, and minerals. In this way, stones are enlightened. But these ecocentric relations of interbeing do not simply collapse the nonhuman natural world into the human world or vice versa. As I have described, teachers at Magnolia Grove implicitly and explicitly recognize a separation of human lives from the nonhuman natural world, albeit an ambiguous separation in relationship. Further, careful readers will have noted that practices and teachings are intended for humans alone. No one at Magnolia Grove teaches meditation to daffodils, rabbits, or other natural forms, although humans clearly are taught it. In these ways in Magnolia Grove teachings and practices, one embraces human existence and meaning through, rather than in spite of, deep experiences of interbeing with a broad array of natural forms.

"Trees must be protected for their own sakes," Chan Hy Nghiem told me. In valuing water, stones, plants, and animals for themselves like this, Magnolia Grove embraces a colorful and creative sense of ecocentrism. But this valuation is not without restrictions. A limitation of ecocentric perspectives everywhere involves practicality; having ecocentric ideals is one thing, but humans still need to live, eat, and flourish, and human flourishing can conflict with ecocentric ideals. Let us take the extreme example as instructive: if every last thing in the natural world is sacred, including plants and stones, and thus deserves respect and nonviolent protection, what then does one eat? How does one make clothing? How does one make medicine? In one way or another, limits like these appear in every ecocentric form of religion. Because of these limits, despite the intense ecocentrism of Magnolia Grove religion, we also find some attitudes of human superiority, just as we have found anthropocentric attitudes in all religions in this book.

There exist several examples of this principle, in which anthropocentrism appears along with ecocentrism. First, I just mentioned that no one teaches meditation to daffodils or rabbits at Magnolia Grove. The instructions and practices at Magnolia Grove are completely oriented toward the development of human religious experience, and no attention is paid to cultivating the possible religious experiences of natural forms. Humans may learn love from tigers, but the question of how tigers learn Buddhist love sits unanswered. Magnolia Grove practices are human-oriented, and natural forms often just serve as tools for this task.

Discussing the use of symbols may clarify what I mean here. Animals, plants, and minerals may function as spiritual exemplars at Magnolia Grove, and community members often express a deep and genuine respect for natural forms. But when nature is referenced in conversations or teachings, we sometimes find a different story. Often when humans use natural beings as symbols, their implementation says more about the humans than about the natural beings themselves, and this remains true at Magnolia Grove. For example, one teacher who taught the community to learn from animals also symbolically portrayed problematic human minds as "more frightening than snakes or ferocious animals" or as uncontrollable "as a jumping monkey." On these occasions natural beings remain unimportant for their own sakes and are stereotyped into negative images for purely human benefit, like the ungrateful lion and pompous elephants of the Jatakas.

Furthermore, often the need to protect the environment is explained not in terms of the benefit for natural beings but simply for the benefit of humans. The oft-heard statement "We need to protect nature so that humans can live," as laudable as this environmental sensibility is, does not evince much intrinsic concern for gazelles or poplar trees. Yet, as I recounted, sometimes we find this approach at Magnolia Grove, so that environment-friendly activities are done not for the sake of nature alone. For example, a senior monastic told me that one reason for the ecologically friendly lifestyle of not using paper napkins was simply to save money, as monasteries often run on very tight budgets. So, as wonderful as the ecological lifestyles at the monastery are, they are not without some human concern for humans alone.

We also find that practical realities constrain the practice of nonviolence. Chan Hy Nghiem, whose nonviolent encounter with a rattlesnake was recounted above, finds that it is difficult to undertake everyday activities without entering a gray area concerning nonviolence. For instance, small beings are at risk every time she cuts the grass. Because of this, she approaches cutting the grass as a meditation practice and tries to mind her breath, remain present with the activity, and manifest compassion for anything lurking in the lawn. Also she offers a daily prayer for the good rebirth of any little creatures that she might accidentally harm that day. In so doing, she does everything she can to remain true to her practice of nonviolence. However, since the mower undoubtedly kills small beings, there simply is no way to cut the lawn with perfect nonviolence. And it is humans, not snakes or gophers, who desire having a manicured lawn.

Sometimes nonviolence is more intentionally compromised than with the accidents of lawn mowing, as we see in the reality of fire ant control. The imported red fire ant (*Solenopsis invicta*) is a nonnative, invasive species found throughout the southern United States, including at Magnolia Grove. Unlike other ants, whose behavior is innocuous, fire ants make their presence known. Grass often hides fire ant mounds, making them easy to disturb, and when their mounds are disturbed, fire ants aggressively swarm with stinging bites and injections of alkaloid venom. These bites can be very painful, can kill small animals, and may be fatal to humans with allergies. Biological controls are unproven and expensive, leaving poison as the main form of fire ant control, and Magnolia Grove uses such poison to control fire ants near high-traffic areas to avoid risk and discomfort to humans. Monastics may lament using these pesticides, but the fact remains that in fire ant control, the monastery chooses to value humans far more than fire ants.

Moreover, to probe limits on nonharm I asked several monastics a hypothetical question: "If a monk is attacked by a tiger, is it acceptable to kill the tiger to save the human life?" Every monastic hesitated to answer this question but, when pressed, responded that it would be good to kill the tiger if it meant saving a human life, each time stressing that the tiger would have to be killed "with compassion." So just as fire ants lose their lives to the practicalities of living at Magnolia Grove, so do hypothetical tigers, despite the fact that tigers also teach us how to love.

In my experience the nuns and monks of Magnolia Grove often regret such human-centered compromises of their ideals, and my point here is not to demean their lifestyle, which may be the most nature-friendly that we have seen in this book. What I wish to highlight is the fact that, looking across religious forms, ecocentrism always seems to be compromised by some form of practical human concern, because humans' material requirements eventually demand some form of anthropocentric response. Examples of this point are numerous, including in this book's chapter on the Maya, but let me describe the traditional religion of the Cheyenne group, a Native American people whose historical home was in Minnesota and later on the Great Plains of the United States.

Traditional Cheyenne religion was highly ecocentric, as it valued animals, plants, and rocks as manifest expressions of sacredness. In the Cheyenne worldview, everything in nature, including rocks and streams, was suffused with holiness. It was, in the words the scholar of religion Howard Harrod, a "sacred ecology," in which a variety of natural beings, even stony ones, served as gods, culture heroes, Masters of Animals, and lesser spirits. One of the most holy of these beings was the bison, which like the Hindu Mother Cow once provided many of the essentials for Cheyenne subsistence: food, clothing, medicine, housing, and so on.[15]

But unlike the contemporary Hindu Mother Cow, bison, as well as other sacred animals and plants, historically were killed for their gifts. Bison meat, which provided a major source of protein, and medicines made from bison organs could be procured only with the animals' slaughter. So with bison, the Cheyenne were on the horns of a dilemma (if the pun may be excused): Bison were sacred, and thus demanded respect and protection, but bison also had to sacrifice their lives for the human community. The Cheyenne resolved this dilemma through mythological stories and hunting rituals that religiously sanctified taking lives and materials from nature.

According to Cheyenne legend, animals for food were the gift of the divine Master of Animals named Coyote Man, who presented the Cheyenne with corn, bison, elk, deer, and birds as food. This gift was sealed when, at the request of Coyote Man, a young Cheyenne man took Coyote Man's daughter, Yellow-Haired Woman, as his bride. This part of the story informed the Cheyenne that it is permitted to kill for food, despite their ecocentric worldview, as they did so by divine mandate. But a taboo was attached: Coyote Man warned Yellow-Haired Woman that she should never, ever pity animals who were taken as food. Eventually Yellow-Haired Woman forgot this advice and felt sorry for a young bison calf. That day all the bison disappeared, and they remained gone for a long time. Thus the Cheyenne were mythically instructed not to feel bad about killing the animals that were given to them by Coyote Man.[16]

But as the tension between human use and sacred respect for nature remained, Cheyenne hunts became religious, ritual affairs, most unlike the secular hunting found in modern Western societies. By ritualizing the hunt through a ceremony called Massaum, the Cheyenne were able to maintain holy attitudes toward nature yet still take what they needed to live. At the beginning of the hunting season the Cheyenne would arrange their camp in the shape of a crescent, with the open end facing the sacred hillock Bear Butte. The Cheyenne placed a circle of lodges, or temples, with one for each of the game animals that the Cheyenne hunted, inside the camp circle. These lodges symbolically represented the underground place from which Coyote Man first released animals for human hunting. The Cheyenne built lanes for driving animals that led into this circular ritual layout. At the end of the lanes stood a corral and the Massaum lodge, which contained human impersonators of the spirits of Yellow-Haired Woman and many animals, all appropriately dressed and painted.

The ritual itself unfolded over five days. On the last day all the animal-spirit impersonators filled the central circle, and the symbolic Yellow-Haired Woman stood in the middle, raised her sacred pipe, and called the animal impersonators into the drive lanes and eventually to the corral by the Massaum lodge. When the animals were in the corral, they were ritually hunted and theatrically killed by men dressed as the Thunder spirits.[17]

In this way Cheyenne hunters were blessed to hunt by the sacred power of Yellow-Haired Woman. After the ritual, the Cheyenne scattered to their fall hunting territories, but they still made certain that when they killed a bison, they butchered it in a ritualized way that left the holy head, backbone, and tail intact. Otherwise they would use every part of the animal but try to take only as many animals as they needed. When the Cheyenne killed a bison, the bison's spirit and perhaps also Coyote Man were thanked for their gifts. Through this ritualized hunting and butchering the Cheyenne hoped to please Coyote Man so that he would continue to send gifts and properly prepare the animals for renewal. Such renewal came through the annual Sun Dance ritual, a major theme of which was restoring the natural world after its depredation by humans.[18]

In this religious complex we see that, for the Cheyenne, the dilemma between regarding a wide variety of natural forms as sacred and the need to take materials for survival was resolved through myth, ritual, and a moral code. Animals for food were divine gifts, provided that one followed the ethical principles that the animals should not be pitied, that animals were taken for need rather than for mere desire, and that ritual injunctions be followed. These ritual injunctions involved divine blessings for hunters, patterned shows of respect for slaughtered natural forms, and atonement for killing through attempts at renewal. The Cheyenne thereby handled violations of their ecocentric worldview by religiously sanctifying these violations.

All ecocentric forms of religion appear to end up finding their own ways to sanctify practical violations of their worldviews, just as the Cheyenne did, and Magnolia Grove is no different. Chan Hy Nghiem's prayers and meditations surrounding cutting the grass exhibit this dynamic, and there is the same ethic that natural beings may be utilized for human need but not for simple desire. Using poison on fire ants is justified by appeals to compassion for humans, which situationally is understood as a higher ethical obligation than compassion for ants. The killing of hypothetical tigers is justified for the same reason. Thus human-centered concerns enter and are embraced by an ecocentric form of religion that ritually and morally sanctifies them but otherwise is happy to consider stones to be Buddhas.

In the end Magnolia Grove presents us with a beautiful example of sacred ecocentric regard for the entire natural world. Humans inherently interconnect with animals, plants, and minerals, and deep religious experiences of this interconnection are encouraged. These experiences result in an ethic of nonviolent protection even for water and stones. Yet, despite their enlightened qualities, natural beings sometimes must be sacrificed on the altar of human benefit. Even in this highly ecocentric religious form, attitudes of human-centeredness appear, just as such attitudes appear in one way or another in all religious settings.

Epilogue

The Mountain Peaks Leaped and Danced

The Buddhists at Magnolia Grove from the last chapter are not the only ones to learn spiritual lessons from trees. A poem contained within one of the oldest compilations of Chinese poetry, the third-century-B.C.E. anthology *Chu ci,* or *Songs of the South,* provides us with another example. In the *Jiu zhang* section of the *Songs of the South* we find the poem "In Praise of the Orange Tree," which includes the following passage:[1]

> Alone and unmoving you [orange tree] stand: how can one not admire you?
> Deep-rooted, hard to shift: truly you have no peer!
> Alert to this world's ways you hold your ground, unyielding against the vulgar tide.
> You have sealed your heart; you guard yourself with care; have never fallen into error;
> Holding a nature free from bias, impartial even as Heaven and Earth are.
> I would fade as you fade with the passing years and ever be your friend.
> Pure and apart and free from sin, and strong in the order of your ways:
> Though young in years, fit to be a teacher of people.

This passage reflects undertones involving primordial Chinese experiences with nature that run through the *Songs of the South* collection, coloring its often beautiful verses. For example, the text offers us a lovely example of shamanic soul travel in nature:[2]

> Harnessing steeds of the rainbow to my chariot, I ride transfigured
>   above the clouds.
> The *jiao-ming* bird clears the way before me; green snakes follow in my
>   train.
> We gallop through the cassia woods, we vault over dangerous places.
> The mountain peaks leaped and danced, the valleys sang for joy,
> And the words of the sacred books were chanted in harmony to the
>   tune.
> I alone was there to enjoy it: such pleasure none could add to.
> I turned and looked back at the foolish world, lost in destruction's nets.

In previous chapters I explored the importance of sun worship in India and Central America. Solar veneration appeared in China as well, and the *Songs of the South* gives us a terrific ancient Chinese travelogue from the point of view of the Sun, the divine Lord of the East:[3]

> With a faint flush I start to come out of the east,
> Shining down on my threshold, Fu-sang [mythical eastern mulberry
>   tree].
> As I urge my horses slowly forwards,
> The night sky brightens, and day has come.
>
> I ride a dragon car and chariot on the thunder,
> With cloud-banners fluttering on the wind.
> I heave a long sigh as I start the ascent,
> Reluctant to leave, and looking back longingly;
> For the beauty and the music are so enchanting,
> The beholder, delighted, forgets that he must go.
>
> In my cloud-coat and my skirt of the rainbow,
> Grasping my bow I soar high up in the sky.
> I aim my long arrow and shoot the Wolf of Heaven [Sirius];
> I seize the Dipper to ladle cinnamon wine.
> Then holding my reins, I plunge down to my setting,
> On my gloomy night journey back to the east.

But the *Songs of the South* contains many voices, and not all are so respect-ful of nature's spiritual powers. For instance, another poem bemoans exile into a wilderness abode:[4]

> When we entered Xu-pu, I halted uncertainly,
> Too distraught to think where I was going.
> Amid the deep woods there, amid the twilight gloom,
> Are the haunts where monkeys live.
> The mountains' awful height screens the noonday sun,
> And below it is dark and dim with perpetual rain;
> Sleet and snow fall there unendingly,
> And the heavy clouds begin where the roof-tops end.
> Alas, that my life should be so devoid of pleasure!
> That I should live here, alone and obscure, among the mountains!
> But I cannot change my heart and follow the vulgar crowd,
> And so I must face bitter sorrow and a hopeless end as my lot.

How far this last passage takes us from the mountain mystic John Muir! In these selections from the *Songs of the South,* some of which hail nature as sacred and some of which rue her as desolate, we see the same theme that has arisen repeatedly in this book: ambivalent, multifaceted interactions with nature. One *Songs of the South* author offers a paean to an orange tree, whereas another abhors monkeys and misty mountains. Every religion that we have surveyed follows this same pattern in its own ways, as each religious form possesses multiple and sometimes divergent models of relationship with the natural world. Each religion does so because it provides a unique blend of attitudes of human-centeredness combined with various attitudes of nonhuman nature–centeredness.

The Christian world alone reveals a variety of orientations and per-mutations. Euro-American churches tend to promote the myth of human superiority, virtually barring natural beings from religious belief and practice other than human-centered blessing rituals. But Ethiopian churches offer more ecocentric perspectives on church grounds; Paul baptizes a lion; and birds pray and prophesy for Brendan. A little further afield, we find John Muir inventing a heterodox form of Christian nature mysticism and the Maya integrating sincere devotion to Christianity with their own culturally appropriate nature mysticism of the sun, the mountains, the fields, jaguars, and so on. In the Islamic world one finds anthropocentric attitudes that contribute to animal sacrifice coexisting with demands for humane treatment of animals, the recognition that animals have communities like humans, and things like a mosque being founded by a camel, resulting in a quirky exposition in *The Case of the Animals versus Humans*. Hinduism offers homage to natural entities as our mothers yet allows some use and killing of natural beings for the sake of humans and their religions. The folklore surrounding the yetis of the Himalayas teaches us that natural beings may be humanlike, tame, religiously pious, godly, strong, or terrifyingly violent, depending on whom you ask. And the Buddhists of Magnolia Grove, so genuinely motivated to lead sacred lives in concert with natural beings, discover that the demands of human existence always seem to result in some form of human-centered compromise, even if that compromise is sacralized.

Recognizing these connections allows me to comment on one of my original questions: Why are religious experiences with the natural world so diverse? The material here highlights how religious experiences with nature arise from cultural attitudes toward nature that shape religious experiences from the ground up, as our mental presumptions strongly color how we encounter the natural world. A European Christian may perceive the same outstanding qualities of the sun—warmth, brightness, nurturance, and so forth—as a Mayan Christian, but it may never occur to the European Christian to consider the sun sacred because she has never substantially encountered or been taught such a belief, as a Maya has. The anthropocentrism in Clement's early Christian milieu helped him to decry the Egyptian "wallowing animals," yet the missionary fervor and emphasis on the universality of Jesus's love within Paul's early Christian environment led him to baptize a lion, or at least a literary lion. Prompted by religious theory, Muslims sacrifice cattle during the Id al-Adha ritual whereas, also on the basis of religious theory, Vietnamese Buddhists actively avoid killing cattle, and New Talavana Hindus energetically protect them. Yet as a result of their own distinctive worldviews, the Hindus kill snakes, mosquitoes, and other creatures, whereas the Buddhists avoid doing the same, thus highlighting differences of nature-friendliness in meatless realms. From such examples, we learn that our operative cultural, psychological, and social models of relationship with the natural world strongly impact who has religious experiences with nature and what forms those experiences take. Therefore, if we wish to have more authentically compassionate and spiritual relationships with nature, we must begin with honest, self-critical assessments of the essentials of our inner attitudes and presumptions, no matter how commonsensical they may seem, toward the natural world.

In terms of my second question—What does the diversity of experiences with nature mean?—we have seen that expressions of religious experiences with nature alter historical and cultural realities and thus bear a variety of real-world meanings. Christian pet blessing ceremonies may be very fulfilling for pet caregivers, thus bringing animals closer to the church than ever before. But in part because influential leaders like Aquinas and Descartes did not decry animal cruelty as a sin, nonpet animals in the Christian world often endure miserable lives rife with cruel behavior—not to mention the realities of plants, water resources, and minerals, which never have held religious or ethical value. Plants, water, and minerals do not merit spiritual respect or value in the Islamic world either, which simultaneously boasts an animal-rights movement that makes solid and positive claims against animal cruelty while factory farms mushroom in number. The Hindus whom we saw create positive outcomes for their revered cattle, plants, and rivers, yet human need nonetheless results in cut timber, dead snakes, and river goddesses who are badly polluted. Mayan nature mystics beautifully embody an ethic of reciprocity with natural beings yet still sometimes overplant, overgraze, and overhunt. In the Himalayas experiences with yetis lead residents to both revere and fear the legendary creatures while Tibetan Buddhism flexes to embrace the sacred animal-human hybrids by including them in the wheel of reincarnation. And at a Vietnamese Buddhist monastery, religious experiences with nature prompt practices of nonharm, learning from natural beings as religious teachers, and meditation on one's sacred interconnections with the natural world, but also the killing of fire ants. These diverse outcomes teach us that it is not enough to survey the contours of religious belief to understand religious experiences with nature; we also must take the real-world meanings of those experiences into account.

Another interesting outcome of these religious experiences with nature involves the many instances in which animals appear to practice religion. These events raise the question whether animals can practice religion in species-specific ways, even if it is not religion as conceptualized and practiced by humans. This question regarding religiosity in animals is hardly new, having occupied various thinkers across cultures since antiquity as a possible criterion for asserting human superiority to the natural world. Of course, the very notion of animal religion will strike some people as odd. If so, the skeptic may consider some insights from contemporary science before unscientifically dismissing the possibility out of hand. Although no current studies substantially support the idea that animals may have religion, quite a few of them indicate that some animals may have the cognitive, emotional, and moral capacities that religious experiences as we know them appear to require.

For a long time students of animal behavior, in the name of avoiding anthropomorphism, strongly resisted attributing things like thinking, feeling, or consciousness to animals. To a point this effort must be applauded, as animals' thoughts and feelings certainly must be different from human thoughts and feelings, given our differing anatomies and social environments. But a growing body of research shows that animals can have what we want to call "feelings," even if they are not exactly like human feelings; and so presuming that animals cannot have feelings at all, as many studies of animal behavior have done, goes too far. As put succinctly by the eminent primatologist Franz de Waal:

"Sometimes I read about someone saying with great authority that animals have no intentions and no feelings, and I wonder, 'Doesn't this guy have a dog?'"[5]

Increasingly, animal-studies scholars side with de Waal, and each year more investigations appear that describe the notable mental and emotional equipment of many different species. An interesting example of this is the book *How Dogs Love Us,* by the neuroscientist Gregory Berns. Berns used MRI scans on alert, unsedated dogs in relatively natural states to detect their brain activity. On the basis of the brain scans that he captured, Berns showed that canine brain structures and activities share a number of similarities to those of humans, allowing advanced social-learning skills and feelings of affection for caregivers, as well as a canine sense of empathy.[6]

But it is not just dogs who appear to possess such capacities. The scholar of animal behavior Marc Bekoff broadly asserts: "Animals feel a wide range of emotions, including each of Darwin's six universal emotions: anger, happiness, sadness, disgust, fear, and surprise." These feelings occur in species-specific ways and vary across individuals within species. It is especially important to the study of religion that, in highlighting that many animals have the same brain architecture that in humans facilitates posttraumatic stress, Bekoff informs us that animals may suffer from loss: "There is no question that animals grieve and ... the universal signs of grief are seen most keenly when animals respond to the death of a mate, family member, or friend." He continues by describing mourning expressions in gorillas, baboons, dogs, llamas, and wolves, and he ends by leaving us with a portrayal of three elephants who respond to the death of a family member who has been killed by a gun:[7]

> Teresia and Trista became frantic and knelt down and tried to lift her up. They worked their tusks under her back and under her head. At one point they succeeded in lifting her into a sitting position but her body flopped back down. Her family tried everything to rouse her, kicking and tusking her, and Tullulah even went off and collected a trunkful of grass and tried to stuff it in her mouth.

Since religious experiences in humans involve an emotional component, the presence of emotion in animals conceivably could hint at the
capacity for religious experience, as Donovan O. Schaefer argued in
Religious Affects. This remains especially true when we consider the centrality of grief. Commentators far too numerous to name tell us that our
struggle with the inevitability of death strongly motivates human religiosity. Thus, it is possible that animals' capacity for grief may indicate
their ability to be religiously sensitive in their own ways.[8]

Besides exhibiting affect in these ways, animals also can experience
rich mental lives. Donald R. Griffin, a leader in cognitive ethology (the
study of animal thinking), accords perceptive consciousness (but not
human reflective consciousness) to a wide variety of species. One example of this principle, among many, comes from the dance of the honeybee. Unappreciated by those who claim that only humans build structures, honeybee hives are engineering marvels that require organized
labor, many resources, and social communication in order to create and
maintain. Part of this communication occurs chemically, but part of it
occurs through what researchers call "waggle dances." Bees who return
from resource-scouting expeditions do repeated, patterned dances that
involve rapid, purposive shaking of the abdomen. Researchers have
demonstrated that these waggle dances communicate with great accu-
racy the type of resource the scout bee has found, as well as its direction, distance, quantity, and even quality. On the basis of these commu-
nicative dances, other specialized bees respond by quickly finding and
exploiting these resources, which hive-worker bees then use to equip
the hive and feed and its inhabitants. In humans, such organized, inten-
tional behavior would be taken as proof of thinking and planning along
with communication and social cooperation.[9]

Further, religion as we know it also involves morality, which we may
distinguish from ethical theorizing. The primatologist Franz de Waal
tells us that many animals possess apparent senses of morality; in his
studies he describes numerous experiences in which primates exhibit

moral virtues like sympathy or community-regarding discipline that at least resemble human social ethics. He says:[10]

> A chimpanzee stroking and patting the victim of attack or sharing her food with a hungry companion shows attitudes that are hard to distinguish from those of a person picking up a crying child or doing volunteer work in a soup kitchen. To classify the chimpanzee's behavior as based on instinct and the person's behavior as proof of moral decency is misleading, and probably incorrect. First of all, it is uneconomic in that it assumes different processes for similar behavior in two closely related species. Second, it ignores the growing body of evidence for mental complexity in the chimpanzee, including the possibility of empathy. I hesitate to call the members of any species other than our own "moral beings," yet I also believe that many of the sentiments and cognitive abilities underlying human morality antedate the appearance of our species on this planet.

But it is not just primates who manifest what appear to be senses of morality, as the scientific literature contains examples of members of numerous species who engage in behaviors that in humans would be described as moral. Let us take, for example, the familiar scenario of dogs at play. The canine-behavior specialist Alexandra Horowitz suggests that dogs always structure their play through implicitly shared values, especially the value of fairness. When a very large dog plays with a very small dog, the large dog does not just dominate, as it could, but instead generously alters the rules to level the playing field. The large dog even levels itself, crouching to look smaller, and then matches the small dog in ferocity, strength, and dexterity rather than overwhelming it. The larger dog actively avoids harming the smaller by extending play bites only. As part of play, usually the larger dog will even adopt postures of submissiveness out of step with normal pack hierarchy. Such fairness enhancements allow dogs with different characteristics and abilities still to play together; Horowitz tells us that dogs who will not seek fairness like this in their play become ostracized. Thus, everyday dog play emerges following unwritten rules of fairness and a canine version of social morality. Incidentally, the dog-bow posture, in which a dog has her front end down low, hind end raised, and tail at alert, communicates an invitation to other dogs to play. Given regularized behaviors like these, if ritual is patterned outer behavior, then dogs who instigate play with the dog bow engage in ritual, although we have no overt reason to call that ritual religious.[11]

In these ways science informs us that animals may have the emotive, thinking, and moral capacities for religious experience, or at least science gives us no reason to rule out the possibility because of a lack of such capacities. We know that many animals and plants communicate, but in ways different from how humans do; could it be that at least some natural beings practice religion, but without the chapels and scriptures?

An influential current scientific voice on the question of animal religion belongs to the famous ethologist Jane Goodall, who supports the notion that animals may have spiritual sensibilities. Having lived for years in the wild, Goodall describes what she considers a sense of religious awe expressed in ritualized dances done by chimpanzees:[12]

> The chimpanzees, I believe, know feelings akin to awe. In the Kakombe valley is a magnificent waterfall. There is a great roar as the water cascades down through the soft green air from the stream bed above. Over countless aeons the water has worn a perpendicular groove in the sheer rock. Ferns move ceaselessly in the wind created by the falling water, and vines hang down on either side. For me it is a magical place, and a spiritual one. And sometimes, as they approach, the chimpanzees display in slow, rhythmic motion along the river-bed. They pick up and throw great rocks and branches. They leap to seize the hanging vines, and swing out over the stream in the spray-drenched wind until it seems the slender stems must snap or be torn from their lofty moorings.
>
> Then one or more of the adult males starts this rhythmic display, much of which is an upright movement. Very, very slow—slapping and slapping and slapping—and stamping and stamping and stamping—and standing up, and swaying and swaying and swaying—and moving rhythmically from foot to foot to foot.... The amazing thing is that afterwards they occasionally stamp in the water, whereas normally they hate getting their feet wet.

For ten minutes or more they may perform this magnificent "dance." Why? Is it not possible that the chimpanzees are responding to some feeling like awe? A feeling generated by the mystery of water: water that seems alive, always rushing past yet never going, always the same yet ever different. Was it perhaps similar feelings of awe that gave rise to the first animistic religions, the worship of the elements and the mysteries of nature over which there was no control?

Having briefly surveyed what science may say about animal religion, let us return to what the religions of the world have to say about this issue. As we have seen in this book, human religions are ambiguous on the question of animal religion, befitting their diversity of perspectives. On the negative side, Christianity almost exclusively follows Augustine's teaching that animals lack souls and therefore the capacity for religion, so Skipper the husky dog was denied Communion. Mainline Islam defines religion in terms of making moral choices, a capacity denied to animals. In Hinduism cows may be objects of veneration but do not practice religion themselves. The Mayan world gave us the *Popol Vuh*'s claim that animals cannot properly praise the gods but humans can. In the mountains of Asia, yetis may be peaceful Buddhist bodhisattvas, but only when they are at their most human. And although our Vietnamese Buddhists do not explicitly deny animals the ability to practice religion, they implicitly do so by making no provision for the spiritual lives of natural beings. Everywhere in the realm of religion we may find explicit or implicit denials of the abilities of animals to practice religion, or at least human religion. Of course in this book I have been able to examine only humanlike religiosity, which may not be a fair standard for judging the religiosity of nonhumans.

But it is rather startling that we also find alternative perspectives in which animals practice religion in humanlike ways. Christian animals at times get baptized, pray, perform Mass, venerate saints, prophesy, or show spiritual insight. Under Islam bees receive revelation, donkeys have mystical experiences, camels locate sacred places, deer help with conversion, and pigeons meditate. The Hindu Chaitanya's tigers and deer kiss in spiritual ecstasy, and Krishna's calves shed tears of transcendent joy. For the Maya, animals were among the first gods, and some jaguars participate in shamanism. Himalayan yetis are not purely human, and yet they may be temple keepers or disciples of yogis. And among Vietnamese Buddhists, religious teachers include tigers who demonstrate spiritual love and trees who exemplify hallowed patience. Today many people claim that the practice of religion makes humans superior, yet these examples prompt us to rethink this part of the myth of human superiority.

Thus preliminary evidence for answering the question of whether animals may possess religion remains muddy. Along with assertions of animal religion we have denials. Moreover, the stories here use the practice of human religion as an essential yardstick, obscuring the fact that animal religions, should they exist at all, assuredly take forms different from human religions. Further, in this book we primarily have stories, or anecdotal data, rather than the hard data from the natural sciences that any serious claim for animal religiosity needs for establishment. So, in the end, this book's peek at the possibility of animal religiosity has been somewhat provocative but leaves much undetermined.

In light of this lack of clarity, Michel de Montaigne, who lived in France in the sixteenth century, just before Descartes, offers us a helpful philosophical voice on the question of animal religiosity. Montaigne described elephants as being very close to humans, closer to some humans than humans may be with each other, so that they possess religious sensibilities. Of elephant religion Montaigne said:[13]

> Elephants have some notion of religion since, after ablutions and purifications, they can be seen waving their trunks like arms upraised, while gazing intently at the rising sun; for long periods at fixed times in the day (by instinct, not from teaching or precept) they stand rooted in meditation and contemplation; there may be no obvious similarities in other animals, but that does not allow us to make judgments about their total lack of religion. When matters are hidden from us, we cannot in any way conceive them.

A willingness to conceive of animals as religious marked part of Montaigne's frequent arguments against the myth of human superiority. Although animals may be thieves, Montaigne taught, so may humans; but unlike sinful humans, animals regulate their problematic desires by time and seasons. Further, the sun, moon, and stars are "free from corruption" but humans are not. Moreover, like Balaam's ass in the Bible, Montaigne's animals may perceive spirits that humans cannot. Montaigne's animals also have extraordinary abilities to sense time and coming weather and to change color, as the octopus and chameleon show.

Montaigne attacks other pillars of the myth of human superiority, including language use. Montaigne mentions that animals do not understand human language but points out that we do not understand animal communications, either. But animals often may communicate among themselves through nonverbal methods, a horse who understands a barking dog highlighting this point for Montaigne. Further, Montaigne resembles Donald Griffin in insisting on animals' possession of a quality that we want to call "reason," for Montaigne the flight of birds alone indicating this. Animals also use tools, recognize natural medicines, construct homes, and create coherent social organizations. They often are more beautiful than humans and, intriguingly, Montaigne says that animals have better marriages than humans. In these ways, through his discourse Montaigne seeks to dethrone various reasons for human superiority given in his time, as some still are now.

For Montaigne, in the end notions of human superiority boil down to human self-centeredness, as he repeatedly attacks humans for being "the most vain," "inherently presumptuous," "treacherous," and "arrogant" of creatures. He says that we do many of the same things that animals do, but these similar actions, when done by a human rather than an animal, are taken to reflect possession of a soul. For Montaigne this is an incoherent view, revealing the myth of human superiority as just a conceited human projection.

But Montaigne does not wish to elevate animals above humans. He wrote that "we are neither above nor below" animals, because humans and animals alike fundamentally seek food, water, sleep, safety, health, and happiness. Moreover, other animals treasure their own species just as humans do, as we previously saw with Xenophanes. Montaigne tells us: "No creature holds anything dearer than the kind of being that it is (lions, eagles, dolphins value nothing above their own species) and … every species reduces the qualities of everything else to analogies of its own." He continues on to say: "Why should a gosling not argue thus: 'All the parts of the universe are there for me: the earth serves me to waddle upon, the sun to give me light; the heavenly bodies exist to breathe their influences upon me; the winds help me this way, the waters, that way: there is nothing which the vault of heaven treats with greater favor than me.'" By dislodging the myth of human superiority, Montaigne simply wants us to enact more peerlike interactions with natural beings by recognizing in them greater value and a sense of personhood.[14]

Montaigne thus helps us to see that the real question is not what distinguishes humans *from* animals but what distinguishes humans *among* animals. To this question the philosopher Mary Midgley adds: "In certain respects, all social mammals, including us, are far more like one another than any is like a snake or a codfish, or even a bee.… What is special about each creature is not a single, unique quality but a rich and complex arrangement of powers and qualities, some of which it will certainly share with its neighbors." Montaigne and Midgley want us to be more cognizant that we live in a mixed community of humans and nonhuman natural beings so that we may more clearly understand ourselves and the natural beings who surround us while generating greater concord in the universe.[15]

A story from the classic Chinese novel *The Journey to the West* nicely illustrates this final point. In this fictional tale a man named Chen was a brilliant scholar with a beautiful new wife, Wenjiao. In recognition of his talents, the emperor named Chen as the new governor of Jiangzhou, and Chen set out with Wenjiao for the new post. On the way, Chen bought a fabulous golden carp, which he intended to feed to his sick mother. But noticing a special look in the eye of the fish, Chen thought the carp must be a superior being who had taken fish form, and so he changed his meal plan and released the carp into river freedom. Chen and his wife then continued their journey. To their misfortune, when crossing a river they found out the hard way that their ferryman, Liu Hong, was a criminal. Liu Hong killed Chen, tossing his lifeless body into the water. He then purloined Chen's belongings, abducted Wen-jiao, and falsely posed as the new governor. Eventually Wenjiao freed herself and alerted the emperor, who had the impostor Liu Hong deposed and killed. Wenjiao, now released from the fraudulent tyrant, finally got to offer the riverbank funeral sacrifices that tradition obliged her to perform for her dead husband.

Chen's dutiful wife did not know at that time that Chen actually was not dead. His body had fallen to the bottom of the river, where it was quickly discovered by an assistant to the dragon king of the river. Inspecting the body, the dragon recognized Chen as his friend, as previously the dragon had temporarily taken up the form of the golden carp that Chen had compassionately released. Since Chinese dragons have magical powers, the dragon king was able to keep Chen alive as a minister in his underwater court while the fraudulent Liu occupied the governor's office. Then one day the dragon king noticed the demise of Liu Hong and Wenjiao's performance of her riverside mourning ritual, and the dragon king thereupon restored Chen with his human body. Chen emerged from the water unhurt and reunited with his wife, much to her astonishment and joy.[16]

In this story Chen looks deeply into nature (the golden carp) and so gains superior insight into the workings of the universe where others would simply have seen dinner's main dish. Gaining respect for the carp as a being in its own right, he then frees the fish out of compassion. This self-sacrificial act, so insignificant and foolish to some, then becomes a positive boon for Chen. Through his profound perceptiveness regarding nature and warmheartedness for natural entities, Chen acts perhaps eccentrically but also positively and effectively, in the end preserving his life and his family. In his warmheartedness toward the natural world, Chen is a model for us all. If we, like Chen, are willing to set aside our preconceptions and look more deeply into ourselves and the natural world, like Chen we may find unforeseen, mutually beneficial ways in which we may respond to and live with our animal, plant, and mineral neighbors.

NOTES

INTRODUCTION

1. John Muir, *John Muir: Spiritual Writings*, ed. Tim Flinders (Maryknoll, N.Y.: Orbis Books, 2013), 35. For the sake of increasing accessibility for general readers, my citations in this book do not follow strict scholarly methods, instead reflecting a citation method that is common to books for nonscholarly audiences. Citations to in-line sources are found collected in footnotes at the ends of the paragraphs in which they are relevant. For reasons of book design, reference notes for block quotations are found immediately preceding those texts, outside the block text itself.

2. Muir, *John Muir: Spiritual Writings*, 107.

3. Muir, *John Muir: Spiritual Writings*, 30, 43–44.

4. Muir, *John Muir: Spiritual Writings*, 50, 54, 79.

5. Muir, *John Muir: Spiritual Writings*, 51; John Muir, *John Muir: Nature Writings*, ed. William Cronon (New York: The Library of America, 1997), 558; Rudolf Otto, *The Idea of the Holy*, trans. John W. Harvey (New York: Oxford University Press, 1958).

6. Muir, *John Muir: Spiritual Writings*, 52.

7. John Muir, *My First Summer in the Sierras* (New York: Random House, 2003), 90.

8. Thurman Wilkins, *John Muir: Apostle of Nature* (Norman: University of Oklahoma Press, 1995), 113.

9. Mary Midgley, *Beast and Man: The Roots of Human Nature* (Ithaca: Cornell University Press, 1978), 18.

10. Paul Shepard, *The Others: How Animals Made Us Human* (Washington, D.C.: Island Press, 1996), 9; Eugenia Shanklin, "Sustenance and Symbol: Anthropological Studies of Domesticated Animals," *Annual Review of Anthropology* 14 (1985), 375, doi: 10.1146/annurev.an.14.100185.002111; David Gordon White, *Myths of the Dog-man* (Chicago: University of Chicago Press, 1991), 12–13.

11. Jeffrey Cohn, "How Wild Wolves Became Domestic Dogs," *BioScience* 47:11 (1997): 726, doi: 10.2307/1313093; Adam R. Boyko et al., "Complex Population Structure in African Village Dogs and Its Implications for Inferring Dog Domestication History," *Proceedings of the National Academy of Sciences of the United States of America* 106:33 (2009), 13903–8, doi: 10.1073/pnas.0902129106; O. Thalmann et al., "Complete Mitochondrial Genomes of Ancient Canids Suggest a European Origin of Domestic Dogs," *Science* 342:6160 (2013), 871–74, doi: 10.1126/science.1243650; Harriet Ritvo, "Pride and Pedigree: The Evolution of the Victorian Dog Fancy," *Victorian Studies* 29:2 (1986), 227–53.

12. A. Irving Hallowell, "Bear Ceremonialism in the Northern Hemisphere," *American Anthropologist* 28:1 (1926), doi: 10.1525/aa.1926.28.1.02a00020; Lydia T. Black, "Bear in Human Imagination and in Ritual," *Ursus* 10 (1998), 343–47.

13. Steven T. Katz, ed., *Mysticism and Philosophical Analysis* (New York: Oxford University Press, 1978).

14. William Warren, *History of the Ojibway People* (St. Paul: Minnesota Historical Society, 1984), 41–53.

15. Katherine Wills Perlo, *Kinship and Killing: The Animal in World Religions* (New York: Columbia University Press, 2009).

16. Jeremy Rapport, "Eating for Unity: Vegetarianism in the Early Unity School of Christianity," *Gastronomica: The Journal of Food and Culture* 9:2 (2009), 35.

17. Michel de Montaigne, *An Apology for Raymond Sebond,* trans. M. A. Screech (London: Penguin Books, 1993), 51.

18. Wilkins, 16, 77, 79; Muir, *John Muir: Nature Writings,* 109; Catherine L. Albanese, *Nature Religion in America* (Chicago: University of Chicago Press, 1990), 95.

19. Muir, *John Muir: Spiritual Writings,* 54; Aaron Honori Katcher and Alan M. Beck, "Health and Caring for Living Things," in *Animals and People Sharing the World,* ed. Andrew N. Rowan (Hanover: University Press of New England, 1988), 69.

20. Muir, *John Muir: Spiritual Writings,* 83, 90–91.

21. Muir, *John Muir: Spiritual Writings,* 45–46.

22. Muir, *My First Summer in the Sierras,* 197.

23. Wilkins, 195.

24. Muir, *My First Summer in the Sierras,* 319, 326.

25. Muir, *My First Summer in the Sierras,* 331; Muir, *John Muir: Spiritual Writings,* 88.

26. Muir, *John Muir: Spiritual Writings,* 61, 89; W. T. Stace, *Mysticism and Philosophy* (New York: Jeremy P. Tharcher, 1987), 78–81.

27. Brian Morris, *Animals and Ancestors: An Ethnography* (Oxford: Berg, 2000), 34.

28. Wilhelm Schneemelcher, ed., *New Testament Apocrypha,* vol. 2 (Louisville: Westminster John Knox Press, 2003), 296, 298; Keith Thomas, *Man and the Natural World* (London: Penguin Books, 1984), 16; Arthur Waley, trans., *Monkey* (New York: The John Day Company, 1943), 277.

29. Quoted in James Serpell, *In the Company of Animals: A Study of Human-Animal Relationships* (Cambridge: Cambridge University Press, 1986), 32.

30. Montaigne, 17. The quotation from Xenophanes: Laura Hobgood-Oster, *Holy Dogs and Asses: Animals in the Christian Tradition* (Urbana: University of Illinois Press, 2008), 13.

1. ALL THE CHRISTIAN BIRDS CHANTED

1. All biblical quotations are from National Council of Churches of Christ in America, *Bible: Revised Standard Version,* accessed 2014, http://quod.lib.umich.edu/r/rsv/browse.html.

2. Frederick Starr, "Popular Celebrations in Mexico," *The Journal of American Folklore* 9:34 (1896), 168; Laura Hobgood-Oster, *Holy Dogs and Asses: Animals in the Christian Tradition* (Urbana: University of Illinois Press, 2008), 107.

3. Hobgood-Oster, 4, 6.

4. Heimo Hohneck, "Animal Mummies and the Worship of Animals in Ancient Egypt," in *Mummies of the World,* ed. Alfried Wieczorek and Wilfried Rosendahl (Munich: Prestel Verlag, 2010), 94; H. te Velde, "A Few Remarks upon the Religious Significance of Animals in Ancient Egypt," *Numen* 27:1 (1980): 81; Geraldine Pinch, *Egyptian Mythology* (Oxford: Oxford University Press, 2002).

5. te Velde, 80; Eric A. Powell, "Messengers to the Gods," *Archaeology* 67:2 (2014), 49.

6. Roberta Kalechofsky, "Hierarchy, Kinship, and Responsibility: The Jewish Relationship to the Animal World," in *A Communion of Subjects: Animals*

in Religion, Science, and Ethics, ed. Paul Waldau and Kimberly Patton (New York: Columbia University Press, 2006), 93.

7. Rod Preece and David Fraser, "The Status of Animals in Biblical and Christian Thought: A Study in Colliding Values," *Society & Animals* 8:3 (2000), 251, doi: 10.1163/156853000X00165.

8. John Binns, "Out of Ethiopia—A Different Way of Doing Theology," *International Journal for the Study of the Christian Church* 13:1 (2013), 35, doi: 10.1080/1474225X.2012.754137; Ulrich Braukämper, "Aspects of Religious Syncretism in Southern Ethiopia," *Journal of Religion in Africa* 22:3 (1992), 198; Tom Boylston, "The Shade of the Divine: Approaching the Sacred in an Ethiopian Orthodox Christian Community" (Ph.D. dissertation, London School of Economics, 2012); Gebrehiwot Gebreslassie Zesu, *The Sacred and the Profane: Environmental Anthropology of Ethiopian Orthodox Christianity* (Hamburg: Anchor Academic Publishing, 2013).

9. Andrew Linzey and Tom Regan, eds., *Animals and Christianity* (Eugene: Wipf and Stock, 1990), 87.

10. Peter Dinzelbacher, "Animal Trials: A Multidisciplinary Approach," *The Journal of Interdisciplinary History* 32:3 (2002), 405–21, doi: 10.1162/002219502753364191; Hobgood-Oster, 103–4.

11. Ralph Waldo Emerson, *The Essential Writings of Ralph Waldo Emerson,* ed. Brooks Atkinson (New York: Modern Library, 2000), 25.

12. Catherine L. Albanese, *Nature Religion in America* (Chicago: University of Chicago Press, 1990), 43.

13. Elizabeth A. Johnson, "Losing and Finding Creation in the Christian Tradition," in *Christianity and Ecology,* ed. Dieter T. Hessel and Rosemary Radford Ruether (Cambridge, Mass.: Harvard University Press, 2000), 7.

14. Michel de Montaigne, *An Apology for Raymond Sebond,* trans. M. A. Screech (London: Penguin Books, 1993), 86; Mary Midgley, *Animals and Why They Matter* (Athens, Ga.: University of Georgia Press, 1984), 79.

15. Lynn White, Jr., "The Historical Roots of Our Ecologic Crisis," *Science* 155:3767 (1967), 1203–7, doi: 10.1126/science.155.3767.1203. The block quotation from Descartes is cited in Hobgood-Oster, 33.

16. Descartes cited from Linzey and Regan, 18; Daniel Cowdin, "The Moral Status of Otherkind in Christian Ethics," in *Christianity and Ecology,* ed. Dieter T. Hessel and Rosemary Radford Ruether (Cambridge, Mass.: Harvard University Press, 2000), 265; Matthew Scully, *Dominion* (New York: St. Martin's Press, 2002), 15.

17. Arnobius of Sicca discussed by Ingvild Sælid Gilhus in *Animals, Gods, and Humans* (London: Routledge, 2006), 148; Animal sacrifice discussed by Selva J. Raj in "Transgressing Boundaries, Transcending Turner: The Pilgrimage Tradition at the Shrine of St. John de Britto," in *Popular Christianity in India,* ed. Selva J. Raj and Corinne G. Dempsey (Albany: State University of New York Press, 2002), 86–89.

18. Lynn White, Jr., 1205; Keith Thomas, *Man and the Natural World* (London: Penguin Books, 1984), 22.

19. Wilhelm Schneemelcher, ed., *New Testament Apocrypha,* vol. 2 (Louisville: Westminster John Knox Press, 2003), 264–65.

20. Schneemelcher, 253; Susan Power Bratton, *Christianity, Wilderness, and Wildlife* (Scranton: University of Scranton Press, 1993), 168.

21. Hobgood-Oster, 58; Gilhus, 248; Thomas, 47; Helen Waddell, trans., *Beasts and Saints* (London: Constable and Co., 1960), 30–38; Glenn E. Snyder, *Acts of Paul* (Tübingen: Mohr Siebeck, 2013), 226.

22. François Bovon and Christopher R. Matthews, trans., *Acts of Philip* (Waco: Baylor University Press, 2012), 79–80.

23. Bovon and Matthews, 85–86.

24. Hobgood-Oster, 69.

25. Waddell, 103–6.

26. Jay Hansford C. Vest, "Will-of-the-Land: Wilderness among Primal Indo-Europeans," *Environmental History Review* 9:4 (1985), 323–29, doi: 10.2307/3984462; John J. O'Meara, trans., *The Voyage of Saint Brendan: Journey to the Promised Land* (Atlantic Highlands: Humanities Press, 1976), 23; Marie-Louise Sjoestedt, *Celtic Gods and Heroes* (Mineola: Dover Publications, 2000), 33. The block quotation is cited from O'Meara, 37-38.

27. O'Meara, 21–22.

28. O'Meara, 49–50.

29. J. F. Webb, trans., *Lives of the Saints* (Baltimore: Penguin Books, 1965), 85–115; Waddell, 53.

30. Waddell, 90–91.

31. Waddell, 74–91.

32. Raphael Brown, trans., *The Little Flowers of Saint Francis* (Garden City: Image Books, 1958), 91–92, 177–78.

33. Brown, 76–78.

34. Brown, 75, 185.

35. Hobgood-Oster, 69; Brown, 88–91.

36. James Serpell, *In the Company of Animals: A Study of Human-Animal Relationships* (Cambridge: Cambridge University Press, 1986), 48.

37. Peter Harrison, "Descartes on Animals," *The Philosophical Quarterly* 42:167 (1992), 223, doi: 10.2307/2220217; David Weissman, ed., *Discourse on the Method and Meditations on First Philosophy* (New Haven: Yale University Press, 1996), 36; Linzey and Regan, 51.

38. Johnson, "Losing and Finding Creation," 10.

39. James Serpell, "Pet-keeping in Non-Western Societies: Some Popular Misconceptions," in *Animals and People Sharing the World,* ed. Andrew N. Rowan (Hanover, N.H.: University Press of New England, 1988), 42.

40. Aaron Honori Katcher and Alan M. Beck, "Health and Caring for Living Things," in *Animals and People Sharing the World,* ed. Andrew N. Rowan (Hanover, N.H.: University Press of New England, 1988), 56.

41. Serpell, *In the Company of Animals;* Paul Shepard, *The Others: How Animals Made Us Human* (Washington, D.C.: Island Press, 1996).

42. The Episcopal Church, *The Book of Common Prayer* (New York: Church Publishing Incorporated, 2007), 13.

43. Dave Cunningham, "So Why Was Earl the Slug Shunned?" *Alberta Report* 24:30 (1997), 34; Hobgood-Oster, 122.

44. Elizabeth A. Johnson, *Ask the Beasts: Darwin and the God of Love* (London: Bloomsbury, 2014), 6. The following block quotation from Saint Basil the Great is cited from Scully, 13.

45. Marthinus L. Daneel, "Earthkeeping Churches at the African Grass Roots," in *Christianity and Ecology,* ed. Dieter T. Hessel and Rosemary Radford Ruether (Cambridge, Mass.: Harvard University Press, 2000), 531–52.

2. THE DONKEY WHO COMMUNED WITH ALLAH

1. Richard Kool, "'What Goes Around Comes Around': Prohibitions to Cruelty against Animals in Judaism," *Worldviews* 14 (2010), 88, doi: 10.1163 /156853510x498050.

2. Richard C. Foltz, *Animals in Islamic Tradition and Muslim Cultures* (Oxford: OneWorld Publications, 2006), 20; Kristen Stilt, *Animal Welfare in Islamic Law* (Cairo: Animal People, 2008), 8–9.

3. All Quranic references are taken from Tarif Khalidi, *The Quran* (New York: Viking, 2008).

4. Foltz, *Animals in Islamic Tradition,* 103; S. Nomanul Haq, "Islam and Ecology: Toward Retrieval and Reconstruction," *Daedalus* 130:4 (2001), 162; N.J.

Dawood, trans., *Tales from the Thousand and One Nights* (London: Penguin Books, 1973), 113.

5. L. Clarke, "The Universe Alive: Nature in the *Masnavī* of Jalal al-Din Rumi," in *Islam and Ecology*, ed. Richard C. Foltz, Frederick M. Denny, and Azizan Baharuddin (Cambridge, Mass.: Harvard University Press, 2003), 39–65.

6. Foltz, *Animals in Islamic Tradition*, 17.

7. A.J. Arberry, trans., *Muslim Saints and Mystics* (London: Arkana, 1966), 65; Foltz, *Animals in Islamic Tradition*, 23–25, 34, 94; Kimberley C. Patton, "'He Who Sits in the Heavens Laughs': Recovering Animal Theology in the Abrahamic Traditions," *The Harvard Theological Review* 93:4 (2000), 415. The block quotation below: Assad Nimer Busool, *Animal Rights and Ecology in Islam* (Chicago: Al-Huda, 1995), 52–53.

8. Carlos A. Driscoll et al., "The Near Eastern Origin of Cat Domestication," *Science* 317:5837 (2007), 519–23, doi: 10.1126/science.1139518; J.-D. Vigne et al., "Early Taming of the Cat in Cyprus," *Science* 304:5668 (2004), 259, doi: 10.1126/science.1095335; Lorraine Chittock, *Cats of Cairo: Egypt's Enduring Legacy* (New York: Abbeville Press, 1999); Stilt, 37. The block quotation that follows is cited from Chittock, 40.

9. Hussein Keshani, "Engaging Islamic Views on Human-Animal Relations: Towards an Adab-centred Approach," *Worldviews* 14 (2010), 7, doi: 10.1163/15685350X490003; Yassin Dutton, "Natural Resources in Islam," in *Islam and Ecology*, ed. Fazlun M. Khalid and Joanne O'Brien (London: Cassell Publishers Limited, 1992), 63; Othman Llewellyn, "Desert Reclamation and Conservation in Islamic Law," in *Islam and Ecology*, ed. Fazlun M. Khalid and Joanne O'Brien (London: Cassell Publishers, Ltd., 1992), 91; Foltz, *Animals in Islamic Tradition*, 20–21.

10. Seyyid Hossein Nasr, "The Cosmos and the Natural Order," in *Islamic Spirituality: Foundations*, ed. Seyyid Hossein Nasr (New York: Crossroad, 1991), 354; Foltz, *Animals in Islamic Tradition*, 6–7.

11. Elsebeth Thomsen, "New Light on the Origin of the Holy Black Stone of the Ka'ba," *Meteoritics* 15:1 (1980), 87, doi: 10.1111/j.1945-5100.1980.tb00176.x.

12. Ibrahim Abdul-Matin, *Green Deen: What Islam Teaches Us about Protecting the Planet* (San Francisco: Berrett-Koehler Publishers, 2010), 136–39; Haq, 162.

13. Harvey Neo, "'They hate pigs, Chinese farmers, . . . everything!' Beastly Racialization in Multiethnic Malaysia," *Antipode* 44:3 (2012), 950–70, doi: 10.1111/j.1467-8330.2011.00922.x.

14. Foltz, *Animals in Islamic Tradition*, 129–30.

15. Foltz, *Animals in Islamic Tradition*, 131–39.

16. Richard Foltz, "Zoroastrian Attitudes toward Animals," *Society and Animals* 18 (2010), 367–78, doi: 10.1163/156853010X524325.

17. Stilt, 29; G.R. Smith and M.A.S. Abdel Haleem, trans., *The Book of the Superiority of Dogs over Many of Those Who Wear Clothes* (Warminster: Aris and Phillips, 1978), 3, 9, 29, 33–34.

18. Maggie Caldwell, "How Big Is the Factory Farm Economy?" *Mother Jones* 38: 6 (2013), 37; Lisa Kemmerer, *Animals and World Religions* (New York: Oxford University Press, 2012).

19. Rose Zuzworsky, "From the Marketplace to the Dinner Plate: The Economy, Theology, and Factory Farming," *Journal of Business Ethics* 29:1–2 (2001), 177–88, doi: 10.1023/A:1006419715108.

20. Florence Bergeaud-Blackler, "New Challenges for Islamic Ritual Slaughter: A European Perspective," *Journal of Ethnic and Migration Studies* 33:6 (2007), 965–80, doi: 10.1080/13691830701432871; Asmi Wood, "Animal Welfare under the Shari'a," *Macquarie Law Journal* 12 (2013): 155–72.

21. Muhammad Iqbal Siddiqui, *The Ritual of Animal Sacrifice in Islam* (New Delhi: Idara Isha'at-E-Diniyat, 2000), vii, 3, 27.

22. Siddiqui, 17–24.

23. Siddiqui, 27–34.

24. Marietta T. Stepaniants, *Sufi Wisdom* (Albany: SUNY Press, 1994), 39.

25. Foltz, *Animals in Islamic Tradition*, 47.

26. Annemarie Schimmel, *Mystical Dimensions of Islam* (Chapel Hill: University of North Carolina Press, 1975), 208; Arberry, 71.

27. Arberry, 228.

28. Arberry, 118.

29. Sarra Tlili, *Animals in the Qur'an* (New York: Cambridge University Press, 2012), 80. The block quotation: Arberry, 44–45.

30. Margaret Smith, *Rabia* (Oxford: One World, 1994), 56.

31. Arberry, 228–29.

32. Arberry, 158. The block quotation: Mojdeh Bayat and Mohammad Ali Jamnia, *Tales from the Land of the Sufis* (Boston: Shambhala, 1994), 44.

33. Arberry, 273.

34. Margaret Smith, 56, 179.

35. Arberry, 232.

36. Busool, 43–44.

37. Arberry, 64–65; Laura Hobgood-Oster, *Holy Dogs and Asses: Animals in the Christian Tradition* (Urbana: University of Illinois Press, 2008), 69.

38. Foltz, *Animals in Islamic Tradition*, 96–97.

39. Ruslan Seferbekov, "Patron Deities of the Hunt and Wild Animals in Dagestan," *Iran and the Caucasus* 16 (2012), 301–7; doi: 10.2307/41723268.

40. Joseph Hellweg, "Manimory and the Aesthetics of Mimesis: Forest, Islam and State in Ivoirian dozoya," *Africa: Journal of the International African Institute* 76:4 (2006), 461–84, doi: 10.3366/afr.2006.0065.

41. Lenn E. Goodman and Richard McGregor, trans., *The Case of the Animals versus Man before the King of the Jinn* (Oxford: Oxford University Press, 2009), 114.

42. Goodman and McGregor, 244–45.

43. Goodman and McGregor, 255–56.

44. Goodman and McGregor, 250.

45. Goodman and McGregor, 312–13.

3. HINDU TREES TREMBLE WITH ECSTASY

1. Andrew George, trans., *The Epic of Gilgamesh* (London: Penguin Books, 1999), 48–54; Brett A. Strawn, *What Is Stronger Than a Lion? Leonine Image and Metaphor in the Hebrew Bible and the Ancient Near East* (Göttingen: Vandenhoeck & Ruprecht, 2005), 258.

2. Harold Coward, "The Ecological Implications of Karma Theory," in *Purifying the Earthly Body of God: Religion and Ecology in Hindu India,* ed. Lance E. Nelson (New Delhi: D.K. Printworld, 2000), 39; David L. Haberman, *River of Love in an Age of Pollution* (Berkeley and Los Angeles: University of California Press, 2006), 38; David L. Haberman, *People Trees: Worship of Trees in Northern India* (New York: Oxford University Press, 2013), 29.

3. A.C. Bhaktivedanta Swami Prabhupāda, trans., *Īśopaniṣad,* accessed 9/5/2014, http://vedabase.net/iso/en.

4. June McDaniel, *The Madness of the Saints: Ecstatic Religion in Bengal* (Chicago: University of Chicago Press, 1989), 33; A.C. Bhaktivedanta Swami Prabhupāda, *Teachings of Lord Caitanya* (Los Angeles: The Bhaktivedanta Book Trust, 1968), 27.

5. A.C. Bhaktivedanta Swami Prabhupāda, trans., *Caitanya Caritāmṛta,* accessed 8/29/2014, http://vedabase.net/cc/madhya/17/en.

6. Thomas J. Hopkins, "The Social and Religious Background for Transmission of Gaudiya Vaisnavism to the West," in *Krishna Consciousness in the West,* ed. David G. Bromley and Larry D. Shinn (Lewisburg, Penn.: Bucknell University Press, 1989), 35–54.

7. E. Burke Rochford, Jr., *Hare Krishna in America* (New Brunswick: Rutgers University Press, 1991), 10; Prema A. Kurien, *A Place at the Multicultural Table:*

The Development of an American Hinduism (New Brunswick: Rutgers University Press, 2007).

8. Haberman, *River of Love,* 53.

9. A. C. Bhaktivedanta Swami Prabhupāda, *Bhagavad-gītā as It Is* (Los Angeles: The Bhaktivedanta Book Trust, 1986), 144. The block quotation below is cited from Prabhupāda, *Īśopaniṣad,* accessed 9/5/2014, http://vedabase.net/iso/en.

10. A. C. Bhaktivedanta Swami Prabhupāda, trans., *Śrīmad Bhāgavatam,* accessed 9/1/2014, http://vedabase.net/sb/10/21/en.

11. Prabhupāda, *Śrīmad Bhāgavatam,* accessed 9/3/2014, http://vedabase.net /sb/10/22/en.

12. A. C. Bhaktivedanta Swami Prabhupāda, *Kṛṣṇa* (Los Angeles: The Bhaktivedanta Book Trust, 1971), 87, 691, 710; Ranchor Prime, *Hinduism and Ecology* (London: Cassell Publishers, Ltd., 1992), 101.

13. Deryck O. Lodrick, *Sacred Cows, Sacred Places: Origins and Survivals of Animal Homes in India* (Berkeley and Los Angeles: University of California Press, 1981), 25.

14. Deryck O. Lodrick, "Symbol and Sustenance: Cattle in South Asian Culture," *Dialectical Anthropology* 29:1 (2005), 63, doi: 10.1007/s10624-005-5809-8; W. Crooke, "The Veneration of the Cow in India," *Folklore* 23:3 (1912), 283, doi: 10.1080/0015587X.1912.9719531.

15. Prabhupāda, *Kṛṣṇa,* 60; Andy Dobson et al., "Sacred Cows and Sympathetic Squirrels: The Importance of Biological Diversity to Human Health," *PLoS Medicine* 3:6 (2006), 714, doi: 10.1371/journal.pmed.0030231; Suresvara Dasa, "Milk—Religion You Can Drink," accessed 8/15/2014, http://back2godhead .com/simple-living-high-thinking-10.

16. Prabhupāda, *Bhagavad-gītā as It Is,* 452; Steven J. Rosen, *Holy Cow: The Hare Krishna Contribution to Vegetarianism and Animal Rights* (New York: Lantern Books, 2004), 2.

17. Christopher Key Chapple, *Nonviolence to Animals, Earth, and Self in Asian Traditions* (Albany: State University of New York Press, 1993), 79; Rosen, *Holy Cow,* 79; Prabhupāda, *Kṛṣṇa,* 413.

18. Michael A. Cremo and Mukunda Goswami, *Divine Nature: A Spiritual Perspective on the Environmental Crisis* (Los Angeles: The Bhaktivedanta Book Trust, 1995), 19.

19. Wendy Doniger, trans., *The Laws of Manu* (London: Penguin Books, 1991), 103.

20. Amy L. Allocco, "Fear, Reverence, and Ambivalence: Divine Snakes in Contemporary South India," in *Charming Beauties and Frightful Beasts: Non-*

Human Animals in South Asian Myth, Ritual and Folklore, ed. Fabrizio M. Ferrari and Thomas Dähnhardt (Sheffield: Equinox, 2013), 217–35.

21. Lodrick, *Sacred Cows, Sacred Places*, 14.

22. Crooke 303; Vijaya Rettakudi Nagarajan, "The Earth as Goddess Bhū Devi," in *Purifying the Earthly Body of God: Religion and Ecology in Hindu India*, ed. Lance E. Nelson (New Delhi: D. K. Printworld, 2000), 271.

23. K. D. Upadhyaya, "Indian Botanical Folklore," *Asian Folklore Studies* 23:2 (1964), 21.

24. Amala-bhakta Dasa, *The Life of Tulasī Devi and Her Care and Worship* (Sandy Ridge, N.C.: Krishna Productions, Inc., 1997), 77. The block quotation: ibid. 47–51.

25. A. C. Bhaktivedanta Swami Prabhupāda, *The Nectar of Devotion* (Los Angeles: The Bhaktivedanta Book Trust, 1970), 100. The block quotation is cited from Amala-bhakta Dasa, *The Life of Tulasī Devi*, 99–100.

26. Amala-bhakta Dasa, *The Life of Tulasī Devi*, 79.

27. Doniger, *The Laws of Manu*, 8.

28. Daniel Chamovitz, *What a Plant Knows* (New York: Scientific American, 2012), 137–38.

29. Brian J. Ford, *The Secret Language of Life* (New York: Fromm International, 2000), 185, 189.

30. A. Irving Hallowell, *Contributions to Anthropology* (Chicago: University of Chicago Press, 1976), 357–90.

31. Diana L. Eck, "Gaṅgā: The Goddess Ganges in Hindu Sacred Geography," in *Devi: Goddesses of India*, ed. John Stratton Hawley and Donna Marie Wulff (Delhi: Motilal Banarsidass, 1998), 149; Anne Feldhaus, *Water and Womanhood: Religious Meanings of Rivers in Maharashtra* (New York: Oxford University Press, 1995), 47; Haberman, *River of Love*, 41, 60.

32. Haberman, *River of Love*, 39, 71–72.

33. David Kinsley, "Learning the Story of the Land: Reflections on the Liberating Power of Geography and Pilgrimage in the Hindu Tradition," in *Purifying the Earthly Body of God: Religion and Ecology in Hindu India*, ed. Lance E. Nelson (New Delhi: D. K. Printworld, 2000), 239; Haberman, *River of Love*, 59–60, 118, 123.

34. Haberman, *River of Love*, 99.

4. SHARING MAYAN NATURAL SOULS

1. Arthur W. Ryder, trans., *The Panchatantra* (Chicago: University of Chicago Press, 1956), 331–32.

2. Roy Willis, *Man and Beast* (New York: Basic Books, 1974); Kristina Jennbert, *Animals and Humans: Recurrent Symbiosis in Archaeology and Old Norse Religion* (Lund: Nordic Academic Press, 2011); Edward O. Wilson, *Biophilia* (Cambridge, Mass.: Harvard University Press, 1984), 86, 93; Laurie Cozad, *Sacred Snakes* (Aurora, Colo.: The Davies Group, 2004), 7.

3. C. F. Oldham, *The Sun and the Serpent: A Contribution to the History of Serpent Worship* (New Delhi: Asian Educational Services, 1988), 86–96.

4. J. Eric S. Thompson, *Maya History and Religion* (Norman: University of Oklahoma Press, 1970), 165.

5. Jean Molesky-Poz, *Contemporary Maya Spirituality* (Austin: University of Texas Press, 2006), 42; Nicholas J. Saunders, *People of the Jaguar* (London: Souvenir Press, 1989), 45. The block quotation is cited from Gary H. Gossen, *Chamulas in the World of the Sun: Time and Space in a Maya Oral Tradition* (Prospect Heights, Ill.: Waveland Press, 1974), 317.

6. Molesky-Poz, 97.

7. E. N. Anderson, *Animals and the Maya in Southeast Mexico* (Tucson: University of Arizona Press, 2005), 71–72.

8. Thompson, 162–63.

9. David Freidel, Linda Schele, and Joy Parker, *Maya Cosmos* (New York: William Morrow and Company, 1993), 43; Thompson, 242.

10. Robert M. Laughlin, *Of Cabbages and Kings: Tales from Zinacantán* (Washington: Smithsonian Institution Press, 1977), 327.

11. Gossen, *Chamulas;* Davíd Carrasco, *Religions of Mesoamerica* (San Francisco: HarperSanFrancisco, 1990), 104; Laughlin, 253–54.

12. Freidel, Schele, and Parker, 252, 254.

13. Carrasco, 101.

14. Pedro Pitarch, *The Jaguar and the Priest* (Austin: University of Texas Press, 2010), 163.

15. Gossen, *Chamulas,* 266–67.

16. Dennis Tedlock, *Breath on the Mirror* (San Francisco: HarperSanFrancisco, 1993), 70.

17. Pitarch, 25–30.

18. Evon Z. Vogt, "Zinacanteco 'Souls,'" *Man* 65 (1965), 34.

19. Gary H. Gossen, "Animal Souls and Human Destiny in Chamula," *Man* 10:3 (1975), 452.

20. Lucille N. Kaplan, "Tonal and Nagual in Coastal Oaxaca, Mexico," *The Journal of American Folklore* 69:274 (1956), 364.

21. Weston La Barre, "Old and New World Narcotics: A Statistical Question and an Ethnological Reply," *Economic Botany* 24:1 (1970), 76, doi: 10.1007/BF02860640; Josef Paz, "The Vicissitude of the Alter Ego Animal in Mesoamerica: An Ethnohistorical Reconstruction of Tonalism," *Anthropos* 90:4–6 (1995), 445–65.

22. Vogt, 34. The block quotation appears originally in Pitarch, 43.

23. Pitarch, 51.

24. Allen J. Christenson, trans., *Popul Vuh: The Sacred Book of the Maya* (Norman: University of Oklahoma Press, 2007), 76–77.

25. Gary H. Gossen, *Telling Maya Tales: Tzotzil Identities in Modern Mexico* (New York: Routledge, 1999), 121–22.

26. Gossen, *Telling Maya Tales,* 127.

27. Thompson, 343.

28. Gossen, "Animal Souls," 451.

29. Marianna Appel Kunow, *Maya Medicine* (Albuquerque: University of New Mexico Press, 2003), 2; Frank J. Lipp, "A Comparative Analysis of Southern Mexican and Guatemalan Shamans," in *Mesoamerican Healers,* ed. Brad R. Huber and Alan R. Sandstrom (Austin: University of Texas Press, 2001), 95–116; R. John McGee, *Life, Ritual, and Religion among the Lacandon Maya* (Belmont, Calif.: Wadsworth Publishing Company, 1990), 8.

30. Saunders, 128.

31. Pieter Jolly, "Therianthropes in San Rock Art," *The South African Archaeological Bulletin* 57:176 (2002), 85–103, doi: 10.2307/3888859; Paul Stoller, *Fusion of the Worlds* (Chicago: University of Chicago Press, 1989), 23, 24; Piers Vitebsky, *The Reindeer People* (Boston: Houghton-Mifflin Company, 2005), 12.

32. Jill Leslie McKeever Furst, "The nahualli of Christ: The Trinity and the Nature of the Soul in Ancient Mexico," *RES: Anthropology and Aesthetics* 33 (1998), 215, doi: 10.2307/20167009.

33. Gossen, *Chamulas,* 330.

34. Martín Prechtel, *Secrets of the Talking Jaguar* (New York: Jeremy P. Tarcher, 1998), 151.

35. Prechtel, 152.

36. Prechtel, 157.

37. Prechtel, 157–58; italics original.

38. Prechtel, 161.

39. Prechtel, 10.

40. Gossen, "Animal Souls," 456.

41. Stefano Beggiora, "Tigers, Tiger Spirits, and Were-Tigers in Tribal Orissa," in *Charming Beauties and Frightful Beasts: Non-Human Animals in South Asian Myth, Ritual and Folklore,* ed. Fabrizio M. Ferrari and Thomas Dähnhardt (Sheffield: Equinox, 2013), 82–95.

42. Thompson, 287.

43. Thompson, 286, 290.

44. Michael D. Coe, *The Maya* (New York: Thames and Hudson, 1999), 31.

45. Charles L. Redman, *Human Impact on Ancient Environments* (Tucson: University of Arizona Press, 1999), 8–11.

46. Burton Watson, trans., *The Complete Works of Zhuangzi* (New York: Columbia University Press, 2013), 18.

5. FRIENDLY YETIS

1. David Noel Freedman, ed., *The Anchor Bible Dictionary,* vol. 2 (New York: Doubleday, 1992), 1–2; Rabbi Natan Slifkin, *Sacred Monsters* (Brooklyn: Zoo Torah Books, 2007), 85, 87.

2. Michael J. Curley, trans., *Physiologus* (Chicago: University of Chicago Press, 1979), 13–14.

3. Robert C. Gregg, trans., *Athanasius: The Life of Antony and the Letter to Marcellinus* (New York: Paulist Press, 1980), 70; Mircea Eliade, *Occultism, Witchcraft, and Cultural Fashions* (Chicago: University of Chicago Press, 1976), 77.

4. James Serpell, *In the Company of Animals: A Study of Human-Animal Relationships* (Cambridge: Cambridge University Press, 1986), 19; Daniel Capper, "The Friendly Yeti," *Journal for the Study of Religion, Nature, and Culture* 6:1 (2012), 71–87, doi: 10.1558/jsrnc.v6i1.71.

5. B.H. Hodgson, "On the Mammalia of Nepal," *The Journal of the Royal Asiatic Society of Bengal* 1:8 (1832): 339; Myra Shackley, *Still Living? Yeti, Sasquatch, and the Neanderthal Enigma* (New York: Thames and Hudson, 1983), 52, 54.

6. Shackley, 52–53; René de Nebesky-Wojkowitz, *Oracles and Demons of Tibet: The Cult and Iconography of the Tibetan Protective Deities* (Graz: Akademische Druck und Verlagsanstalt, 1975), 344.

7. David L. Snellgrove, *Buddhist Himalaya* (Kathmandu: Himalayan Book Sellers, 1995), 214; Shackley, 52; Charles Stonor, *The Sherpa and the Snowman* (London: Hollis and Carter, 1955), 64, 158.

8. René de Nebesky-Wojkowitz, *Where the Gods Are Mountains* (New York: Reynal and Company, 1957), 157; Nebesky-Wojkowitz, *Oracles and Demons,* 344; Shackley, 52; Stonor, 5.

9. Geoffrey Gorer, *Himalayan Village: An Account of the Lepchas of Sikkim* (New York: Basic Books, 1967), 79; H. Siiger, "The 'Abominable Snowman': Himalayan Religion and Folklore from the Lepchas of Sikkim," in *Himalayan Anthropology: The Indo-Tibetan Interface*, ed. James F. Fisher (The Hague: Mouton, 1978): 421–30.

10. Stonor, 30, 34, 45, 54.

11. Nebesky-Wojkowitz, *Where the Gods Are Mountains*, 158, 160; Shackley, 62; Reinhold Messner, *My Quest for the Yeti* (New York: St. Martin's Press, 2000); Jeff Meldrum, *Sasquatch: Legend Meets Science* (New York: Tom Doherty Associates, 2006).

12. Nebesky-Wojkowitz, *Where the Gods Are Mountains*, 160; Shackley, 62–63; Stonor, 45; Ivan T. Sanderson, *Abominable Snowmen: Legend Come to Life* (New York: Pyramid Books, 1968), 271, 277.

13. Shackley, 62; Nebesky-Wojkowitz, *Where the Gods Are Mountains*, 160; Kunsang Choden, *Bhutanese Tales of the Yeti* (Bangkok: White Lotus Company, 1997), x–xi; Tribhuvan Nath and Madan M. Gupta, *On the Yeti Trail* (New Delhi: UBS Publishers' Distributors, 1994), 100–101; John Napier, *Bigfoot: The Yeti and Sasquatch in Myth and Reality* (New York: E.P. Dutton and Co., 1973), 53.

14. Stonor, 38–39.

15. Stonor, 152–53.

16. Stonor, 5.

17. Larry G. Peters, *The Yeti: Spirit of Himalayan Forest Shamans* (Delhi: Nirala Publications, 2004), 30–31; R.A. Stein, *Tibetan Civilization* (Stanford: Stanford University Press, 1972), 28, 46.

18. Garma C.C. Chang, trans., *The Hundred Thousand Songs of Milarepa*, vol. 1 (Boston: Shambhala, 1962), 24–25.

19. Stonor, 136–37.

20. Messner, 98–101.

21. Snellgrove, 214.

22. Jamyang Wangmo, *Dancing in the Clouds: The Mani Rimdu, Dumche, and Tsogchen Festivals of the Khumbu Sherpas* (Kathmandu: Vajra Publications, 2008), 124–25.

23. Sir Edmund Hillary, *View from the Summit* (London: Corgi Books, 2000), 197; David Chidester, *Authentic Fakes: Religion and American Popular Culture* (Berkeley and Los Angeles: University of California Press, 2005), vii.

24. Choden, 137–39.

25. Surya Das, *The Snow Lion's Turquoise Mane* (San Francisco: HarperSanFrancisco, 1992), 229–31.

26. Wangmo, 162–73.

27. Stonor, 137–38.

28. Gorer, 79; Stonor, 171.

29. Myra Shackley, "Monastic Ritual and Extinct Animals: The Significance of a Meh-teh Mask at the Nqon-Ga Janqhub Ling Monthang Choedhe Gompa, Nepal/Tibet," *Anthrozoös* 7:2 (1994): 82–84.

30. B.C. Dietrich, "Peak Cults and Their Place in Minoan Religion," *Historia: Zeitschrift für Alte Geschichte* 18:3 (1969), 257–75.

31. Scott Schnell, "Are Mountain Gods Vindictive? Competing Images of the Japanese Alpine Landscape," *The Journal of the Royal Anthropological Institute* 13:4 (2007), 863–80, doi: 10.1111/j.1467-9655.2007.00461.x.

32. Snellgrove, 314; Stonor, 172; Inger-Marie Bjonness, "Mountain Hazard Perception and Risk-Avoiding Strategies among the Sherpas of Khumbu Himal, Nepal," *Mountain Research and Development* 6.4 (1986): 277–92; Patrick Newman, *Tracking the Weretiger: Supernatural Man-eaters of India, China, and Southeast Asia* (Jefferson, N.C.: Mcfarland and Company, 2012), 42; Paul Shepard and Barry Sanders, *The Sacred Paw: The Bear in Nature, Myth, and Literature* (New York: Viking Penguin, 1985), 98.

33. Snellgrove, 314; Stonor, 97–98; Nath and Gupta, 62; Meldrum, 73–86.

34. Toni Huber, *The Cult of Pure Crystal Mountain: Popular Pilgrimage and Visionary Landscape in Southeast Tibet* (New York: Oxford University Press, 1999), 122.

35. Choden, 133–35.

36. Choden, 69–73.

37. Gerald Carson, *Men, Beasts, and Gods* (New York: Charles Scribner's Sons, 1972), vii.

6. ENLIGHTENED BUDDHIST STONES

1. Howard L. Harrod, *The Animals Came Dancing* (Tucson: University of Arizona Press, 2000), 42–43; Åke Hultkrantz, *The Religions of the American Indians* (Berkeley and Los Angeles: University of California Press, 1967), 61.

2. Paul Waldau, *The Specter of Speciesism: Buddhist and Christian Views of Animals* (Oxford: Oxford University Press, 2002); Ian Harris, "'A vast unsupervised recycling plant': Animals and the Buddhist Cosmos," in *A Communion of Subjects: Animals in Religion, Science, and Ethics,* ed. Paul Waldau and Kimberly Patton (New York: Columbia University Press, 2006), 207–17; James P. McDermott, "Animals and Humans in Early Buddhism," *Indo-Iranian Journal* 32 (1989), 274, doi: 10.1007/BF00203863; Daniel Capper, "The Trees, My Lungs: Self Psy-

chology and the Natural World at an American Buddhist Center," *Zygon* 49:3 (2014): 554–71, doi: 10.1111/zygo.12101.

3. Peter Khoroche, trans., *Once the Buddha was a Monkey* (Chicago: University of Chicago Press, 1989), 6.

4. Khoroche, 151, 144.

5. Khoroche, 249–53.

6. Susan M. Darlington, "The Ordination of a Tree: The Buddhist Ecology Movement in Thailand," *Ethnology* 37:1 (1998), 1–15; Susan M. Darlington, "The Good Buddha and the Fierce Spirits: Protecting the Northern Thai Forest," *Contemporary Buddhism* 8:2 (2007), 169–85, doi: 10.1080/14639940701636133.

7. J. Baird Callicott, *Earth's Insights: A Multicultural Survey of Ecological Ethics from the Mediterranean Basin to the Australian Outback* (Berkeley and Los Angeles: University of California Press, 1994); Christopher Key Chapple, *Nonviolence to Animals, Earth, and Self in Asian Traditions* (Albany: State University of New York Press, 1993).

8. Carl Bielefeldt, trans., "Mountains and Waters Sutra," accessed August 11, 2014, http://scbs.stanford.edu/sztp3/translations/shobogenzo/-translations /sansuikyo/sansuikyo.translation.html.

9. Sallie B. King, "Thich Nhat Hanh and the Unified Buddhist Church of Vietnam: Nondualism in Action," in *Engaged Buddhism: Buddhist Liberation Movements in Asia,* ed. Christopher S. Queen and Sallie B. King (Albany: State University of New York Press, 1996), 321–63; Patricia Hunt-Perry and Lyn Fine, "All Buddhism Is Engaged: Thich Nhat Hanh and the Order of Interbeing," in *Engaged Buddhism in the West,* ed. Christopher S. Queen (Boston: Wisdom Publications, 2000), 35–66; John Chapman, "The 2005 Pilgrimage and Return to Vietnam of Exiled Zen Master Thich Nhat Hanh," in *Modernity and Re-enchantment: Religion in Post-revolutionary Vietnam,* ed. Philip Taylor (Singapore: Institute of Southeast Asian Studies, 2007), 297–341.

10. Thich Nhat Hanh, *Being Peace* (Berkeley: Parallax Press, 1987), 87–88; Thich Nhat Hanh, *Interbeing: Fourteen Guidelines for Engaged Buddhism* (Berkeley: Parallax Press, 1998), 3.

11. Thich Nhat Hanh, *The Diamond That Cuts through Illusion: Commentaries on the Prajñaparamita Diamond Sutra* (Berkeley: Parallax Press, 1992), 4, 89; Thich Nhat Hanh, *The World We Have* (Berkeley: Parallax Press, 2008), 70, 73, 107.

12. Thich Nhat Hanh, "Letter from Thich Nhat Hanh," *The Mindfulness Bell* 47 (2008): 13–14.

13. Thich Nhat Hanh, *Touching the Earth* (Berkeley: Parallax Press, 2008), 64.

14. Katherine Wills Perlo, *Kinship and Killing: The Animal in World Religions* (New York: Columbia University Press, 2009), 128.

15. Harrod, xiv.

16. Harrod, 47–49.

17. Harrod, 86–87.

18. Harrod, 86, 111–12.

EPILOGUE

1. David Hawkes, trans., *The Songs of the South: An Ancient Chinese Anthology of Poems by Qu Yuan and Other Poets* (London: Penguin Classics, 2011), 179.

2. Hawkes, 277.

3. Hawkes, 113.

4. Hawkes, 160–61.

5. Marc Bekoff, *The Emotional Lives of Animals: A Leading Scientist Explores Animal Joy, Sorrow, Empathy—and Why They Matter* (Novato, Calif.: New World Library, 2007), 111.

6. Gregory Berns, *How Dogs Love Us* (Boston: New Harvest, 2013), 192–93, 204.

7. Bekoff, 67.

8. Donovan O. Schaefer, *Religious Affects: Animality, Evolution, and Power* (Durham: Duke University Press, 2015).

9. Donald R. Griffin, *Animal Minds* (Chicago: University of Chicago Press, 2001), 194–209.

10. Frans de Waal, *Good Natured: The Origins of Right and Wrong in Humans and Other Animals* (Cambridge, Mass.: Harvard University Press, 1996), 210.

11. Alexandra Horowitz, *Inside of a Dog* (New York: Scribner, 2009), 196–207.

12. Jane Goodall, "The Dance of Awe," in *A Communion of Subjects: Animals in Religion, Science, and Ethics,* ed. Paul Waldau and Kimberly Patton (New York: Columbia University Press, 2006), 653–54.

13. Michel de Montaigne, *An Apology for Raymond Sebond,* trans. M.A. Screech (London: Penguin Books, 1993), 33.

14. Montaigne, 105–6.

15. Mary Midgley, *Beast and Man: The Roots of Human Nature* (Ithaca: Cornell University Press, 1978), 206–7.

16. Anthony C. Yu, ed. and trans., *The Journey to the West,* vol. 1 (Chicago: University of Chicago Press, 2012), 218–29.

BIBLIOGRAPHY

Abdul-Matin, Ibrahim. *Green Deen: What Islam Teaches Us about Protecting the Planet.* San Francisco: Berrett-Koehler Publishers, 2010.

Albanese, Catherine L. *Nature Religion in America.* Chicago: University of Chicago Press, 1990.

Allocco, Amy L. "Fear, Reverence, and Ambivalence: Divine Snakes in Contemporary South India." In *Charming Beauties and Frightful Beasts: Non-Human Animals in South Asian Myth, Ritual and Folklore,* edited by Fabrizio M. Ferrari and Thomas Dähnhardt. Sheffield: Equinox, 2013.

Amala-bhakta Dasa. *The Life of Tulasī Devi and Her Care and Worship.* Sandy Ridge, N.C.: Krishna Productions, Inc., 1997.

Anderson, E. N. *Animals and the Maya in Southeast Mexico.* Tucson: University of Arizona Press, 2005.

Arberry, A. J., trans. *Muslim Saints and Mystics.* London: Arkana, 1966.

Bayat, Mojdeh, and Mohammad Ali Jamnia. *Tales from the Land of the Sufis.* Boston: Shambhala, 1994.

Beggiora, Stefano. "Tigers, Tiger Spirits, and Were-Tigers in Tribal Orissa." In *Charming Beauties and Frightful Beasts: Non-Human Animals in South Asian Myth, Ritual and Folklore,* edited by Fabrizio M. Ferrari and Thomas Dähnhardt. Sheffield: Equinox, 2013.

Bekoff, Marc. *The Emotional Lives of Animals: A Leading Scientist Explores Animal Joy, Sorrow, Empathy—and Why They Matter.* Novato, Calif.: New World Library, 2007.

Bergeaud-Blackler, Florence. "New Challenges for Islamic Ritual Slaughter: A European Perspective." *Journal of Ethnic and Migration Studies* 33:6 (2007), 965–80. doi: 10.1080/13691830701432871.

Berns, Gregory. *How Dogs Love Us.* Boston: New Harvest, 2013.

Bielefeldt, Carl, trans. "Mountains and Waters Sutra." Accessed August 11, 2014. http://scbs.stanford.edu/sztp3/translations/shobogenzo/-translations/sansuikyo/sansuikyo.translation.html.

Binns, John. "Out of Ethiopia—A Different Way of Doing Theology." *International Journal for the Study of the Christian Church* 13:1 (2013), 33–47. doi: 10.1080/1474225X.2012.754137.

Bjonness, Inger-Marie. "Mountain Hazard Perception and Risk-Avoiding Strategies among the Sherpas of Khumbu Himal, Nepal." *Mountain Research and Development* 6:4 (1986), 277–92.

Black, Lydia T. "Bear in Human Imagination and in Ritual." *Ursus* 10 (1998), 343–47.

Bovon, François, and Christopher R. Matthews, trans. *Acts of Philip.* Waco: Baylor University Press, 2012.

Boyko, Adam R., et al. [Boyko, Adam R., Ryan H. Boyko, Corin M. Boyko, Heidi G. Parker, Marta Castelhano, Liz Corey, Jeremiah D. Degenhardt, Adam Auton, Marius Hedimbi, Robert Kityo, Elaine A. Ostrander, Jeffrey Schoenebeck, Rory J. Todhunter, Paul Jones, and Carlos D. Bustamante.] "Complex Population Structure in African Village Dogs and Its Implications for Inferring Dog Domestication History." *Proceedings of the National Academy of Sciences of the United States of America* 106:33 (2009), 13903–8. doi: 10.1073/pnas.0902129106.

Boylston, Tom. "The Shade of the Divine: Approaching the Sacred in an Ethiopian Orthodox Christian Community." Ph.D. dissertation, London School of Economics, 2012.

Bratton, Susan Power. *Christianity, Wilderness, and Wildlife.* Scranton: University of Scranton Press, 1993.

Braukämper, Ulrich. "Aspects of Religious Syncretism in Southern Ethiopia." *Journal of Religion in Africa* 22:3 (1992), 194–207.

Brown, Raphael, trans. *The Little Flowers of Saint Francis.* Garden City: Image Books, 1958.

Busool, Assad Nimer. *Animal Rights and Ecology in Islam.* Chicago: Al-Huda, 1995.

Caldwell, Maggie. "How Big Is the Factory Farm Economy?" *Mother Jones* 38:6 (2013), 37.

Callicott, J. Baird. *Earth's Insights: A Multicultural Survey of Ecological Ethics from the Mediterranean Basin to the Australian Outback.* Berkeley and Los Angeles: University of California Press, 1994.

Capper, Daniel. "The Friendly Yeti." *Journal for the Study of Religion, Nature, and Culture* 6:1 (2012), 71–87. doi: 10.1558/jsrnc.v6i1.71.

———. "The Trees, My Lungs: Self Psychology and the Natural World at an American Buddhist Center." *Zygon* 49:3 (2014), 554–71. doi: 10.1111/zygo .12101.

Carrasco, Davíd. *Religions of Mesoamerica.* San Francisco: HarperSanFrancisco, 1990.

Carson, Gerald. *Men, Beasts, and Gods.* New York: Charles Scribner's Sons, 1972.

Chamovitz, Daniel. *What a Plant Knows.* New York: Scientific American, 2012.

Chang, Garma C. C., trans. *The Hundred Thousand Songs of Milarepa.* Volume 1. Boston: Shambhala, 1962.

Chapman, John. "The 2005 Pilgrimage and Return to Vietnam of Exiled Zen Master Thich Nhat Hanh." In *Modernity and Re-enchantment: Religion in Post-revolutionary Vietnam,* edited by Philip Taylor. Singapore: Institute of Southeast Asian Studies, 2007.

Chapple, Christopher Key. *Nonviolence to Animals, Earth, and Self in Asian Traditions.* Albany: State University of New York Press, 1993.

Chidester, David. *Authentic Fakes: Religion and American Popular Culture.* Berkeley and Los Angeles: University of California Press, 2005.

Chittock, Lorraine. *Cats of Cairo: Egypt's Enduring Legacy.* New York: Abbeville Press, 1999.

Choden, Kunsang. *Bhutanese Tales of the Yeti.* Bangkok: White Lotus Company, 1997.

Christenson, Allen J., trans. *Popul Vuh: The Sacred Book of the Maya.* Norman: University of Oklahoma Press, 2007.

Clarke, L. "The Universe Alive: Nature in the *Masnavī* of Jalal al-Din Rumi." In *Islam and Ecology,* edited by Richard C. Foltz, Frederick M. Denny, and Azizan Baharuddin. Cambridge, Mass.: Harvard University Press, 2003.

Coe, Michael D. *The Maya.* New York: Thames and Hudson, 1999.

Cohn, Jeffrey. "How Wild Wolves Became Domestic Dogs." *BioScience* 47:11 (1997), 725–28. doi: 10.2307/1313093.

Coward, Harold. "The Ecological Implications of Karma Theory." In *Purifying the Earthly Body of God: Religion and Ecology in Hindu India,* edited by Lance E. Nelson. New Delhi: D. K. Printworld, 2000.

Cowdin, Daniel. "The Moral Status of Otherkind in Christian Ethics." In *Christianity and Ecology*, edited by Dieter T. Hessel and Rosemary Radford Ruether. Cambridge, Mass.: Harvard University Press, 2000.

Cozad, Laurie. *Sacred Snakes*. Aurora, Colo.: The Davies Group, 2004.

Cremo, Michael A., and Mukunda Goswami. *Divine Nature: A Spiritual Perspective on the Environmental Crisis*. Los Angeles: The Bhaktivedanta Book Trust, 1995.

Crooke, W. "The Veneration of the Cow in India." *Folklore* 23:3 (1912), 275–306. doi: 10.1080/0015587X.1912.9719531.

Cunningham, Dave. "So Why Was Earl the Slug Shunned?" *Alberta Report* 24:30 (1997), 34.

Curley, Michael J., trans. *Physiologus*. Chicago: University of Chicago Press, 1979.

Daneel, Marthinus L. "Earthkeeping Churches at the African Grass Roots." In *Christianity and Ecology*, edited by Dieter T. Hessel and Rosemary Radford Ruether. Cambridge, Mass.: Harvard University Press, 2000.

Darlington, Susan M. "The Good Buddha and the Fierce Spirits: Protecting the Northern Thai Forest." *Contemporary Buddhism* 8:2 (2007), 169–85. doi: 10.1080/14639940701636133.

———. "The Ordination of a Tree: The Buddhist Ecology Movement in Thailand." *Ethnology* 37:1 (1998), 1–15.

Das. *See* Surya Das.

Dasa. *See* Amala-bhakta Dasa, Suresvara Dasa.

Dawood, N.J., trans. *Tales from the Thousand and One Nights*. London: Penguin Books, 1973.

de Waal, Frans. *Good Natured: The Origins of Right and Wrong in Humans and Other Animals*. Cambridge, Mass.: Harvard University Press, 1996.

Dietrich, B.C. "Peak Cults and Their Place in Minoan Religion." *Historia: Zeitschrift für Alte Geschichte* 18:3 (1969), 257–75.

Dinzelbacher, Peter. "Animal Trials: A Multidisciplinary Approach." *The Journal of Interdisciplinary History* 32:3 (2002), 405–21. doi: 10.1162/002219502753364191.

Dobson, Andy, et al. [Dobson, Andy, Isabella Cattadori, Robert D. Holt, Richard S. Ostfeld, Felicia Keesing, Kristle Krichbaum, Jason R. Rohr, Sarah E. Perkins, and Peter J. Hudson.] "Sacred Cows and Sympathetic Squirrels: The Importance of Biological Diversity to Human Health." *PLoS Medicine* 3:6 (2006), 714–18. doi: 10.1371/journal.pmed.0030231.

Doniger, Wendy, trans. *The Laws of Manu*. London: Penguin Books, 1991.

Driscoll, Carlos A., et al. [Driscoll, Carlos A., Marilyn Menotti-Raymond, Alfred L. Roca, Karsten Hupe, Warren E. Johnson, Eli Geffen, Eric H.

Harley, Miguel Delibes, Dominique Pontier, Andrew C. Kitchener, Nobuyuki Yamaguchi, Stephen J. O'Brien, and David W. Macdonald.] "The Near Eastern Origin of Cat Domestication." *Science* 317:5837 (2007), 519–23. doi: 10.1126/science.1139518.

Dutton, Yassin. "Natural Resources in Islam." In *Islam and Ecology,* edited by Fazlun M. Khalid and Joanne O'Brien. London: Cassell Publishers, Ltd.,1992.

Eck, Diana L. "Gaṅgā: The Goddess Ganges in Hindu Sacred Geography." In *Devi: Goddesses of India,* edited by John Stratton Hawley and Donna Marie Wulff. Delhi: Motilal Banarsidass, 1998.

Eliade, Mircea. *Occultism, Witchcraft, and Cultural Fashions.* Chicago: University of Chicago Press, 1976.

Emerson, Ralph Waldo. *The Essential Writings of Ralph Waldo Emerson,* edited by Brooks Atkinson. New York: Modern Library, 2000.

Episcopal Church, The. *The Book of Common Prayer.* New York: Church Publishing, Inc., 2007.

Feldhaus, Anne. *Water and Womanhood: Religious Meanings of Rivers in Maharashtra.* New York: Oxford University Press, 1995.

Foltz, Richard C. *Animals in Islamic Tradition and Muslim Cultures.* Oxford: One-World Publications, 2006.

———. "Zoroastrian Attitudes toward Animals." *Society and Animals* 18 (2010), 367–78. doi: 10.1163/156853010x524325.

Ford, Brian J. *The Secret Language of Life.* New York: Fromm International, 2000.

Freedman, David Noel, ed. *The Anchor Bible Dictionary.* Volume 2. New York: Doubleday, 1992.

Freidel, David, Linda Schele, and Joy Parker. *Maya Cosmos.* New York: William Morrow and Company, 1993.

Furst, Jill Leslie McKeever. "The nahualli of Christ: The Trinity and the Nature of the Soul in Ancient Mexico." *RES: Anthropology and Aesthetics* 33 (1998), 208–24. doi: 10.2307/20167009.

George, Andrew, trans. *The Epic of Gilgamesh.* London: Penguin Books, 1999.

Gilhus, Ingvild Sælid. *Animals, Gods, and Humans.* London: Routledge, 2006.

Goodall, Jane. "The Dance of Awe." In *A Communion of Subjects: Animals in Religion, Science, and Ethics,* edited by Paul Waldau and Kimberly Patton. New York: Columbia University Press, 2006.

Goodman, Lenn E., and Richard McGregor, trans. *The Case of the Animals versus Man before the King of the Jinn.* Oxford: Oxford University Press, 2009.

Gorer, Geoffrey. *Himalayan Village: An Account of the Lepchas of Sikkim.* New York: Basic Books, 1967.

Gossen, Gary H. "Animal Souls and Human Destiny in Chamula." *Man* 10:3 (1975), 448–61.

———. *Chamulas in the World of the Sun: Time and Space in a Maya Oral Tradition.* Prospect Heights, Ill.: Waveland Press, 1974.

———. *Telling Maya Tales: Tzotzil Identities in Modern Mexico.* New York: Routledge, 1999.

Gregg, Robert C., trans. *Athanasius: The Life of Antony and the Letter to Marcellinus.* New York: Paulist Press, 1980.

Griffin, Donald R. *Animal Minds.* Chicago: University of Chicago Press, 2001.

Haberman, David L. *People Trees: Worship of Trees in Northern India.* New York: Oxford University Press, 2013.

———. *River of Love in an Age of Pollution.* Berkeley and Los Angeles: University of California Press, 2006.

Hallowell, A. Irving. "Bear Ceremonialism in the Northern Hemisphere." *American Anthropologist* 28:1 (1926), 1–175. doi: 10.1525/aa.1926.28.1.02a00020.

———. *Contributions to Anthropology.* Chicago: University of Chicago Press, 1976.

Haq, S. Nomanul. "Islam and Ecology: Toward Retrieval and Reconstruction." *Daedalus* 130:4 (2001), 141–77.

Harris, Ian. "'A vast unsupervised recycling plant': Animals and the Buddhist Cosmos." In *A Communion of Subjects: Animals in Religion, Science, and Ethics,* edited by Paul Waldau and Kimberly Patton. New York: Columbia University Press, 2006.

Harrison, Peter. "Descartes on Animals." *The Philosophical Quarterly* 42:167 (1992), 219–27. doi: 10.2307/2220217.

Harrod, Howard L. *The Animals Came Dancing.* Tucson: University of Arizona Press, 2000.

Hawkes, David, trans. *The Songs of the South: An Ancient Chinese Anthology of Poems by Qu Yuan and Other Poets.* London: Penguin Classics, 2011.

Hellweg, Joseph. "Manimory and the Aesthetics of Mimesis: Forest, Islam and State in Ivoirian dozoya." *Africa: Journal of the International African Institute* 76:4 (2006), 461–84. doi: 10.3366/afr.2006.0065.

Hillary, Sir Edmund. *View from the Summit.* London: Corgi Books, 2000.

Hobgood-Oster, Laura. *Holy Dogs and Asses: Animals in the Christian Tradition.* Urbana: University of Illinois Press, 2008.

Hodgson, B.H. "On the Mammalia of Nepal." *The Journal of the Royal Asiatic Society of Bengal* 1:8 (1832), 335–49.

Hohneck, Heimo. "Animal Mummies and the Worship of Animals in Ancient Egypt." In *Mummies of the World,* edited by Alfried Wieczorek and Wilfried Rosendahl. Munich: Prestel Verlag, 2010.

Hopkins, Thomas J. "The Social and Religious Background for Transmission of Gaudiya Vaisnavism to the West." In *Krishna Consciousness in the West,* edited by David G. Bromley and Larry D. Shinn. Lewisburg, Penn.: Bucknell University Press, 1989.

Horowitz, Alexandra. *Inside of a Dog.* New York: Scribner, 2009.

Huber, Toni. *The Cult of Pure Crystal Mountain: Popular Pilgrimage and Visionary Landscape in Southeast Tibet.* New York: Oxford University Press, 1999.

Hultkrantz, Å l. *The Religions of the American Indians.* Berkeley and Los Angeles: University of California Press, 1967.

Hunt-Perry, Patricia, and Lyn Fine. "All Buddhism Is Engaged: Thich Nhat Hanh and the Order of Interbeing." In *Engaged Buddhism in the West,* edited by Christopher S. Queen. Boston: Wisdom Publications, 2000.

Jennbert, Kristina. *Animals and Humans: Recurrent Symbiosis in Archaeology and Old Norse Religion.* Lund: Nordic Academic Press, 2011.

Johnson, Elizabeth A. *Ask the Beasts: Darwin and the God of Love.* London: Bloomsbury, 2014.

———. "Losing and Finding Creation in the Christian Tradition." In *Christianity and Ecology,* edited by Dieter T. Hessel and Rosemary Radford Ruether. Cambridge, Mass.: Harvard University Press, 2000.

Jolly, Pieter. "Therianthropes in San Rock Art." *The South African Archaeological Bulletin* 57:176 (2002), 85–103. doi: 10.2307/3888859.

Kalechofsky, Roberta. "Hierarchy, Kinship, and Responsibility: The Jewish Relationship to the Animal World." In *A Communion of Subjects: Animals in Religion, Science, and Ethics,* edited by Paul Waldau and Kimberly Patton. New York: Columbia University Press, 2006.

Kaplan, Lucille N. "Tonal and Nagual in Coastal Oaxaca, Mexico." *The Journal of American Folklore* 69:274 (1956), 363–68.

Katcher, Aaron Honori, and Alan M. Beck. "Health and Caring for Living Things." In *Animals and People Sharing the World,* edited by Andrew N. Rowan. Hanover, N.H.: University Press of New England, 1988.

Katz, Steven T., ed. *Mysticism and Philosophical Analysis.* New York: Oxford University Press, 1978.

Kemmerer, Lisa. *Animals and World Religions.* New York: Oxford University Press, 2012.

Keshani, Hussein. "Engaging Islamic Views on Human-Animal Relations: Towards an Adab-centred Approach." *Worldviews* 14 (2010), 6–25. doi: 10.1163/156853510X490003.

Khalidi, Tarif, trans. *The Quran.* New York: Viking, 2008.

Khoroche, Peter, trans. *Once the Buddha Was a Monkey.* Chicago: University of Chicago Press, 1989.

King, Sallie B. "Thich Nhat Hanh and the Unified Buddhist Church of Vietnam: Nondualism in Action." In *Engaged Buddhism: Buddhist Liberation Movements in Asia,* edited by Christopher S. Queen and Sallie B. King. Albany: State University of New York Press, 1996.

Kinsley, David. "Learning the Story of the Land: Reflections on the Liberating Power of Geography and Pilgrimage in the Hindu Tradition." In *Purifying the Earthly Body of God: Religion and Ecology in Hindu India,* edited by Lance E. Nelson. New Delhi: D. K. Printworld, 2000.

Kool, Richard. "'What Goes Around Comes Around': Prohibitions to Cruelty against Animals in Judaism." *Worldviews* 14 (2010), 83–95. doi: 10.1163 /156853510X498050.

Kunow, Marianna Appel. *Maya Medicine.* Albuquerque: University of New Mexico Press, 2003.

Kurien, Prema A. *A Place at the Multicultural Table: The Development of an American Hinduism.* New Brunswick: Rutgers University Press, 2007.

La Barre, Weston. "Old and New World Narcotics: A Statistical Question and an Ethnological Reply." *Economic Botany* 24:1 (1970), 73–80. doi: 10.1007/ BF02860640.

Laughlin, Robert M. *Of Cabbages and Kings: Tales from Zinacantán.* Washington: Smithsonian Institution Press, 1977.

Linzey, Andrew, and Tom Regan, eds. *Animals and Christianity.* Eugene: Wipf and Stock, 1990.

Lipp, Frank J. "A Comparative Analysis of Southern Mexican and Guatemalan Shamans." In *Mesoamerican Healers,* edited by Brad R. Huber and Alan R. Sandstrom. Austin: University of Texas Press, 2001.

Llewellyn, Othman. "Desert Reclamation and Conservation in Islamic Law." In *Islam and Ecology,* edited by Fazlun M. Khalid and Joanne O'Brien. London: Cassell Publishers, Ltd., 1992.

Lodrick, Deryck O. *Sacred Cows, Sacred Places: Origins and Survivals of Animal Homes in India.* Berkeley and Los Angeles: University of California Press, 1981.

———. "Symbol and Sustenance: Cattle in South Asian Culture." *Dialectical Anthropology* 29:1 (2005), 61–84. doi: 10.1007/s10624-005-5809-8.

McDaniel, June. *The Madness of the Saints: Ecstatic Religion in Bengal.* Chicago: University of Chicago Press, 1989.

McDermott, James P. "Animals and Humans in Early Buddhism." *Indo-Iranian Journal* 32 (1989), 269–80. doi: 10.1007/BF00203863.

McGee, R. John. *Life, Ritual, and Religion among the Lacandon Maya.* Belmont, Calif.: Wadsworth Publishing Company, 1990.

Meldrum, Jeff. *Sasquatch: Legend Meets Science.* New York: Tom Doherty Associates, 2006.

Messner, Reinhold. *My Quest for the Yeti.* New York: St. Martin's Press, 2000.

Midgley, Mary. *Animals and Why They Matter.* Athens, Ga.: University of Georgia Press, 1984.

———. *Beast and Man: The Roots of Human Nature.* Ithaca: Cornell University Press, 1978.

Molesky-Poz, Jean. *Contemporary Maya Spirituality.* Austin: University of Texas Press, 2006.

Montaigne, Michel de. *An Apology for Raymond Sebond.* Translated by M. A. Screech. London: Penguin Books, 1993.

Morris, Brian. *Animals and Ancestors: An Ethnography.* Oxford: Berg, 2000.

Muir, John. *John Muir: Nature Writings.* Edited by William Cronon. New York: The Library of America, 1997.

———. *John Muir: Spiritual Writings.* Edited by Tim Flinders. Maryknoll, N.Y.: Orbis Books, 2013.

———. *My First Summer in the Sierras.* New York: Random House, 2003.

Nagarajan, Vijaya Rettakudi. "The Earth as Goddess Bhū Devi." In *Purifying the Earthly Body of God: Religion and Ecology in Hindu India,* edited by Lance E. Nelson. New Delhi: D. K. Printworld, 2000.

Napier, John. *Bigfoot: The Yeti and Sasquatch in Myth and Reality.* New York: E. P. Dutton and Company, 1973.

Nasr, Seyyid Hossein. "The Cosmos and the Natural Order." In *Islamic Spirituality: Foundations,* edited by Seyyid Hossein Nasr. New York: Crossroad, 1991.

Nath, Tribhuvan, and Madan M. Gupta. *On the Yeti Trail.* New Delhi: UBS Publishers' Distributors, 1994.

National Council of Churches of Christ in America. *Bible: Revised Standard Version.* Accessed 2014. http://quod.lib.umich.edu/r/rsv/browse.html.

Nebesky-Wojkowitz, René de. *Oracles and Demons of Tibet: The Cult and Iconography of the Tibetan Protective Deities.* Graz: Akademische Druck und Verlagsanstalt, 1975.

————. *Where the Gods Are Mountains*. New York: Reynal and Company, 1957.

Neo, Harvey. "'They hate pigs, Chinese farmers, … everything!' Beastly Racialization in Multiethnic Malaysia." *Antipode* 44:3 (2012), 950–70. doi: 10.1111/j.1467-8330.2011.00922.x.

Newman, Patrick. *Tracking the Weretiger: Supernatural Man-eaters of India, China, and Southeast Asia.* Jefferson, N.C.: Mcfarland and Company, 2012.

Oldham, C. F. *The Sun and the Serpent: A Contribution to the History of Serpent Worship.* New Delhi: Asian Educational Services, 1988.

O'Meara, John J., trans. *The Voyage of Saint Brendan: Journey to the Promised Land.* Atlantic Highlands: Humanities Press, 1976.

Otto, Rudolf. *The Idea of the Holy.* Translated by John W. Harvey. New York: Oxford University Press, 1958.

Patton, Kimberly C. "'He Who Sits in the Heavens Laughs': Recovering Animal Theology in the Abrahamic Traditions." *The Harvard Theological Review* 93:4 (2000), 401–34.

Paz, Josef. "The Vicissitude of the Alter Ego Animal in Mesoamerica: An Ethnohistorical Reconstruction of Tonalism." *Anthropos* 90:4–6 (1995), 445–65.

Perlo, Katherine Wills. *Kinship and Killing: The Animal in World Religions.* New York: Columbia University Press, 2009.

Peters, Larry G. *The Yeti: Spirit of Himalayan Forest Shamans.* Delhi: Nirala Publications, 2004.

Pinch, Geraldine. *Egyptian Mythology.* Oxford: Oxford University Press, 2002.

Pitarch, Pedro. *The Jaguar and the Priest.* Austin: University of Texas Press, 2010.

Powell, Eric A. "Messengers to the Gods." *Archaeology* 67:2 (2014), 47–52.

Prabhupāda, A. C. Bhaktivedanta Swami. *Bhagavad-gītā as It Is.* Los Angeles: The Bhaktivedanta Book Trust, 1986.

————, trans. *Caitanya Caritāmṛta.* Accessed 8/29/2014. http://vedabase.net /cc/madhya/17/en.

————, trans. *Īśopaniṣad.* Accessed 9/5/2014. http://vedabase.net/iso/en.

————. *Kṛṣṇa.* Los Angeles: The Bhaktivedanta Book Trust, 1971.

————. *The Nectar of Devotion.* Los Angeles: The Bhaktivedanta Book Trust, 1970.

————, trans. *Śrīmad Bhāgavatam.* Accessed 9/1/2014. http://vedabase.net /sb/10/21/en.

————. *Teachings of Lord Caitanya.* Los Angeles: The Bhaktivedanta Book Trust, 1968.

Prechtel, Martín. *Secrets of the Talking Jaguar.* New York: Jeremy P. Tarcher, 1998.

Preece, Rod, and David Fraser. "The Status of Animals in Biblical and Christian Thought: A Study in Colliding Values." *Society & Animals* 8:3 (2000), 245–63. doi: 10.1163/156853000X00165.

Prime, Ranchor. *Hinduism and Ecology.* London: Cassell Publishers, Ltd., 1992.

Raj, Selva J. "Transgressing Boundaries, Transcending Turner: The Pilgrimage Tradition at the Shrine of St. John de Britto." In *Popular Christianity in India,* edited by Selva J. Raj and Corinne G. Dempsey. Albany: State University of New York Press, 2002.

Rapport, Jeremy. "Eating for Unity: Vegetarianism in the Early Unity School of Christianity." *Gastronomica: The Journal of Food and Culture* 9:2 (2009), 35–44.

Redman, Charles L. *Human Impact on Ancient Environments.* Tucson: University of Arizona Press, 1999.

Ritvo, Harriet. "Pride and Pedigree: The Evolution of the Victorian Dog Fancy." *Victorian Studies* 29:2 (1986), 227–53.

Rochford, E. Burke, Jr. *Hare Krishna in America.* New Brunswick: Rutgers University Press, 1991.

Rosen, Steven J. *Holy Cow: The Hare Krishna Contribution to Vegetarianism and Animal Rights.* New York: Lantern Books, 2004.

Ryder, Arthur W., trans. *The Panchatantra.* Chicago: University of Chicago Press, 1956.

Sanderson, Ivan T. *Abominable Snowmen: Legend Come to Life.* New York: Pyramid Books, 1968.

Saunders, Nicholas J. *People of the Jaguar.* London: Souvenir Press, 1989.

Schaefer, Donovan O. *Religious Affects: Animality, Evolution, and Power.* Durham and London: Duke University Press, 2015.

Schimmel, Annemarie. *Mystical Dimensions of Islam.* Chapel Hill: University of North Carolina Press, 1975.

Schneemelcher, Wilhelm, ed. *New Testament Apocrypha.* Volume 2. Louisville: Westminster John Knox Press, 2003.

Schnell, Scott. "Are Mountain Gods Vindictive? Competing Images of the Japanese Alpine Landscape." *The Journal of the Royal Anthropological Institute* 13:4 (2007), 863–80. doi: 10.1111/j.1467-9655.2007.00461.x.

Scully, Matthew. *Dominion.* New York: St. Martin's Press, 2002.

Seferbekov, Ruslan. "Patron Deities of the Hunt and Wild Animals in Dagestan." *Iran and the Caucasus* 16 (2012), 301–7. doi: 10.2307/41723268.

Serpell, James. *In the Company of Animals: A Study of Human-Animal Relationships.* Cambridge: Cambridge University Press, 1986.

————. "Pet-keeping in Non-Western Societies: Some Popular Misconceptions." In *Animals and People Sharing the World,* edited by Andrew N. Rowan. Hanover, N.H.: University Press of New England, 1988.

Shackley, Myra. "Monastic Ritual and Extinct Animals: The Significance of a Meh-teh Mask at the Nqon-Ga Janqhub Ling Monthang Choedhe Gompa, Nepal/Tibet." *Anthrozoös* 7:2 (1994), 82–84.

————. *Still Living? Yeti, Sasquatch, and the Neanderthal Enigma.* New York: Thames and Hudson, 1983.

Shanklin, Eugenia. "Sustenance and Symbol: Anthropological Studies of Domesticated Animals." *Annual Review of Anthropology* 14 (1985), 375–403. doi: 10.1146/annurev.an.14.100185.002111.

Shepard, Paul. *The Others: How Animals Made Us Human.* Washington, D.C.: Island Press, 1996.

Shepard, Paul, and Barry Sanders. *The Sacred Paw: The Bear in Nature, Myth, and Literature.* New York: Viking Penguin, 1985.

Siddiqui, Muhammad Iqbal. *The Ritual of Animal Sacrifice in Islam.* New Delhi: Idara Isha'at-E-Diniyat, 2000.

Siiger, H. "The 'Abominable Snowman': Himalayan Religion and Folklore from the Lepchas of Sikkim." In *Himalayan Anthropology: The Indo-Tibetan Interface,* edited by James F. Fisher. The Hague: Mouton, 1978.

Sjoestedt, Marie-Louise. *Celtic Gods and Heroes.* Mineola: Dover Publications, 2000.

Slifkin, Rabbi Natan. *Sacred Monsters.* Brooklyn: Zoo Torah Books, 2007.

Smith, G. R., and M. A. S. Abdel Haleem, trans. *The Book of the Superiority of Dogs over Many of Those Who Wear Clothes.* Warminster: Aris and Phillips, 1978.

Smith, Margaret. *Rabia.* Oxford: OneWorld Publications, 1994.

Snellgrove, David L. *Buddhist Himalaya.* Kathmandu: Himalayan Book Sellers, 1995.

Snyder, Glenn E. *Acts of Paul.* Tübingen: Mohr Siebeck, 2013.

Stace, W. T. *Mysticism and Philosophy.* New York: Jeremy P. Tharcher, 1987.

Starr, Frederick. "Popular Celebrations in Mexico." *The Journal of American Folklore* 9:34 (1896), 161–69.

Stein, R. A. *Tibetan Civilization.* Stanford: Stanford University Press, 1972.

Stepaniants, Marietta T. *Sufi Wisdom.* Albany: State University of New York Press, 1994.

Stilt, Kristen. *Animal Welfare in Islamic Law.* Cairo: Animal People, 2008.

Stoller, Paul. *Fusion of the Worlds*. Chicago: University of Chicago Press, 1989.

Stonor, Charles. *The Sherpa and the Snowman*. London: Hollis and Carter, 1955.

Strawn, Brett A. *What Is Stronger Than a Lion? Leonine Image and Metaphor in the Hebrew Bible and the Ancient Near East*. Göttingen: Vandenhoeck & Ruprecht, 2005.

Suresvara Dasa. "Milk—Religion You Can Drink." Accessed 8/15/2014. http://back2godhead.com/simple-living-high-thinking-10.

Surya Das. *The Snow Lion's Turquoise Mane*. San Francisco: HarperSanFrancisco, 1992.

Tedlock, Dennis. *Breath on the Mirror*. San Francisco: HarperSanFrancisco, 1993.

te Velde, H. "A Few Remarks upon the Religious Significance of Animals in Ancient Egypt." *Numen* 27:1 (1980), 76–82.

Thalmann, O., et al. [Thalmann, O., B. Shapiro, P. Cui, V.J. Schuenemann, S.K. Sawyer, D.L. Greenfield, M.B. Germonpré, M.V. Sablin, F. López-Giráldez, X. Domingo-Roura, H. Napierala, H.-P. Uerpmann, D.M. Loponte, A.A. Acosta, L. Giemsch, R.W. Schmitz, B. Worthington, J.E. Buikstra, A. Druzhkova, A.S. Graphodatsky, N.D. Ovodov, N. Wahlberg, A.H. Freedman, R.M. Schweizer, K.-P. Koepfli, J.A. Leonard, M. Meyer, J. Krause, S. Pääbo, R.E. Green, and R.K. Way.] "Complete Mitochondrial Genomes of Ancient Canids Suggest a European Origin of Domestic Dogs." *Science* 342:6160 (2013), 871–74. doi: 10.1126/science.1243650.

Thich Nhat Hanh. *Being Peace*. Berkeley: Parallax Press, 1987.

———. *The Diamond That Cuts through Illusion: Commentaries on the Prajñaparamita Diamond Sutra*. Berkeley: Parallax Press, 1992.

———. *Interbeing: Fourteen Guidelines for Engaged Buddhism*. Berkeley: Parallax Press, 1998.

———. "Letter from Thich Nhat Hanh." *The Mindfulness Bell* 47 (2008), 13–14.

———. *Touching the Earth*. Berkeley: Parallax Press, 2008.

———. *The World We Have*. Berkeley: Parallax Press, 2008.

Thomas, Keith. *Man and the Natural World*. London: Penguin Books, 1984.

Thompson, J. Eric S. *Maya History and Religion*. Norman: University of Oklahoma Press, 1970.

Thomsen, Elsebeth. "New Light on the Origin of the Holy Black Stone of the Ka'ba." *Meteoritics* 15:1 (1980), 87–91. doi: 10.1111/j.1945-5100.1980.tb00176.x.

Tlili, Sarra. *Animals in the Qur'an*. New York: Cambridge University Press, 2012.

Upadhyaya, K.D. "Indian Botanical Folklore." *Asian Folklore Studies* 23:2 (1964), 15–34.

Vest, Jay Hansford C. "Will-of-the-Land: Wilderness among Primal Indo-Europeans." *Environmental History Review* 9:4 (1985), 323–29. doi: 10.2307/3984462.

Vigne, J.-D., et al. [Vigne, J.-D., J. Guilaine, K. Debue, L. Haye and P. Gérard.] "Early Taming of the Cat in Cyprus." *Science* 304: 5668 (2004), 259. doi: 10.1126/science.1095335.

Vitebsky, Piers. *The Reindeer People.* Boston: Houghton-Mifflin Company, 2005.

Vogt, Evon Z. "Zinacanteco 'Souls.'" *Man* 65 (1965), 33–35.

Waddell, Helen, trans. *Beasts and Saints.* London: Constable and Company, 1960.

Waldau, Paul. *The Specter of Speciesism: Buddhist and Christian Views of Animals.* Oxford: Oxford University Press, 2002.

Waley, Arthur, trans. *Monkey.* New York: The John Day Company, 1943.

Wangmo, Jamyang. *Dancing in the Clouds: The Mani Rimdu, Dumche, and Tsogchen Festivals of the Khumbu Sherpas.* Kathmandu: Vajra Publications, 2008.

Warren, William. *History of the Ojibway People.* St. Paul: Minnesota Historical Society, 1984.

Watson, Burton, trans. *The Complete Works of Zhuangzi.* New York: Columbia University Press, 2013.

Webb, J.F., trans. *Lives of the Saints.* Baltimore: Penguin Books, 1965.

Weissman, David, ed. and trans. *Discourse on the Method and Meditations on First Philosophy.* New Haven: Yale University Press, 1996.

White, David Gordon. *Myths of the Dog-man.* Chicago: University of Chicago Press, 1991.

White, Lynn, Jr. "The Historical Roots of Our Ecologic Crisis." *Science* 155:3767 (1967), 1203–7. doi: 10.1126/science.155.3767.1203.

Wilkins, Thurman. *John Muir: Apostle of Nature.* Norman: University of Oklahoma Press, 1995.

Willis, Roy. *Man and Beast.* New York: Basic Books, 1974.

Wilson, Edward O. *Biophilia.* Cambridge, Mass.: Harvard University Press, 1984.

Wood, Asmi. "Animal Welfare under the Shari'a." *Macquarie Law Journal* 12 (2013), 155–72.

Yu, Anthony C., ed. and trans. *The Journey to the West.* Volume 1. Chicago: University of Chicago Press, 2012.

Zesu, Gebrehiwot Gebreslassie. *The Sacred and the Profane: Environmental Anthropology of Ethiopian Orthodox Christianity.* Hamburg: Anchor Academic Publishing, 2013.

Zuzworsky, Rose. "From the Marketplace to the Dinner Plate: The Economy, Theology, and Factory Farming." *Journal of Business Ethics* 29: 1–2 (2001), 177–88. doi: 10.1023/A:1006419715108.

INDEX

Abraham, 68–69, 84, 102
Abrahamic religions, 103, 160, 174;
    animal sacrifices in, 46; and
    animals, 24; anthropocentrism in,
    27; battle nature religion, 101; and
    disregard for minerals, 207; and
    Himalayan worldviews, 179; and
    Hindu approaches to nature, 140;
    human superiority, 26, 38, 70;
    invisible God in, 42; Islamic
    approaches to nature within, 70–71;
    limits of nature-friendliness, 39;
    and stewardship, 76, 156
Abu Said, 90
Acts of Paul, 48–49
Acts of Paul and Thecla, 48
Acts of Peter, 26
Acts of Philip, 49–50, 57, 64
Acts of the Apostles, 46, 48
Adham, Ibrahim ibn, 72, 87, 92
agriculture, 12, 13, 17, 142–43, 147;
    agricultural nature mysticism, 143,
    144, 171–72; and environment, 116;
    and mountain gods, 198; pests, 198;
    slash-and-burn, 171, 173
ahimsa, 114–15, 118; and Abrahamic
    religions, 140; in Jainism, 12, 136;

limits to, 118; and snakes, 118–19. *See
    also* non-harm
angels, 38–39, 47, 54, 75, 97
animals: animal cognition and morality,
    248–50, 253; animal feelings, 246–48;
    animal spirit companion (*vahana*),
    108, 113, 179; animal superiority, 71;
    Balaam's donkey, 47; in Buddhism,
    207; chanting, 51–52, 104; in
    Christianity, 35, 44–47, 57–58;
    cruelty to, 46, 59, 81–82; inherent
    enlightenment in, 221–22; in Islam,
    70, 74–75; mummies, 36, 60, 66; rights,
    73–75, 123; sacrifice, 8, 46, 80–85, 94;
    talking, 26, 47–49, 50–51, 72
animism, 47, 144, 154, 251
antelopes, 165, 191; gazelles, 36, 235
Anthony Abbot, 34, 178–79
anthropocentrism, 16, 27; Biblical, 20;
    Buddhism, 207, 211–12, 234;
    Christianity, 27, 41, 57–58; defined,
    13–14; Islam, 77; and limits of
    ecocentrism, 235–36; Mayan, 175; in
    Muir's childhood Christianity, 19;
    pet keeping, 60–61
ants: fire ants, 236–37; have own social
    groups, 96; in Islam, 73; non-harm

Mayan religion, 142–76, 197, 207, 237; agricultural nature mysticism, 144, 171; animals practice religion, 165; animism in, 144, 154; and Christianity, 147; chulel soul, 153; cross, 150, 151, 154; ecocentrism, 145; and environmental problems, 173; ethic of reciprocity, 144–46, 160; human fulfillment in, 146; jaguar nature mysticism, 164–71; models of human perfection, 172; Moon-Mary, 148; Mountain Lords, 151–52; natural beings as persons, 152; natural shrines, 150; resurgence, 147; shamanism, 155–61, 186; snake veneration, 144; soul mountains, 152–54; soul sharing, 154–58; sun veneration, 148, 236; three souls, 153–54; weather, 151, 154; World Tree, 150

Mayapur Dham Dasa, 112, 114, 116–18, 132

meat eating, 14, 83, 115, 194, 227; acceptable meat in Islam, 85; and animal domestication, 7; Buddhism, 207; Cheyenne, 237; and the environment, 116, 117; leads to larger brains, 6; and negative karma, 118

meditation, 20, 190, 222; Buddhist mindfulness, 215, 224; Buddhists do not teach to nonhumans, 234; by elephants, 252; grass cutting as, 236; and Guru Nanak, 98; through jaguar nature mysticism, 167–69; Milarepa's retreat, 186; mindful eating, 228; Sufi, 87–90, 92; and Tibetan artwork, 188; touching the earth, 225; walking meditation, 224–27, 231, 233

Memorial of the Saints, The, 87–91

mermaid, 177

Messner, Reinhold, 183, 188–89, 191

Midgley, Mary, 6, 28, 44, 254

Milarepa as snow leopard, 186

milk, 9, 93, 109, 112, 114–17; as impure, 113; butterfat content, 119; milking

by hand, 120, 121*fig;* offering to cobra, 142; warm milk river, 137

minerals: with Buddhist ecocentrism, 219, 221; and Buddhist nondiscrimination, 220; and Buddhist non-harm, 233; with Christianity, 39; in Ethiopian Orthodoxy, 39; in Great Chain of Being, 38; and interbeing, 219–20; with Islam, 70, 76, 77; lacking value in biocentrism, 14; recipients of Buddhist gratitude, 224; sacred to Muir, 22; in Tibetan religions, 203

Minoan religion, 112, 197

Mohanasini, 116

monkeys, 158, 184; abhorred, 243; cursed by Sun-Christ, 159; devoted to Buddhist monk, 222; symbolic of negative Buddhist mind states, 235; as Tibetan deity of compassion, 185; were-monkeys, 185

Montaigne, Michel de, 15, 44; animal marriages better than humans, 253; animals as religious, 252; attacks against human superiority, 253; on playing with cat, 28; reason in animals, 253

moon, 43, 71, 132, 151, 187, 253; in Psalms, 37; veneration of, 148

Moon-Mary, 148

Mother Cow, 113–14, 116–17, 123–24, 126, 237

Mountain Lords, 151–53, 197, in agricultural nature mysticism, 171; and kin ecocentrism, 152; offerings to, 150; retaliation for lack of offerings, 152; slave seeking, 161; and snake veneration, 144. *See also* mountains

mountains: Abdal's home, 93; abhorred, 243; as altars, 3; dancing, 242; as deities, 47, 127, 144, 150–54, 197–201; and Dogen, 213; Indian veneration of, 101, 137; judicial functions, 199; Juktas, 198; Kailash, 198; Kalindi,

symbolism of, 44; non-harm
toward, 118–19, 231; Paul unhurt by
snake bite, 53; rattlesnake, 118, 231,
236; sacred in Egypt, 36–37; in
shamanic journey, 242; snake bite
healing, 155; "The Snake Who Paid
Cash," 142–44, 172; symbolic of
Buddhist vices, 235; taming, 90;
water moccasins, 118
"Snake Who Paid Cash, The," 142–44,
172
Songs of the South, 241–43
soul, 19, 21, 77, 242; and Aquinas, 58;
and Augustine, 41; Bird of the
Heart, 153, 160; in cattle, 112;
Christianity, 35, 39–41, 64; chulel,
153–54, 160; compared to unruly
dog, 78; of corn, 154, 171; and
Descartes, 58; with ecocentrism, 16;
in Great Chain of Being, 39; Islamic
animal soul, 74; in Jainism, 11–12;
leopards, 11; Mayan three souls, 153;
Montaigne on, 253; natural
soul-companion, 154; plants, 77, 109;
rational, 41, 45, 58, 63, 74; of rock, 11;
shared natural soul (*lab*), 154; soul
mountains, 152–54, 193; soul sharing,
154–58; soul travel, 153, 161, 166, 169;
of water, 11; Zoroastrianism, 79
spiders, 12, 19, 44, 155
spiritual sky (*vaikuntha*), 107, 108,
118, 130
stars, 1, 43, 71, 253; in Psalms, 37; Venus
the Morning Star, 149
stewardship: Christian, 37–38; Hindu,
111, 140; Islamic, 75–76; Mayan, 158
stones. *See* rocks; minerals
Stonor, Charles, 183, 187, 191
Sufism, 78, 86–94; Abu Said, 90;
Bistami, 88; encounters with lions,
89; Hiri, 91; Khauwas, 91; longing
for God, 93; meditation, 88; nature
as sacred, 86; Rabia, 88–91; saints,
88–91, 93–94; spiritual path, 78,

86–87, 89; trust in God, 89–90; in
United Kingdom, 92
sun, 43, 98, 206; as creator, 165; Mayan
veneration of, 148–49, 151, 159; as
muslim, 71; nature mysticism, 171–72,
242; as person, 16; Shamash, 99;
Sun Dance, 239; watched by
elephants, 252; Yamuna as daughter
of, 138–40
Sun-Christ, 148–49, 159
Sun Dance, 239
surabhis (wish-fulfilling cows), 108, 113
sycamores, 40
symbolic approaches, limits of, 43–46,
85–86

Taj Mahal, 77, 138
talking animals, 26, 47–49, 50–51, 72
Thousand and One Nights, The, 71
tigers, 27, 235; the Buddha sacrifices
himself for, 209; as Buddhist
protectors, 197; as carnivores, 115;
flesh forbidden in Buddhism, 207;
Islam, 73; as judicial instruments,
170, 199; kissing deer, 104; learning
love from, 222; as meditation
distraction, 202; and non-harm,
236–37; offered by yeti, 194;
sabre-toothed, 174
totemism, 10–11, 113; different from
Mayan soul sharing, 156
trees, 42, 144, 174; admired by Krishna,
109; *balché,* 162; Buddhist tree
ordinations, 211–12; Christianity, 40;
as deities, 101, 127–33, 150; deodar
cedar, 144; Easter Island, 174;
ecstasy, 109; in Genesis, 32; and
Guinefort, 42; "In Praise of the
Orange Tree," 241; Indian
reverence toward, 129; inferior to
humans, 110; interconnected with
humans, 219, 223; and Muir, 3, 19, 21,
22; and Nanak, 97–98; and nonharm, 114; protection, 234; in

trees *(continued)*
  Quran, 71, 72; as religious teachers, 3, 222–23, 233; sycamore as holy, 40; Tulsi, 127; wish-granting, 108; World Tree, 150; as yeti tomb, 201. *See also* plants
Tulsi (holy basil), 127–33, 135–36, 139, 140; care for, 132; in offerings, 130; rosaries, 131; wife of Vishnu, 129, 207
turkeys, 157; and factory farms, 81
turtles, 41, 102, 198
tzedakah, 69

United Kingdom Sufis, 92
Unity School of Christianity, 14

Vaishnava tradition, 102, 132
veganism, 227, 232
vegetarianism, 123; Buddhism, 209; Christianity, 14, 15; Hinduism, 106, 115–18; Islam, 88; in Jainism, 12; limits of, 231
Venus, 99, 149
Vishnu, 101, 102, 109; and Garuda, 179; and Narasimha, 179; and *shalagrama* stones, 207; Tulsi as wife, 129
Vrindavan, 104, 109, 131; and Yamuna River, 108, 138; Goverdhan Mountain, 127, 207; Krishna's childhood home, 107
vultures, 121, 165

waggle dances, 248
water: blessed, 33, 39, 130, 140, 212; with Christianity, 39, 40; with ecocentrism, 16, 213; enlightened, 213–14; in Ethiopian Orthodoxy, 39–40; as friend, 220; has a soul, 11–12; with Islam, 70, 74, 76–77; and kin ecocentrism, 100; lacking value in biocentrism, 14; Muir's kin ecocentrism with, 20; Muir's words of God, 19; Nafisa's irrigation miracle, 91; provided by mountain

gods, 198; watering flowers spiritual practice, 223
weasels, 68, 154, 155, 198
weather, 31, 115, 143–44, 186, 201; and Mayan religion, 151, 154; and Montaigne's animals, 253; mountain god control, 151, 199
weeds, 133, 145, 171
were-animals, 178; apes, 185, 187, 188; bears, 165, 187; as divine, 196; jaguars, 164; mermaid, 177; monkeys, 185–86; yetis, 179, 185
White, Lynn, 45, 47
witches, 162, 169; animal soul-companions, 156; shape-shifting, 164, 166; soul capture, 153, 161
wolves, 7, 44, 51, 59, 80, 242, 247; as Buddhist protectors, 197; of Gubbio, 57; and love, 71; werewolves, 179, 187, 199
woodpeckers, 154, 210
World Tree, 150–51

Xenophanes, 28, 254

yaks, 182, 184, 188, 197, 203
Yamuna River, 108, 136–39
yetis, 178–205; as bears, 182–83; as bogeyman, 188; as Buddhist disciples, 190; charismatic relics, 190–91; *chumung,* 182, 196; as deities, 196–203; derivation of name, 181–82; *dzuteh,* 182; as *gigantopithecus,* 183; habitat, 183; history in English language, 180–81; in Himalayan religions, 180; as holy people, 183; in human imagination, 179; inbreeding with humans, 187–88; *miteh,* 182, 197; as Neanderthals, 183; part human, 185–86; as permanent hybrids, 186–87; as pests, 196; physical descriptions, 182–83; practice religion, 189–92; as primates, 182–83, 185, 188, 192, 199; as religious helpers, 193–95; scalps, 179, 190–91; scapegoat,

Lightning Source UK Ltd.
Milton Keynes UK
UKHW041536031022
409846UK00003B/705